THE ALMANAC INVESTOR NEWSLETTER

Now you can get monthly updates of *Almanac* strategies, learn whether seasonal patterns are on course, be warned about upcoming best or worst market periods. Subscribers receive important *Almanac Investor Alerts* via email such as the MACD Seasonal Buy and Sell Signals, important updates, the year-end FREE-LUNCH Menu, Plus much more!

All subscriptions include emailed copies and print copies of the newsletter, emailed interim alerts, plus a FREE copy of the annual *Almanac* for the duration of the subscription!

The Hirsch Organization is proud to enter our second year of publishing the *Almanac Investor*. We have adapted it to the *Almanac* reader's needs and requests and the comments we receive from our subscribers are overwhelmingly positive.

Almanac Investor provides you with all this plus unusual investing opportunities—exciting small-cap growth stocks and seasoned, undervalued equities. We also research special situations, hedging to preserve capital, and safe, high-yield situations.

This is an invitation to try the ***Almanac Investor*** at our expense. We'll send you the first three issues of your subscription as a trial. If you are not convinced it can help you make money and keep money, let me know within 10 days of getting your *third issue*. I'll refund your entire subscription.

Jeff Hirsch
Jeff Hirsch, Publisher

P.S.: For a limited time, Charter Subscriptions are available at <u>37% off</u> the cover price. Order today by calling Toll-Free 800-477-3400, Ext. 20, using the postage-paid order card below or faxing it to 201-767-7337 or go to www.stocktradersalmanac.com.

☐ **Yes**, please enter my subscription to ***Almanac Investor Newsletter*** at the CHARTER RATE of **$155** for one year, 20% off the regular **$195** price. I understand that you'll return the entire **$155** if I am not entirely satisfied after 3 issues.

☐ **Best Deal** I'd like to save even more. Sign me up for 2 years for just **$245** (a 37% savings). I understand that you'll return the entire **$245** if I am not entirely satisfied after 3 issues.

☐ $ _____ payment enclosed
(US funds only, drawn on a US bank)
(Foreign add $20 per year.)

Charge Credit Card (check one)

☐ VISA ☐ MasterCard ☐ AmEx

Name _____

Account # _____ Exp Date _____

Address _____

Phone *(Only in case of a question with your order)*

City _____

Signature _____

State _____ Zip _____

Email *(For Email delivery and important* Almanac Investor *Alerts)*

Update your Almanac EVERY MONTH

Now you can find out what seasonal trends are on schedule
and which are not...how to take advantage of them...
what market-moving events are coming up...
what the indicators say about the next move.
All of the important *Almanac Investor Alerts* via email
such as the MACD Seasonal Buy and Sell Signals, important
updates, the year-end FREE-LUNCH Menu, Plus much more!

PLUS...Stock research focused on high-potential issues
Wall Street hasn't yet discovered...
Special situations with hidden value...
Yield-enhancing strategies and more.
See the other side for a special offer on
our new monthly newsletter.

NO POSTAGE
NECESSARY
IF MAILED
IN THE
UNITED STATES

BUSINESS REPLY MAIL
FIRST CLASS   PERMIT NO. 239   WESTWOOD, NJ

POSTAGE WILL BE PAID BY ADDRESSEE:

The Hirsch Organization Inc.
PO Box 2069
River Vale, NJ 07675-9988

Yale Hirsch & Jeffrey A. Hirsch

The Hirsch Organization Inc. ♦ 184 Central Avenue ♦ Old Tappan NJ 07675
www.stocktradersalmanac.com

Editor in Chief	Yale Hirsch
Publisher & Managing Editor	Jeffrey A. Hirsch
Holistics	J. Taylor Brown
Director of Research	Robert Cardwell
Data Coordination	Scott Barrie
Software Development	Gecko Software
Graphic Design	B&W Creative Group

The *Stock Trader's Almanac*® is an organizer. Its wealth of information is presented on a calendar basis. The Almanac puts investing in a business framework and makes investing easier because it:

- updates investment knowledge and informs you of new techniques and tools.
- is a monthly reminder and refresher course.
- alerts you to both seasonal opportunities and dangers.
- furnishes an historical viewpoint by providing pertinent statistics on past market performance.
- supplies forms necessary for portfolio planning, record keeping and tax preparation.

We are constantly searching for new insights and nuances about the stock market and welcome any suggestions from our readers.

Have a healthy and prosperous 2003!

Copyright © 2002 Yale Hirsch and Jeffrey A. Hirsch.
All Rights Reserved.
Published by The Hirsch Organization Inc.
Printed and bound by Quebecor World Inc.

Except as permitted under the United States Copyright Act of 1976, no part of this publication may be reproduced or distributed in any form or by any means, or stored in a database or retrieval system, without the prior written consent of the publisher.

ISBN 1-889223-03-4

 Signifies THIRD FRIDAY OF THE MONTH on calendar pages and alerts you to extraordinary volatility due to expiration of equity and index options and index futures contracts. Triple-witching days appear during March, June, September and December.

 The BULL SYMBOL on calendar pages signifies very favorable trading days based on the S&P 500 rising 60% or more of the time on a particular trading day during the 21-year period January 1981 to December 2001 (see Recent S&P 500 Market Probability Calendar 2003, page 123). Market Probability Calendars for the NASDAQ, Dow and S&P for other time periods appear on pages 120-122. Other seasonalities near the ends, beginnings and middles of months; options expirations, around holidays and other times are noted for Almanac investors' convenience on the weekly planner pages.

This Thirty-Sixth Edition is respectfully dedicated to:

Louis Rukeyser

A phenomenon of Wall Street, who set the standard for integrity and quality in financial-economic-political reporting for over a third of a century and continues to bring his keen wit and wisdom into America's homes every week. Appearing as a guest on Lou's show remains one of Yale's fondest and proudest experiences.

INTRODUCTION TO THE THIRTY-SIXTH EDITION

We are pleased and proud to introduce the Thirty-Sixth Edition of the *Stock Trader's Almanac*. The Almanac provides you with the necessary tools to invest successfully in the twenty-first century.

J.P. Morgan's classic retort "Stocks will fluctuate" is often quoted with a wink-of-the-eye implication that the only prediction one can make about the stock market is that it will go up, down, or sideways. Many investors agree that no one ever really knows which way the market will move. Nothing could be further from the truth. We discovered that while stocks do indeed fluctuate, they do so in well-defined, often predictable patterns. These patterns recur too frequently to be the result of chance or coincidence. How else do we explain that since 1950 practically all the gains in the market were made during November through April compared to a loss in the May through October periods. (See page 50.)

The Almanac is a practical investment tool. Its wealth of information is organized on a calendar basis. It alerts you to those little-known market patterns and tendencies on which shrewd professionals enhance profit potential.

You will be able to forecast market trends with accuracy and confidence when you use the Almanac to help you understand:

- How our presidential elections affect the economy and the stock market—just as the moon affects the tides. Many investors have made fortunes following the political cycle. You can be sure that money managers who control many billions of dollars are also political cycle watchers. Astute people do not ignore a pattern that has been working effectively throughout most of our economic history.
- How the passage of the Twentieth Amendment to the Constitution fathered the January Barometer. This barometer has an outstanding record for predicting the general course of the stock market each year and had a perfect record since 1937 in odd-numbered years until 2001 (with the rare two interest rate cuts that pushed January up and the 9/11 attack that drove the market sharply lower).
- Why there is a significant market bias at certain times of the day, week, month and year.

Even if you are an investor who pays scant attention to cycles, indicators and patterns, your investment survival could hinge on your interpretation of one of the recurring patterns found within these pages. One of the most intriguing and important patterns is the symbiotic relationship between Washington and Wall Street. Aside from the potential profitability in seasonal patterns, there's the pure joy of seeing the market very often do just what you expected.

2003 promises to be a positive year for the stock market for at least a few reasons. The post-millennial hangover investors suffered after the bursting of the "bubble" market and economy in 2000 ought to have worn off by the latter part of 2002, and the devastation consumers and investors felt from 9/11 should be lifted. Looking at the track record of pre-election years gives us something to look forward to in 2003 as well. Not one pre-presidential election year has lost ground in 64 years since the outset of WWII in 1939. By the time you read this edition when it comes off press in the fall of 2002, markets will likely already be in the midst of rally off the midterm election-year low. There is a potential for a 50% move from that midterm election-year bottom to the high in 2003. (See page 78.)

Presidential elections every four years have a profound impact on the economy and the stock market. Wars, recessions and bear markets tend to start or occur in the first half of the term; prosperous times and bull markets, in the latter half. (See page 127.)

It is no mere coincidence that the last two years (pre-election year and election year) of the 43 administrations since 1833 produced a total net market gain of 717.5%, dwarfing the 244.4% gain of the first two years of these administrations.

THE 2003 STOCK TRADER'S ALMANAC

CONTENTS

- 8 2003 Strategy Calendar
- 10 Prognosticating Tools And Patterns For 2003
- 12 January Almanac
- 14 January's First Five Days An "Early Warning" System
- 16 The Incredible January Barometer (Devised 1972) Only Four Significant Errors In 52 Years
- 18 January Barometer In Graphic Form Since 1950
- 20 February Almanac
- 22 Hot January Industries Beat S&P 500 Next 11 Months
- 24 1933 "Lame Duck" Amendment Reason January Barometer Works
- 26 The Third Year Of Decades
- 28 March Almanac
- 30 Market Charts Of Pre-Presidential Election Years
- 32 Profit On Day Before St. Patrick's Day
- 34 Hubris: Pride Cometh Before The Fall (In Stock Price)
- 36 Eight Days A Month Now Outperform Rest Of Month Eight To One
- 38 April Almanac
- 40 Add The December Low Indicator To Your Prognosticating Arsenal
- 42 Pre-Presidential Election Years: No Losers in 64 Years
- 44 Down Januarys: A Remarkable Record
- 46 May Almanac
- 48 Top Performing Months Past 52½ Years S&P 500 & Dow Industrials
- 50 Our "Best Six Months" Discovery (In 1986) Continues to Rack Up Phenomenal Gains
- 52 "Best Six Months" Record Skyrockets With A Simple Market-Timing Indicator
- 54 June Almanac
- 56 Top Performing NASDAQ Months Past 31½ Years
- 58 NASDAQ's "Best Six Months Strategy Beats Dow "Best Eight" Even Better, "Worst Four A Bust
- 60 NASDAQ's "Best Eight Months" Shoot The Moon With A Simple MACD Timing Indicator

62	First-Trading-Day-Of-The-Month Phenomenon
64	July Almanac
66	2001 Daily Dow Point Changes
68	Take Advantage Of Down Friday/Down Monday Warning
70	A Rally For All Seasons
72	August Almanac
74	First Month Of First Three Quarters Is The Most Bullish
76	Down Triple Witching Weeks Trigger More Weakness Week After
78	Why A 50.2% Gain In The Dow Is Possible From Its 2002 Low To Its High In 2003
80	Don't-Sell-Stocks-On-Monday Mantra May Be Back
82	September Almanac
84	A Correction For All Seasons
86	Market Behavior Three Days Before And Three Days After Holidays
88	End-Of-Month Bullish Seasonality Shifting
90	October Almanac
92	First Came The Prime Five Days; Now End, Beginning, And Mid-Month Are Strongest
94	*Trading Classic Chart Patterns:* Best Investment Book Of The Year
98	Year's Top Investment Books
102	November Almanac
104	Be Contrary! Go Against Bullish/Bearish Fervor
106	Most Of The So-Called "January Effect" Takes Place In December's Last Two Weeks
108	Trading The Thanksgiving Market
110	December Almanac
112	Wall Street's Only Free Lunch Now Served In Late December
114	January Effect Starts In Mid-December
116	If Santa Claus Should Fail To Call Bears May Come To Broad And Wall
118	Sector Seasonality: Selected Percentage Plays
120	NASDAQ Market Probability Calendar 2003
121	Dow Jones Industrials Market Probability Calendar 2003
122	S&P 500 Market Probability Calendar 2003
123	Recent S&P 500 Market Probability Calendar 2003
124	2004 Strategy Calendar
126	Decennial Cycle: A Market Phenomenon
127	Presidential Election/Stock Market Cycle The 169-Year Saga Continues
128	Bull And Bear Markets Since 1900

DIRECTORY OF TRADING PATTERNS & DATABANK

- 130 A Typical Day In The Market
- 131 Through the Week On A Half-Hourly Basis
- 132 Monday Reverts To Its Old Bear Market Pattern Worst Day Of Week Last Two Years
- 133 NASDAQ Days Of The Week
- 134 S&P Daily Performance Each Year Since 1952
- 135 NASDAQ Daily Performance Each Year Since 1971
- 136 Monthly Cash Inflows Into S&P Stocks
- 137 Monthly Cash Inflows Into NASDAQ Stocks
- 138 November, December, January-Year's Best Three Month Span
- 139 November Through June-NASDAQ's Eight-Month Run
- 140 Standard & Poor's 500 Monthly Percent Changes
- 142 Standard & Poor's 500 Monthly Closing Prices
- 144 Dow Jones Industrials Monthly Percent Changes
- 146 Dow Jones Industrials Monthly Point Changes
- 148 Dow Jones Industrials Monthly Closing Prices
- 150 NASDAQ Composite Monthly Percent Changes
- 152 NASDAQ Composite Monthly Closing Prices
- 154 Largest One-Day Dow Gains And Losses
- 155 Largest One-Day NASDAQ Gains And Losses
- 156 Largest Weekly Dow Gains And Losses
- 157 Largest Weekly NASDAQ Gains And Losses
- 158 Largest Monthly Dow Gains And Losses
- 159 Largest Monthly NASDAQ Gains And Losses
- 160 Largest Yearly Dow & NASDAQ Gains And Losses

STRATEGY PLANNING AND RECORD SECTION

- 162 Portfolio At Start Of 2003
- 164 Additional Purchases
- 167 Short-Term Transactions
- 173 Long-Term Transactions
- 177 Interest/Dividends Received During 2003/Brokerage Account Data 2003
- 178 Portfolio At End Of 2003
- 180 Weekly Portfolio Price Record 2003 (First Half)
- 182 Weekly Portfolio Price Record 2003 (Second Half)
- 184 Weekly Indicator Data 2003
- 186 Monthly Indicator Data 2003
- 187 If You Don't Profit From Your Investment Mistakes Someone Else Will/Performance Record Of Recommendations
- 188 IRA: Most Awesome Mass Investment Incentive Ever Devised
- 189 Option Trading Codes & Top Sixty-Nine Exchange Traded Funds
- 190 G.M. Loeb's "Battle Plan" For Investment Survival
- 191 G.M. Loeb's Investment Survival Checklist
- 192 Important Contacts

2003 STRATEGY CALENDAR
(Option expiration dates encircled)

	MONDAY	TUESDAY	WEDNESDAY	THURSDAY	FRIDAY	SATURDAY	SUNDAY
JANUARY	30	31	1 JANUARY New Year's Day	2	3	4	5
	6	7	8	9	10	11	12
	13	14	15	16	(17)	18	19
	20 Martin Luther King Day	21	22	23	24	25	26
	27	28	29	30	31	1 FEBRUARY	2
FEBRUARY	3	4	5	6	7	8	9
	10	11	12	13	14 ♥	15	16
	17 Presidents' Day	18	19	20	(21)	22	23
	24	25	26	27	28	1 MARCH	2
MARCH	3	4	5 Ash Wednesday	6	7	8	9
	10	11	12	13	14	15	16
	17 ♣ St. Patrick's Day	18	19	20	(21)	22	23
	24	25	26	27	28	29	30
APRIL	31	1 APRIL	2	3	4	5	6
	7	8	9	10	11	12	13
	14	15	16	(17) Passover	18 Good Friday	19	20 Easter
	21	22	23	24	25	26	27
	28	29	30	1 MAY	2	3	4
MAY	5	6	7	8	9	10	11 Mother's Day
	12	13	14	15	(16)	17	18
	19	20	21	22	23	24	25
	26 Memorial Day	27	28	29	30	31	1 JUNE
JUNE	2	3	4	5	6	7	8
	9	10	11	12	13	14	15 Father's Day
	16	17	18	19	(20)	21	22
	23	24	25	26	27	28	29

Market closed on shaded weekdays; closes early when half-shaded.

2003 STRATEGY CALENDAR
(Option expiration dates encircled)

MONDAY	TUESDAY	WEDNESDAY	THURSDAY	FRIDAY	SATURDAY	SUNDAY	
30	1 JULY	2	3	4 Independence Day	5	6	JULY
7	8	9	10	11	12	13	
14	15	16	17	(18)	19	20	
21	22	23	24	25	26	27	
28	29	30	31	1 AUGUST	2	3	
4	5	6	7	8	9	10	AUGUST
11	12	13	14	(15)	16	17	
18	19	20	21	22	23	24	
25	26	27	28	29	30	31	
1 SEPTEMBER Labor Day	2	3	4	5	6	7	SEPTEMBER
8	9	10	11	12	13	14	
15	16	17	18	(19)	20	21	
22	23	24	25	26	27 Rosh Hashanah	28	
29	30	1 OCTOBER	2	3	4	5	
6 Yom Kippur	7	8	9	10	11	12	OCTOBER
13 Columbus Day	14	15	16	(17)	18	19	
20	21	22	23	24	25	26	
27	28	29	30	31	1 NOVEMBER	2	
3	4 Election Day	5	6	7	8	9	NOVEMBER
10	11 Veteran's Day	12	13	14	15	16	
17	18	19	20	(21)	22	23	
24	25	26	27 Thanksgiving	28	29	30	
1 DECEMBER	2	3	4	5	6	7	DECEMBER
8	9	10	11	12	13	14	
15	16	17	18	(19)	20 Chanukah	21	
22	23	24	25 Christmas	26	27	28	
29	30	31					

PROGNOSTICATING TOOLS AND PATTERNS FOR 2003

For 36 years, Almanac readers have profited from being able to predict the timing of the Political Market Cycle. To help you gain perspective in 2003, a pre-presidential election year, a valuable array of tables, charts and pertinent information can be found on the pages noted.

THE INCREDIBLE JANUARY BAROMETER
ONLY FOUR MAJOR ERRORS IN 52 YEARS

Since 1937 the January Barometer has compiled a very impressive record. In odd-numbered years (when new Congresses convene) the record was perfect until 2001 with the rare two interest rate cuts that pushed January up and the 9/11 attack that drove the market sharply lower. *Pages 16 and 24.*

THE THIRD YEAR OF DECADES

Graphic presentation reveals that "third" years have a mixed record. But since the market rose from the ashes in 1933, only 1973—in the wake of Watergate, Vietnam, Mideast Turmoil and an Oil Embargo—posted a substantial loss. Third years that precede election years have fared rather well, making 2003's prospects optimistic. *Page 26.*

MARKET CHARTS OF PRE-PRESIDENTIAL ELECTION YEARS

Individual charts for each of the last 21 pre-presidential election years, including sitting presidents. *Page 30.*

PRE-PRESIDENTIAL ELECTION YEARS: NO LOSERS IN 64 YEARS

Market charts of pre-presidential election years are presented, along with capsule comments on each pre-presidential election year since 1915. Twelve double-digit gains on the S&P, eleven on the Dow, in the last fifteen pre-presidential election years. NASDAQ racked up monstrous gains in seven of the last eight pre-election years. *Page 42.*

WHY A 50.2% GAIN IN THE DOW IS POSSIBLE
FROM ITS 2002 LOW TO ITS HIGH IN 2003

An average gain of 50.2% has been recorded since 1914 between the Dow's midterm-year low and its high in the following pre-election year. *Page 78.*

PRESIDENTIAL ELECTIONS AND STOCK GYRATIONS
THE 169-YEAR SAGA CONTINUES

Stock prices have been impacted by the presidential election cycle for 169 years, gaining 717.5% in the second halves of presidential terms vs. 244.4% in the first halves. *Page 127.*

DECEMBER 2002

Watch upcoming Santa Claus Rally (page 116)

MONDAY
23

> *Never overpay for a stock. More money is lost than in any other way by projecting above-average growth and paying an extra multiple for it.*
> — Charles Neuhauser (Reich & Tang)

(Shortened Trading Day)
Day before Christmas Dow up 8 of last 12

TUESDAY
24

> *There is no tool to change human nature...people are prone to recurring bouts of optimism and pessimism that manifest themselves from time to time in the buildup or cessation of speculative excesses.*
> — Alan Greenspan (Fed Chairman, July 18, 2001 monetary policy report to the Congress)

Christmas Day
(Market Closed)

WEDNESDAY
25

> *Of 120 companies from 1987 to 1992 that relied primarily on cost cutting to improve the bottom line, 68 percent failed to achieve profitable growth during the next five years.*
> — Mercer Management Consulting (*Smart Money Magazine*, August 2001)

Day after Christmas Dow up 10 of last 11
New Lows perform better when selected last settlement day of year (page 112)

THURSDAY
26

> *Companies that announce mass layoffs or a series of firings underperform the stock market over a three-year period.*
> — Bain & Company (*Smart Money Magazine*, August 2001)

Almanac Investor FREE LUNCH Menu of
New Lows served to newsletter subscribers,
email service@hirschorg.com for details

FRIDAY
27

> *Life does not consist mainly of facts and happenings. It consists mainly of the storm of thoughts that are forever blowing through one's mind.*
> — Mark Twain (1835-1910, pen name of Samuel Langhorne Clemens, American novelist and satirist)

SATURDAY
28

January Sector Seasonalities: Bullish:
SOX; Bearish: XNG (page 118)

SUNDAY
29

JANUARY ALMANAC

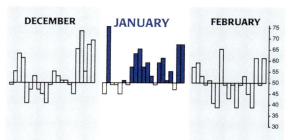

Market Probability Chart above is a graphic representation of the Market Probability Calendar on page 122.

◆ Since 1937 the January Barometer had a perfect record predicting market direction in odd-numbered years until 2001 with the unusual two interest rate cuts that pushed January up and the 9/11 attack that drove the market sharply lower ◆ Every down January on the S&P since 1950, *without exception*, preceded a new or extended bear market, or a flat market (page 44) ◆ January's first five days usually decline in a new or continuing bear market ◆ November, December and January constitute the year's best three-month span, a 4.96% S&P gain, 21.4% annualized (page 48) ◆ At this rate, $1000 since 1950 grew to over $28 million ◆ January NASDAQ powerful 4.1% since 1971 (page 56) ◆ "January Effect" starts in mid-December and favors small-cap stocks (pages 106, 114)

JANUARY DAILY POINT CHANGES DOW JONES INDUSTRIALS

Previous Month Close	1993	1994	1995	1996	1997	1998	1999	2000	2001	2002
	3301.11	3754.09	3834.44	5117.12	6448.27	7908.25	9181.43	11497.12	10786.85	10021.50
1	H	H	H	H	H	H	H	H	H	H
2	—	—	Closed	60.33	− 5.78	56.79	—	—	− 140.70	51.90
3	—	2.51	4.04	16.62	101.60	—	—	− 139.61	299.60	98.74
4	8.11	27.30	19.17	− 20.23	—	—	2.84	− 359.58	− 33.34	87.60
5	− 1.35	14.92	− 6.73	7.59	—	13.95	126.92	124.72	− 250.40	—
6	− 2.71	5.06	16.49	—	23.09	− 72.74	233.78	130.61	—	—
7	− 36.20	16.89	—	—	33.48	− 3.98	− 7.21	269.30	—	− 62.69
8	− 17.29	—	—	16.25	− 51.18	− 99.65	105.56	—	− 40.66	− 46.50
9	—	—	− 6.06	− 67.55	76.19	−222.20	—	—	− 48.80	− 56.46
10	—	44.74	5.39	− 97.19	78.12	—	—	49.64	31.72	− 26.23
11	11.08	− 15.20	− 4.71	32.16	—	—	− 23.43	− 61.12	5.28	− 80.33
12	1.89	− 1.68	− 3.03	− 3.98	—	66.76	− 145.21	40.02	− 84.17	—
13	− 1.08	− 6.20	49.46	—	5.39	84.95	− 125.12	31.33	—	—
14	4.32	24.77	—	—	53.11	52.56	− 228.63	140.55	—	− 96.11
15	3.24	—	—	− 17.34	− 35.41	− 92.92	219.62	—	H	32.73
16	—	—	23.88	44.44	38.49	61.78	—	—	127.28	− 211.88
17	—	3.09	− 1.68	− 21.32	67.73	—	—	H	− 68.32	137.77
18	3.79	N/C	− 1.68	57.45	—	—	H	− 162.26	93.94	− 78.19
19	− 18.92	14.08	− 46.77	60.33	—	H	14.67	− 71.36	− 90.69	—
20	− 14.04	7.59	− 12.78	—	10.77	119.57	− 19.31	− 138.06	—	—
21	11.07	22.52	—	—	40.03	− 78.72	− 71.83	− 99.59	—	H
22	3.79	—	—	34.68	− 33.87	− 63.52	− 143.41	—	9.35	− 58.05
23	—	—	− 2.02	− 27.09	− 94.28	− 30.14	—	—	71.57	17.16
24	—	− 1.69	− 4.71	50.57	− 59.27	—	—	− 243.54	− 2.84	65.11
25	35.39	− 17.45	8.75	− 26.01	—	—	82.65	21.72	82.55	44.01
26	6.75	12.66	− 1.01	54.92	—	12.20	121.26	3.10	− 69.54	—
27	− 7.56	18.30	− 12.45	—	− 35.79	102.14	− 124.35	− 4.97	—	—
28	14.86	19.13	—	—	− 4.61	100.39	81.10	− 289.15	—	25.67
29	3.78	—	—	33.23	84.66	57.55	77.50	—	42.21	− 247.51
30	—	—	− 25.91	76.23	83.12	− 66.52	—	—	179.01	144.62
31	—	32.93	11.78	14.09	− 10.77	—	—	201.66	6.16	157.14
Close	3310.03	3978.36	3843.86	5395.30	6813.09	7906.50	9358.83	10940.53	10887.36	9920.00
Change	8.92	224.27	9.42	278.18	364.82	− 1.75	177.40	− 556.59	100.51	− 101.50

20th Amendment made "Lame Ducks" disappear
Now, "As January goes, so goes the odd-numbered year"

DECEMBER/JANUARY 2003

MONDAY
30

640K ought to be enough for anybody.
— William H. Gates (Microsoft founder, 1981, We're about 200 times that lately, or 128 megabytes)

Last Day Of Year NASDAQ Up 29 Of 31
Dow down 5 of last 6

TUESDAY
31

Whom the gods would destroy,
they first put on the cover of Business Week.
— Paul Krugman (Economist, referring to CEO of Enron, *NY Times* Op-Ed August 17, 2001, On cover 2/12, gets pie in the face 6/23, and quits 8/16)

New Year's Day
(Market Closed)

WEDNESDAY
1

Whenever you see a successful business, someone once made a courageous decision.
— Peter Drucker (Management Consultant, "The man who invented the corporate society," born in Austria 1909)

Average January gains last 32 years:
NAS 4.1%, Dow 2.2%, S&P 2.1%
January first trading day Dow up 8 of last 12

THURSDAY
2

Brilliant men are often strikingly ineffectual; they fail to realize that the brilliant insight is not by itself achievement. They never have learned that insights become effectiveness only through hard systematic work.
— Peter Drucker

Second Trading Day Dow Up 9 of last 11 with larger gains than first trading day

FRIDAY
3

When teachers held high expectations of their students that alone was enough to cause an increase of 25 points in the students' IQ scores.
— Warren Bennis (Author, *The Unconscious Conspiracy: Why Leaders Can't Lead*, 1976)

SATURDAY
4

SUNDAY
5

JANUARY'S FIRST FIVE DAYS AN "EARLY WARNING" SYSTEM

Market action during the first five trading days of the month often serves as an excellent "early warning" system for the year as a whole. Early January gains since 1950 (excluding 1994) were matched by whole-year gains with just three war-related exceptions: Vietnam military spending delayed start of 1966 bear market; ceasefire imminence early 1973 raised stocks temporarily; and Saddam Hussein turned 1990 into a bear. Twenty Januarys got off to a bad start and ten of those ended on the downside. Investors pushing taxable gains into the New Year cause many bad starts following great bull years. Remember that five days is a brief span and some extraordinary event could sidetrack this indicator as it did on the fifth day of 1986 and 1998.

THE FIRST-FIVE-DAYS-IN-JANUARY INDICATOR

Chronological Data

	Previous Year's Close	January 5th Day	5-Day Change	Year Change
1950	16.76	17.09	2.0%	21.8%
1951	20.41	20.88	2.3	16.5
1952	23.77	23.91	0.6	11.8
1953	26.57	26.33	– 0.9	– 6.6
1954	24.81	24.93	0.5	45.0
1955	35.98	35.33	– 1.8	26.4
1956	45.48	44.51	– 2.1	2.6
1957	46.67	46.25	– 0.9	– 14.3
1958	39.99	40.99	2.5	38.1
1959	55.21	55.40	0.3	8.5
1960	59.89	59.50	– 0.7	– 3.0
1961	58.11	58.81	1.2	23.1
1962	71.55	69.12	– 3.4	– 11.8
1963	63.10	64.74	2.6	18.9
1964	75.02	76.00	1.3	13.0
1965	84.75	85.37	0.7	9.1
1966	92.43	93.14	0.8	– 13.1
1967	80.33	82.81	3.1	20.1
1968	96.47	96.62	0.2	7.7
1969	103.86	100.80	– 2.9	– 11.4
1970	92.06	92.68	0.7	0.1
1971	92.15	92.19	0.04	10.8
1972	102.09	103.47	1.4	15.6
1973	118.05	119.85	1.5	– 17.4
1974	97.55	96.12	– 1.5	– 29.7
1975	68.56	70.04	2.2	31.5
1976	90.19	94.58	4.9	19.1
1977	107.46	105.01	– 2.3	– 11.5
1978	95.10	90.64	– 4.7	1.1
1979	96.11	98.80	2.8	12.3
1980	107.94	108.95	0.9	25.8
1981	135.76	133.06	– 2.0	– 9.7
1982	122.55	119.55	– 2.4	14.8
1983	140.64	145.23	3.3	17.3
1984	164.93	168.90	2.4	1.4
1985	167.24	163.99	– 1.9	26.3
1986	211.28	207.97	– 1.6	14.6
1987	242.17	257.28	6.2	2.0
1988	247.08	243.40	– 1.5	12.4
1989	277.72	280.98	1.2	27.3
1990	353.40	353.79	0.1	– 6.6
1991	330.22	314.90	– 4.6	26.3
1992	417.09	418.10	0.2	4.5
1993	435.71	429.05	– 1.5	7.1
1994	466.45	469.90	0.7	– 1.5
1995	459.27	460.83	0.3	34.1
1996	615.93	618.46	0.4	20.3
1997	740.74	748.41	1.0	31.0
1998	970.43	956.04	– 1.5	26.7
1999	1229.23	1275.09	3.7	19.5
2000	1469.25	1441.46	– 1.9	– 10.1
2001	1320.28	1295.86	– 1.8	– 13.0
2002	1148.08	1160.71	1.1	??

Ranked By Performance

Rank		5-Day Change	Year Change
1	1987	6.2%	2.0%
2	1976	4.9	19.1
3	1999	3.7	19.5
4	1983	3.3	17.3
5	1967	3.1	20.1
6	1979	2.8	12.3
7	1963	2.6	18.9
8	1958	2.5	38.1
9	1984	2.4	1.4
10	1951	2.3	16.5
11	1975	2.2	31.5
12	1950	2.0	21.8
13	1973	1.5	– 17.4
14	1972	1.4	15.6
15	1964	1.3	13.0
16	1961	1.2	23.1
17	1989	1.2	27.3
18	2002	1.1	??
19	1997	1.0	31.0
20	1980	0.9	25.8
21	1966	0.8	– 13.1
22	1994	0.7	– 1.5
23	1965	0.7	9.1
24	1970	0.7	0.1
25	1952	0.6	11.8
26	1954	0.5	45.0
27	1996	0.4	20.3
28	1959	0.3	8.5
29	1995	0.3	34.1
30	1992	0.2	4.5
31	1968	0.2	7.7
32	1990	0.1	– 6.6
33	1971	0.04	10.8
34	1960	– 0.7	– 3.0
35	1957	– 0.9	– 14.3
36	1953	– 0.9	– 6.6
37	1974	– 1.5	– 29.7
38	1998	– 1.5	26.7
39	1988	– 1.5	12.4
40	1993	– 1.5	7.1
41	1986	– 1.6	14.6
42	2001	– 1.8	– 13.0
43	1955	– 1.8	26.4
44	2000	– 1.9	– 10.1
45	1985	– 1.9	26.3
46	1981	– 2.0	– 9.7
47	1956	– 2.1	2.6
48	1977	– 2.3	– 11.5
49	1982	– 2.4	14.8
50	1969	– 2.9	– 11.4
51	1962	– 3.4	– 11.8
52	1991	– 4.6	26.3
53	1978	– 4.7	1.1

Based on S&P 500

JANUARY

MONDAY 6

Everyone wants to make the same three things: money, a name, and a difference. What creates diversity in the human race is how we prioritize the three.
— Roy H. Williams
(Author, *Secret Formulas of the Wizard of Ads*)

TUESDAY 7

So at last I was going to America! Really, really going, at last! The boundaries burst. The arch of heaven soared! A million suns shone out for every star. The winds rushed in from outer space, roaring in my ears, "America! America!"
— Mary Antin (1881-1949, Immigrant writer, *The Promised Land*, 1912)

January's First Five Days, an "Early Warning" System (page 14)

WEDNESDAY 8

The time to buy is when blood is running in the streets.
— Baron Nathan Rothschild (London financier, 1777-1836)

THURSDAY 9

Successful innovation is not a feat of intellect, but of will.
— Joseph A. Schumpeter (Austrian-American economist, *Theory of Economic Development*, 1883-1950)

FRIDAY 10

You can't grow long-term if you can't eat short-term. Anybody can manage short. Anybody can manage long. Balancing those two things is what management is.
— Jack Welch (CEO of General Electric, *Business Week*, June 8, 1998)

SATURDAY 11

SUNDAY 12

INCREDIBLE JANUARY BAROMETER (DEVISED 1972) ONLY FOUR SIGNIFICANT ERRORS IN 52 YEARS

Since 1950 January has predicted the annual course of the stock market with amazing precision, registering only four major errors for a 92.3% accuracy ratio. The January Barometer, devised by Yale Hirsch in 1972, is based on whether the S&P 500 is up or down in January. Most years, stocks continue the course set in January. Of the four major errors two (1966 and 1968) were affected by Vietnam, one (1982) by the start of the powerful bull market that began in August 1982, and in 2001 the Fed's two January rate cuts unnaturally buoyed the market higher. The 9/11 attacks, despite the subsequent rally, still likely held the market down in 2001.

However, there was **only one error in odd years** (2001) when new congresses convened. **Bear markets began or continued when Januarys had a loss** (see page 44). The six flat years switched directions in the year's final months.

AS JANUARY GOES, SO GOES THE YEAR

	Market Performance In January				Ranked By Performance			
	Previous Year's Close	January Close	January Change	Year Change	Rank		January Change	Year Change
1950	16.76	17.05	1.7%	21.8%	1	1987	13.2%	2.0%
1951	20.41	21.66	6.1	16.5	2	1975	12.3	31.5
1952	23.77	24.14	1.6	11.8	3	1976	11.8	19.1
1953	26.57	26.38	– 0.7	– 6.6	4	1967	7.8	20.1
1954	24.81	26.08	5.1	45.0	5	1985	7.4	26.3
1955	35.98	36.63	1.8	26.4	6	1989	7.1	27.3
1956	45.48	43.82	– 3.6	2.6	7	1961	6.3	23.1
1957	46.67	44.72	– 4.2	– 14.3	8	1997	6.1	31.0
1958	39.99	41.70	4.3	38.1	9	1951	6.1	16.5
1959	55.21	55.42	0.4	8.5	10	1980	5.8	25.8
1960	59.89	55.61	– 7.1	– 3.0	11	1954	5.1	45.0
1961	58.11	61.78	6.3	23.1	12	1963	4.9	18.9
1962	71.55	68.84	– 3.8	– 11.8	13	1958	4.3	38.1
1963	63.10	66.20	4.9	18.9	14	1991	4.2	26.3
1964	75.02	77.04	2.7	13.0	15	1999	4.1	19.5
1965	84.75	87.56	3.3	9.1	16	1971	4.0	10.8
1966	92.43	92.88	0.5	– 13.1 X	17	1988	4.0	12.4
1967	80.33	86.61	7.8	20.1	18	1979	4.0	12.3
1968	96.47	92.24	– 4.4	7.7 X	19	2001	3.5	– 13.0 X
1969	103.86	103.01	– 0.8	– 11.4	20	1965	3.3	9.1
1970	92.06	85.02	– 7.6	0.1	21	1983	3.3	17.3
1971	92.15	95.88	4.0	10.8	22	1996	3.3	20.3
1972	102.09	103.94	1.8	15.6	23	1994	3.3	– 1.5 flat
1973	118.05	116.03	– 1.7	– 17.4	24	1964	2.7	13.0
1974	97.55	96.57	– 1.0	– 29.7	25	1995	2.4	34.1
1975	68.56	76.98	12.3	31.5	26	1972	1.8	15.6
1976	90.19	100.86	11.8	19.1	27	1955	1.8	26.4
1977	107.46	102.03	– 5.1	– 11.5	28	1950	1.7	21.8
1978	95.10	89.25	– 6.2	1.1	29	1952	1.6	11.8
1979	96.11	99.93	4.0	12.3	30	1998	1.0	26.7
1980	107.94	114.16	5.8	25.8	31	1993	0.7	7.1
1981	135.76	129.55	– 4.6	– 9.7	32	1966	0.5	– 13.1 X
1982	122.55	120.40	– 1.8	14.8 X	33	1959	0.4	8.5
1983	140.64	145.30	3.3	17.3	34	1986	0.2	14.6
1984	164.93	163.41	– 0.9	1.4	35	1953	– 0.7	– 6.6
1985	167.24	179.63	7.4	26.3	36	1969	– 0.8	– 11.4
1986	211.28	211.78	0.2	14.6	37	1984	– 0.9	1.4 flat
1987	242.17	274.08	13.2	2.0	38	1974	– 1.0	– 29.7
1988	247.08	257.07	4.0	12.4	39	2002	– 1.6	??
1989	277.72	297.47	7.1	27.3	40	1973	– 1.7	– 17.4
1990	353.40	329.08	– 6.9	– 6.6	41	1982	– 1.8	14.8 X
1991	330.22	343.93	4.2	26.3	42	1992	– 2.0	4.5 flat
1992	417.09	408.79	– 2.0	4.5	43	1956	– 3.6	2.6 flat
1993	435.71	438.78	0.7	7.1	44	1962	– 3.8	– 11.8
1994	466.45	481.61	3.3	– 1.5	45	1957	– 4.2	– 14.3
1995	459.27	470.42	2.4	34.1	46	1968	– 4.4	7.7 X
1996	615.93	636.02	3.3	20.3	47	1981	– 4.6	– 9.7
1997	740.74	786.16	6.1	31.0	48	1977	– 5.1	– 11.5
1998	970.43	980.28	1.0	26.7	49	2000	– 5.1	– 10.1
1999	1229.23	1279.64	4.1	19.5	50	1978	– 6.2	1.1 flat
2000	1469.25	1394.46	– 5.1	– 10.1	51	1990	– 6.9	– 6.6
2001	1320.28	1366.01	3.5	– 13.0 X	52	1960	– 7.1	– 3.0
2002	1148.08	1130.20	– 1.6	??	53	1970	– 7.6	0.1 flat

X = 4 major errors   Based on S&P 500

JANUARY

MONDAY
13

Mate selection is usually a far greater determinant of individual well being than stock selection.
— Ross Miller (President, Miller Risk Advisors, *Paving Wall Street: Experimental Economics and the Quest for the Perfect Market*, December 2001)

TUESDAY
14

Welch's genius was the capacity to energize and inspire hundreds of thousands of people across a range of businesses and countries.
— Warren G. Bennis (USC Business professor, *Business Week*, September 10, 2001, referring to retiring CEO Jack Welch of General Electric)

WEDNESDAY

15

Welch's special genius was to make big changes before the market demanded them and before his competitors saw the need.
— Richard S. Tedlow (Harvard Business School historian, *Business Week*, September 10, 2001)

THURSDAY

16

Welch could change the direction of a huge conglomerate with the speed and agility of a small firm.
— Michael Useem (Wharton School professor, *Business Week*, September 10, 2001)

FRIDAY

17

The biggest change we made was the move to a boundary-less company. We got rid of the corner offices, the bureaucracy, and the not-invented-here syndrome. Instead we got every mind in the game, got the best out of all our people.
— Jack Welch (retiring CEO of General Electric, *Business Week*, September 10, 2001)

SATURDAY
18

SUNDAY
19

JANUARY BAROMETER IN GRAPHIC FORM SINCE 1950

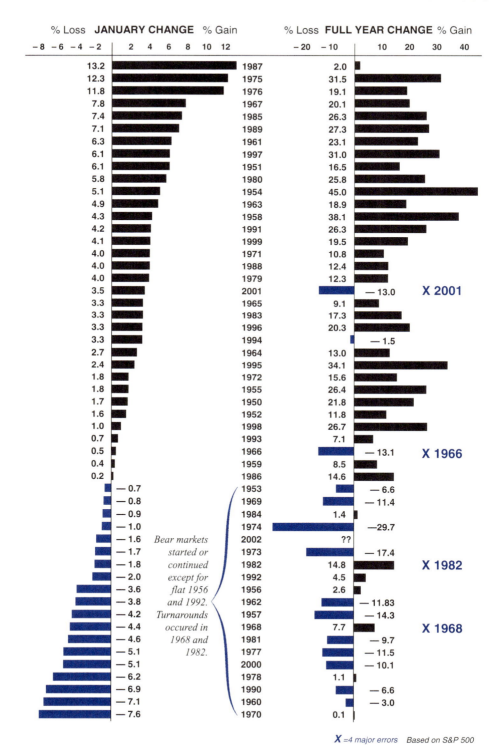

JANUARY

MONDAY 20

Martin Luther King Jr. Day
(Market Closed)

*A fanatic is one who can't change his mind
and won't change the subject.*
— Winston Churchill (British statesman, 1874-1965)

TUESDAY 21

*An appeaser is one who feeds a crocodile—
hoping it will eat him last.*
— Winston Churchill

WEDNESDAY 22

*The world has changed! You can't be an 800-pound gorilla;
you need to be an economic gazelle.
You've got to be able to change directions quickly.*
— Mark Breier (The 10-Second Internet Manager)

THURSDAY 23

*People with a sense of fulfillment think the world is good, while the
frustrated blame the world for their failure.*
— Eric Hoffer (The True Believer, 1951)

FRIDAY 24

*Of a stock's move, 31% can be attributed to the general stock
market, 12% to the industry influence, 37% to the influence of other
groupings, and the remaining 20% is peculiar to the one stock.*
— Benjamin F. King (Market and Industry Factors in Stock Price
Behavior, Journal of Business, January 1966)

SATURDAY 25

SUNDAY 26

FEBRUARY ALMANAC

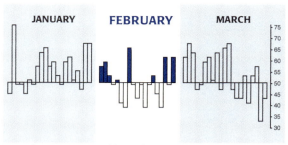

Market Probability Chart above is a graphic representation of the Market Probability Calendar on page 122.

◆ Sharp January moves usually correct or consolidate in February ◆ Compare January and February performance on page 140 ◆ Tends to follow current market trend ◆ RECORD: S&P 28 up, 25 down ◆ Average S&P change -0.04% for 53 years, recent 15 years 0.2% ◆ Seventh best in NASDAQ (page 56) ◆ Eleven dogs in a row day before Presidents' Day weekend, off 295.05 points on Dow in 2000, 91.20 in 2001, 98.95 in 2002; day after no prize either lately (see below and page 86) ◆ Many technicians modify market predictions based on January's market

FEBRUARY DAILY POINT CHANGES DOW JONES INDUSTRIALS

Previous Month Close	1993 3310.03	1994 3978.36	1995 3843.86	1996 5395.30	1997 6813.09	1998 7906.50	1999 9358.83	2000 10940.53	2001 10887.36	2002 9920.00
1	22.15	− 14.35	3.70	9.76	—	—	− 13.13	100.52	96.27	− 12.74
2	− 3.51	11.53	23.21	− 31.07	—	201.28	− 71.58	− 37.85	− 119.53	—
3	45.12	− 7.88	57.87	—	− 6.93	52.57	92.69	10.24	—	—
4	42.95	− 96.24	—	—	27.32	− 30.64	− 62.31	− 49.64	—	− 220.17
5	25.40	—	—	33.60	− 86.58	− 12.46	0.26	—	101.75	− 1.66
6	—	—	9.09	52.02	26.16	72.24	—	—	− 8.43	− 32.04
7	—	34.90	− 0.34	32.51	82.74	—	—	− 58.01	− 10.70	− 27.95
8	− 4.60	− 0.29	− 2.02	47.33	—	—	− 13.13	51.81	− 66.17	118.80
9	− 22.96	25.89	− 2.69	2.17	—	− 8.97	− 158.08	− 258.44	− 99.10	—
10	− 2.16	− 36.58	6.39	—	− 49.26	115.09	44.28	− 55.53	—	—
11	10.27	− 0.56	—	—	51.57	18.94	186.15	− 218.42	—	140.54
12	− 30.26	—	—	58.53	103.52	55.05	− 88.57	—	165.32	− 21.04
13	—	—	15.14	1.08	60.81	0.50	—	—	− 43.45	125.93
14	—	9.28	4.04	− 21.68	− 33.48	—	—	94.63	− 107.91	12.32
15	H	24.21	27.92	− 28.18	—	—	H	198.25	95.61	− 98.95
16	− 82.94	9.00	1.35	− 48.05	—	H	22.14	− 156.68	− 91.20	—
17	2.70	− 14.63	− 33.98	—	—	28.40	− 101.56	− 46.84	—	—
18	− 10.00	− 35.18	—	—	78.50	52.56	103.16	− 295.05	—	H
19	19.99	—	—	H	− 47.33	− 75.48	41.32	—	H	− 157.90
20	—	—	H	− 44.79	− 92.75	38.36	—	—	− 68.94	196.03
21	—	H	10.43	57.44	4.24	—	—	H	− 204.30	− 106.49
22	20.81	24.20	9.08	92.49	—	—	212.73	85.32	0.23	133.47
23	− 19.72	− 19.98	30.28	22.03	—	− 3.74	− 8.26	− 79.11	− 84.91	—
24	33.23	− 51.78	8.41	—	76.58	− 40.10	− 144.75	− 133.10	—	—
25	8.64	− 1.12	—	—	30.01	87.68	− 33.33	− 230.51	—	177.56
26	5.67	—	—	− 65.39	− 55.03	32.89	− 59.76	—	200.63	− 30.45
27	—	—	− 23.17	− 15.89	− 58.11	55.05	—	—	5.65	12.32
28	—	− 6.76	22.48	− 43.00	− 47.33	—	—	176.53	− 141.60	− 21.45
29				− 20.59				89.66		
Close	3370.81	3832.02	4011.05	5485.62	6877.74	8545.72	9306.58	10128.31	10495.28	10106.13
Change	60.78	−146.34	167.19	90.32	64.65	639.22	− 52.25	− 812.22	− 392.08	186.13

*Either go short, or stay away
The day before Presidents' Day*

JANUARY/FERBUARY

MONDAY 27

You don't learn to hold your own in the world by standing on guard, but by attacking and getting well hammered yourself.
— George Bernard Shaw (Irish Dramatist, 1856-1950)

FOMC Meeting (2 days)

TUESDAY 28

The wisdom of the ages are the fruits of freedom and democracy.
— Lawrence Kudlow (Economist, 24th Annual Paulson SmallCap Conference, Waldorf Astoria NYC, 11/8/01)

WEDNESDAY 29

The CROWD is always wrong at market turning points but often times right once a trend sets in. The reason many market fighters go broke is they believe the CROWD is always wrong. There is nothing further from the truth. Unless volatility is extremely low or very high one should think twice before betting against the CROWD.
— Shawn Andrew (Trader, Ricercar Fund /SA, 12/21/01)

THURSDAY **30**

Life is what happens, while you're busy making other plans.
— John Lennon (Beatle)

"January Barometer" 92.3% accurate (page 16) only one error in odd-numbered years since 1937 (page 24) Email service@hirschorg.com for official final results

 FRIDAY 31

Fortune favors the brave.
— Virgil (Roman Poet, Aeneid, 70-19 B.C.)

SATURDAY 1

February Sector Seasonalities: Bullish: XNG; Bearish: MSH, XTC (page 118)

SUNDAY 2

HOT JANUARY INDUSTRIES BEAT S&P NEXT 11 MONTHS

Just as January tends to be a barometer of the market's direction for the whole year, stocks moving quickly out of the starting gate in January outperform the market the rest of the year.

Sam Stovall, Senior Investment Strategist at Standard & Poor's, massaged the data and proved this premise for the Almanac. Since 1970, January's 10 best performing industries within the S&P 500 (Sam calls it the January Barometer Portfolio or JBP) went on to outperform the S&P 500 during the remaining 11 months of the year 72% of the time, 15.7% to 7.1%, on average.

Investing in a top 10 industries portfolio only when the January S&P is up increases the average portfolio gain to 22.0% for the last 11 months of the year vs. 13.0% for the S&P. The best gain after a down January was 37.2% in turnaround year 1982, in the middle of the second year of a bear market. More information about the S&P 500 industries can be found at *www.spglobal.com*.

AS JANUARY GOES, SO GOES THE YEAR FOR TOP PERFORMING INDUSTRIES
January's Top 10 Industries vs. S&P 500 Next 11 Months

	11 Month % Change		S&P Jan	After S&P Up in January		After S&P Down in January	
	Portfolio	S&P	%	Portfolio	S&P	Portfolio	S&P
1970	− 4.7	− 0.3	− 7.6			− 4.7	− 0.3
1971	23.5	6.1	4.0	23.5	6.1		
1972	19.7	13.7	1.8	19.7	13.7		
1973	5.2	− 20.0	− 1.7			5.2	− 20.0
1974	− 29.2	− 30.2	− 1.0			− 29.2	− 30.2
1975	57.3	22.2	12.3	57.3	22.2		
1976	16.3	8.1	11.8	16.3	8.1		
1977	− 9.1	− 9.6	− 5.1			− 9.1	− 9.6
1978	7.3	6.5	− 6.2			7.3	6.5
1979	21.7	8.1	4.0	21.7	8.1		
1980	38.3	20.4	5.8	38.3	20.4		
1981	5.0	− 6.9	− 4.6			5.0	− 6.9
1982	37.2	18.8	− 1.8			37.2	18.8
1983	17.2	13.9	3.3	17.2	13.9		
1984	− 5.0	− 1.1	− 0.9			− 5.0	− 1.1
1985	28.2	20.8	7.4	28.2	20.8		
1986	18.1	19.4	0.2	18.1	19.4		
1987	− 1.5	− 8.9	13.2	− 1.5	− 8.9		
1988	18.4	10.4	4.0	18.4	10.4		
1989	16.1	22.1	7.1	16.1	22.1		
1990	− 4.4	− 3.3	− 6.9			− 4.4	− 3.3
1991	35.7	19.4	4.2	35.7	19.4		
1992	14.6	4.7	− 2.0			14.6	4.7
1993	23.7	7.2	0.7	23.7	7.2		
1994	− 7.1	− 4.6	3.3	− 7.1	− 4.6		
1995	25.6	30.9	2.4	25.6	30.9		
1996	5.4	16.5	3.3	5.4	16.5		
1997	4.7	23.4	6.1	4.7	23.4		
1998	45.2	25.4	1.0	45.2	25.4		
1999	67.9	14.8	4.1	67.9	14.8		
2000	23.6	− 5.3	− 5.1			23.6	− 5.3
2001	− 13.1	− 16.0	3.5	− 13.1	− 16.0		
2002			− 1.6				
Averages	**15.7%**	**7.1%**		**22.0%**	**13.0%**	**3.7%**	**− 4.2%**

FEBRUARY

*"Best Three-Month Span" normally ends here
(pages 48, 56, 138 and 139)*

MONDAY

3

*Individualism, private property, the law of accumulation of wealth
and the law of competition…are the highest result of human
experience, the soil in which, so far, has produced the best fruit.*
— Andrew Carnegie (Scottish-born US industrialist,
philanthropist, The Gospel Of Wealth, 1835-1919)

TUESDAY

4

*It is not how right or how wrong you are that matters,
but how much money you make when right and
how much you do not lose when wrong.*
— George Soros

WEDNESDAY

5

The monuments of wit survive the monuments of power.
— Francis Bacon (English philosopher, essayist,
statesman, 1561-1626)

THURSDAY

6

*Keep me away from the wisdom which does not cry, the philosophy which
does not laugh and the greatness which does not bow before children.*
— Kahlil Gibran (Lebanese-born American mystic,
poet and artist, 1883-1931)

FRIDAY

7

*You're perhaps the most accomplished confidence man since
Charles Ponzi. I'd say you were a carnival barker, except that
wouldn't be fair to carnival barkers. A carnie will at least tell
you up front that he's running a shell game.*
—Senator Peter G. Fitzgerald (In comments to Kenneth L. Lay,
former chairman of Enron, February 13, 2002)

SATURDAY

8

SUNDAY

9

1933 "LAME DUCK" AMENDMENT REASON JANUARY BAROMETER WORKS

Between 1901 and 1933 the market's direction in January was similar to that of the whole year 19 times and different 14 times. Comparing January to the 11 subsequent months, 16 were similar and 17 dissimilar.

A dramatic change occurred in 1934—the Twentieth Amendment to the Constitution! Since then it has essentially been "As January goes, so goes the year." January's direction has correctly forecasted the major trend for the market in most of the subsequent years.

Prior to 1934, newly elected Senators and Representatives did not take office until December of the following year, 13 months later (except when new Presidents were inaugurated). Defeated Congressmen stayed in Congress for all of the following session. They were known as "lame ducks."

Since the Twentieth (Lame Duck) Amendment was ratified in 1933, Congress convenes January 3 and includes those members newly elected the previous November. Inauguration Day was also moved up from March 4 to January 20. As a result several events have been squeezed into January which affect our economy and our stock market and quite possibly those of many nations of the world. During January, Congress convenes, the President gives the State of the Union message, presents the annual budget and sets national goals and priorities. Switch these events to any other month and chances are the January Barometer would become a memory.

The table shows the January Barometer in odd years. In 1935 and 1937, the Democrats already had the most lopsided congressional margins in history, so when these two Congresses convened it was anticlimactic. **The January Barometer in all subsequent odd-numbered years had compiled a perfect record until 2001 with the rare two interest rate cuts that pushed January up and the 9/11 attack that drove the market sharply lower.**

JANUARY BAROMETER (ODD YEARS)

January % Change	12 Month % Change	Same	Opposite
− 4.2%	41.2%		1935
3.8	− 38.6		1937
− 6.9	− 5.4	1939	
− 4.8	− 17.9	1941	
7.2	19.4	1943	
1.4	30.7	1945	
2.4	N/C	1947	
0.1	10.3	1949	
6.1	16.5	1951	
− 0.7	− 6.6	1953	
1.8	26.4	1955	
− 4.2	− 14.3	1957	
0.4	8.5	1959	
6.3	23.1	1961	
4.9	18.9	1963	
3.3	9.1	1965	
7.8	20.1	1967	
− 0.8	− 11.4	1969	
4.0	10.8	1971	
− 1.7	− 17.4	1973	
12.3	31.5	1975	
− 5.1	− 11.5	1977	
4.0	12.3	1979	
− 4.6	− 9.7	1981	
3.3	17.3	1983	
7.4	26.3	1985	
13.2	2.0	1987	
7.1	27.3	1989	
4.1	26.3	1991	
0.7	7.1	1993	
2.4	34.1	1995	
6.1	31.0	1997	
4.1	19.5	1999	
3.5	− 13.0		2001

12 month's % change includes January's % change
Based on S&P 500

FEBRUARY

MONDAY 10

Bill Gates' One-Minus Staffing: *For every project, figure out the bare minimum of people needed to staff it. Cut to the absolute muscle and bones, then take out one more. When you understaff, people jump on the loose ball. You find out who the real performers are. Not so when you're overstaffed. People sit around waiting for somebody else to do it.*
— Quoted by Rich Karlgaard (Publisher, *Forbes* Dec. 25, 2000)

TUESDAY 11

The whole secret to our success is being able to con ourselves into believing that we're going to change the world [even though] we are unlikely to do it.
— Tom Peters (*Fortune*, Nov. 13, 2000)

Two days before more bullish than Valentine's Day
Ah, anticipation

WEDNESDAY 12

I don't think education has a lot to do with the number of years you're incarcerated in a brick building being talked down to.
— Tom Peters (*Fortune*, Nov. 13, 2000)

THURSDAY 13

You get stepped on, passed over, knocked down, but you have to come back.
— 90-year old Walter Watson (MD, *Fortune*, Nov. 13, 2000)

Valentine's Day

Eleven dogs in a row before Presidents Day weekend

FRIDAY 14

When you loved me I gave you the whole sun and stars to play with. I gave you eternity in a single moment, strength of the mountains in one clasp of your arms, and the volume of all the seas in one impulse of your soul.
— George Bernard Shaw (Irish dramatist, *Getting Married*, 1856-1950)

SATURDAY 15

SUNDAY 16

THE THIRD YEAR OF DECADES

Graphic presentation reveals that "third" years have a mixed record. But since the market rose from the ashes in 1933, only 1973—in the wake of Watergate, Vietnam, Mideast Turmoil and an Oil Embargo—posted a substantial loss. Third years that precede election years have fared rather well making 2003's prospects optimistic.

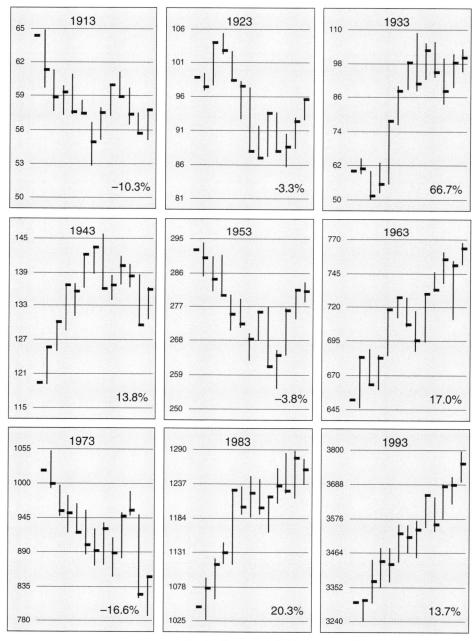

Based on Dow Jones industrial average monthly ranges and closing prices

FEBRUARY

MONDAY

Presidents' Day
(Market Closed)

Vietnam, the original domino in the Cold War, now faces the prospect of becoming, in the words of political scientist Sunai Phasuk of Chulalongkorn University in Bangkok, one of the new "dominos of democracy."
— Quoted by Seth Mydans (*NY Times*, Jan. 6, 2001)

TUESDAY

First Trading Day of Expiration Week Dow up 9 straight
Day after Presidents Day Dow Up 6 of last 9

An autobiography must be such that one can sue oneself for libel.
— Thomas Hoving (Museum Director)

WEDNESDAY

Always grab the reader by the throat in the first paragraph, sink your thumbs into his windpipe in the second, and hold him against the wall until the tag line.
— Paul O'Neil (Marketer, *Writing Changes Everything*)

THURSDAY

Liberal democracies do not fight wars with one another because they see the same human nature and the same rights applicable everywhere and to everyone. Cultures fight wars with one another. Cultures have different perceptions, which determine what the world is. They cannot come to terms.
— Allan Bloom (*The Closing of the American Mind*, 1987)

FRIDAY

If you want to raise a crop for one year, plant corn.
If you want to raise a crop for decades, plant trees.
If you want to raise a crop for centuries, raise men.
If you want to plant a crop for eternities, raise democracies.
— Carl A. Schenk

SATURDAY

SUNDAY
23

MARCH ALMANAC

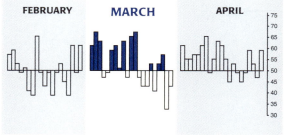

Market Probability Chart above is a graphic representation of the Market Probability Calendar on page 122.

◆ See "In like a lion, out like a lamb" tendency above: surges early in month, then fades towards end—2002 top on 19th perfect example ◆ Three record Dow point gains in a row, a big loss in 2001, then strong in 2002 ◆ RECORD: S&P 35 up, 18 down ◆ Average S&P gain 1.1%, fifth best ◆ March has been taking some mean end-of-quarter hits—revealed below, down 1469 Dow points in ten trading days March 2001 ◆ Last three or four days a net loser nine out of last ten years ◆ NASDAQ hard hit in 2001, down 14.5% after 22.4% drop in February ◆ Market much luckier the day before St. Patrick's Day.

MARCH DAILY POINT CHANGES DOW JONES INDUSTRIALS

Previous Month Close	1993 3370.81	1994 3832.02	1995 4011.05	1996 5485.62	1997 6877.74	1998 8545.72	1999 9306.58	2000 10128.31	2001 10495.28	2002 10106.13
1	−15.40	−22.79	−16.25	50.94	—	—	18.20	9.62	−45.14	262.73
2	45.12	22.51	−14.87	—	—	4.73	−27.17	26.99	16.17	—
3	3.51	−7.32	9.68	—	41.18	34.38	−21.73	202.28	—	—
4	−5.13	7.88	—	63.59	−66.20	−45.59	191.52	—	—	217.96
5	5.67	—	—	42.27	93.13	−94.91	268.68	—	95.99	−153.41
6	—	—	7.95	−12.65	−1.15	125.06	—	−196.70	28.92	140.88
7	—	23.92	−34.93	11.92	56.19	—	—	−374.47	138.38	−48.92
8	64.84	−4.50	16.60	−171.24	—	—	−8.47	60.50	128.65	47.12
9	2.70	1.69	4.16	—	—	−2.25	−33.85	154.20	−213.63	—
10	6.22	−22.79	52.22	—	78.50	75.98	79.08	−81.91	—	—
11	−21.34	32.08	—	110.55	5.77	32.63	124.60	—	—	38.75
12	−29.18	—	—	2.89	−45.79	−16.19	−21.09	—	−436.37	21.11
13	—	—	−10.38	−15.17	−160.48	−57.04	—	18.31	82.54	−130.50
14	—	0.28	23.52	17.34	56.57	—	—	−135.89	−317.34	15.29
15	14.59	−13.39	−10.38	−1.09	—	—	82.42	320.17	57.83	90.09
16	0.54	−1.44	30.78	—	—	116.33	−28.30	499.19	−207.87	—
17	−16.21	16.99	4.50	—	20.02	31.14	−51.06	−35.37	—	—
18	38.90	30.51	—	98.63	−58.92	25.41	118.21	—	—	−29.48
19	5.94	—	—	−14.09	−18.88	27.65	−94.07	—	135.70	57.50
20	—	—	10.03	−14.09	−57.40	103.38	—	85.01	−238.35	−133.68
21	—	−30.80	−11.07	−28.54	−15.49	—	—	227.10	−233.76	−21.73
22	−8.10	−2.30	10.38	9.76	—	—	−13.04	−40.64	−97.52	−52.17
23	−1.62	6.91	4.84	—	—	−90.18	−218.68	253.16	115.30	—
24	−16.48	−48.37	50.84	—	100.46	88.19	−4.99	−7.14	—	—
25	15.94	−46.36	—	7.22	−29.08	−31.64	169.55	—	—	−146.00
26	−21.34	—	—	26.74	4.53	−25.91	−14.15	—	182.75	71.69
27	—	—	18.67	−43.72	−140.11	−50.81	—	−86.87	260.01	73.55
28	—	−12.38	−5.53	3.97	H	—	—	−89.74	−162.19	−22.97
29	15.12	−63.33	8.99	−43.71	—	—	184.54	82.61	13.71	H
30	2.17	−72.27	11.76	—	—	−13.96	−93.52	−38.47	79.72	—
31	−22.16	9.21	−14.87	—	−157.11	17.69	−127.10	−58.33	—	—
Close	3435.11	3635.96	4157.69	5587.14	6583.48	8799.81	9786.16	10921.92	9878.78	10403.94
Change	64.30	−196.06	146.64	101.52	−294.26	254.09	479.58	793.61	−616.50	297.81

March has Ides and St. Patrick's Day
Begins bullishly, then fades away

FEBRUARY/MARCH

MONDAY 24

If you create an act, you create a habit.
If you create a habit, you create a character.
If you create a character, you create a destiny.
— André Maurois (Novelist, biographer, essayist, 1885-1967)

TUESDAY 25

No horse gets anywhere until he is harnessed. No steam or gas ever drives anything until it is confined. No Niagara is ever turned into light and power until it is tunneled. No life ever grows great until it is focused, dedicated, disciplined.
— Harry Emerson Fosdick (Protestant minister, author, 1878-1969)

WEDNESDAY **26**

With globalization, the big [countries] don't eat the small, the fast eat the slow.
— Thomas L. Friedman
(Op-ed columnist, referring to the Arab nations, *New York Times*)

THURSDAY 27

The advice of the elders to young men is very apt to be as unreal as a list of the best books.
— Oliver Wendell Holmes Jr.
(*The Mind and Faith of Justice Holmes,* edited by Max Lerner)

FRIDAY **28**

What is it that attracts me to the young? When I am with mature people I feel their rigidities, their tight crystallizations. They have become...like the statues of the famous. Achieved. Final.
— Anaïs Nin (*The Diaries of Anaïs Nin, Vol. IV*)

SATURDAY 1

March Sector Seasonalities: Bullish: XAL, FPP XOI; Bearish: BTK (page 118)

SUNDAY 2

MARKET CHARTS OF PRE-PRESIDENTIAL ELECTION YEARS

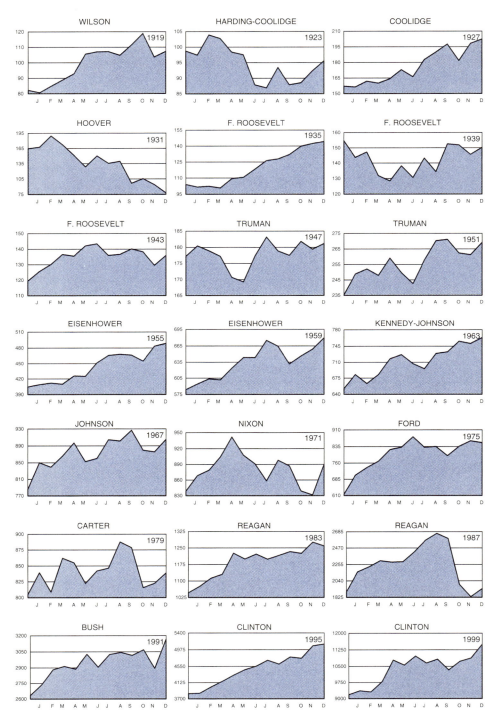

Based on Dow Jones industial average monthly closing prices

MARCH

March first trading day Dow up 6 of last 7

MONDAY

3

> *Every age has a blind eye and sees nothing wrong in practices and institutions, which its successors view with just horror.*
> — Sir Richard Livingston (*On Education*)

TUESDAY

4

> *The only way to even begin to manage this new world is by focusing on…nation building—helping others restructure their economies and put in place decent non-corrupt government.*
> — Thomas L. Friedman (*New York Times*)

Ash Wednesday **WEDNESDAY**

5

> *To an imagination of any scope the most far-reaching form of power is not money, it is the command of ideas.*
> — Oliver Wendell Holmes Jr.
> (*The Mind and Faith of Justice Holmes,* edited by Max Lerner)

THURSDAY

6

> *Six major points of* In Search Of Excellence: *Action beats talk! People Matter! Customers are why we exist! Vision and Values are more important than policy manuals! Keep the structure very simple and radically decentralized! Nurture entrepreneurial spirit, even in the biggest of companies!*
> — Tom Peters

FRIDAY

7

> *The common denominator: Something that matters! Something that counts! Something that defines! Something that is imbued with soul. And with life!*
> — Tom Peters (referring to projects, *Reinventing Work*, 1999)

SATURDAY

8

SUNDAY

9

PROFIT ON DAY BEFORE ST. PATRICK'S DAY

Days before major legal holidays tend to be bullish. Dan Turov, editor of *Turov On Timing*, also tracks the seasonality around St. Patrick's Day. Results appear below.

Note the stellar performance of the market on the day before St. Patrick's Day. It outperforms the days before many legal holidays. The average gain of 0.33% on the S&P is equivalent to more than 30 Dow points (at current levels for the Dow). That's equal to an annualized rate of return of over 100%. Irish luck, or coincidence?

In 2003 St. Patrick's Day falls on Monday. Therefore, Friday, March 14th could provide you with an added edge to make a little extra profit. During the past 49 years St. Patrick's Day itself has posted just a wee gain of 0.05%. But, Monday before Triple-Witching Day has been up 8 of the last 10 times on the Dow. So, if we are lucky, St. Pat's could turn into Triple-Leprechaun Day in 2003.

ST. PATRICK'S DAY TRADING RECORD (DAYS BEFORE AND AFTER)

Year	St. Pat's Day	% Change 2 Days Prior	% Change 1 Day Prior	S&P 500 St. Pat's Day or Next *	% Change St. Patrick's Day *	% Change Day After
1953	Tue	0.19%	0.15%	26.33	0.42%	−0.34%
1954	Wed	−0.45	−0.04	26.62	0.23	0.41
1955	Thu	2.15	0.76	36.12	0.39	0.17
1956	Sat	0.97	0.31	48.59	0.93	0.58
1957	Sun	0.07	−0.05	43.85	−0.45	0.43
1958	Mon	0.12	−0.31	42.04	−0.69	−0.36
1959	Tue	0.12	−1.08	56.52	0.82	−0.23
1960	Thu	0.77	0.55	54.96	−0.15	0.09
1961	Fri	0.30	1.01	64.60	0.61	0.40
1962	Sat	0.21	−0.17	70.85	−0.13	−0.27
1963	Sun	−0.47	0.50	65.61	−0.49	−0.21
1964	Tue	0.08	0.00	79.32	0.23	0.08
1965	Wed	0.03	−0.13	87.02	−0.13	−0.24
1966	Thu	−0.57	0.58	88.17	0.35	0.41
1967	Fri	0.95	1.01	90.25	0.18	−0.06
1968	Sun	−1.90	0.88	89.59	0.55	−0.67
1969	Mon	−0.67	−0.40	98.25	0.26	0.24
1970	Tue	−0.53	−1.08	87.29	0.44	0.29
1971	Wed	1.14	0.50	101.12	−0.09	0.07
1972	Fri	0.13	−0.23	107.92	0.39	−0.31
1973	Sat	−0.75	−0.51	112.17	−1.21	−0.20
1974	Sun	−0.09	−0.37	98.05	−1.24	−0.84
1975	Mon	0.18	1.22	86.01	1.47	−1.02
1976	Wed	−1.05	1.12	100.86	−0.06	−0.41
1977	Thu	0.55	0.19	102.08	−0.09	−0.22
1978	Fri	−0.26	0.44	90.20	0.77	0.69
1979	Sat	0.15	0.83	101.06	0.37	−0.55
1980	Mon	−1.17	−0.18	102.26	−3.01	1.80
1981	Tue	−0.06	1.18	133.92	−0.56	0.22
1982	Wed	0.77	−0.16	109.08	−0.18	1.12
1983	Thu	0.35	−1.03	149.59	−0.14	0.21
1984	Sat	0.41	1.18	157.78	−0.94	0.68
1985	Sun	−0.20	−0.74	176.88	0.20	1.50
1986	Mon	0.28	1.44	234.67	−0.79	0.47
1987	Tue	−0.46	−0.57	292.47	1.47	0.11
1988	Thu	−0.09	0.95	271.22	0.96	−0.04
1989	Fri	0.52	0.93	292.69	−2.25	−0.95
1990	Sat	0.36	1.14	343.53	0.47	−0.57
1991	Sun	−0.29	0.02	372.11	−0.40	−1.48
1992	Tue	0.48	0.14	409.58	0.78	−0.10
1993	Wed	0.36	−0.01	448.31	−0.68	0.80
1994	Thu	−0.08	0.52	470.89	0.31	0.04
1995	Fri	−0.20	0.72	495.52	0.02	0.13
1996	Sun	0.37	0.09	652.65	1.75	−0.15
1997	Mon	−1.83	0.46	795.71	0.32	−0.76
1998	Tue	−0.13	1.00	1080.45	0.11	0.47
1999	Wed	0.98	−0.07	1297.82	−0.65	1.44
2000	Fri	2.43	4.76	1464.47	0.41	−0.54
2001	Sat	0.59	−1.96	1170.81	1.76	−2.41
2002	Sun	−0.09	1.14	1165.55	−0.05	−0.41
Average		**0.09%**	**0.33%**		**0.05%**	**0.01%**

*When St. Patrick's Day falls on Saturday or Sunday the following trading day is used. Based on S&P 500

MARCH

MONDAY

10

One of the more prolonged and extreme periods favoring large-cap stocks was 1994-1999. The tide turned in 2000. A cycle has begun of investors favoring small-cap stocks, which is likely to continue through the next several years.
— Jim Oberweis (*The Oberweis Report*, February 2001)

TUESDAY
11

*Life is like riding a bicycle.
You don't fall off unless you stop peddling.*
— Claude D. Pepper
(1900-1989, U.S. Senator 1937-1950, U.S. House 1963-1989)

WEDNESDAY
12

We are handicapped by policies based on old myths rather than current realities.
— James William Fulbright (1905-1995, U.S. Senator 1944-1974)

THURSDAY

13

Every great advance in natural knowledge has involved the absolute rejection of authority.
— Thomas H. Huxley (British scientist and humanist, defender of Darwinism, 1825-1895)

FRIDAY

14

Market much luckier day before St. Patrick's Day (page 32)

The difference between life and the movies is that a script has to make sense, and life doesn't.
— Joseph L. Mankiewicz (Film director, writer, producer, 1909-1993)

SATURDAY
15

SUNDAY
16

HUBRIS: PRIDE GOETH BEFORE A FALL (IN PRICE)

"Pride goeth before destruction, and an haughty spirit before a fall."
— Proverbs 16:18

Hubris—excessive pride or self-confidence, arrogance—is one of the oldest themes in literature. Heroes of classical Greek tragedies typically become imbued with hubris. Then the gods cut down those individuals who imagine themselves their equal.

These days, divine intervention is not needed—*the market* punishes hubris. In fact, excessive pride and confidence often serve as excellent warning signs of market busts ahead.

One would expect successful companies serving large numbers of customers, depending on the support of shareholders, to act with some restraint. But when they build fancy skyscrapers, have their names put on stadiums, or their top people make outrageous statements, astute shortsellers' mouths water, sensing the best days of these companies may be over.

General Motors, CBS, IBM, and AT&T all erected landmark skyscrapers in Manhattan as their power and profitability were cresting. One of the 100 tallest buildings in the world is named for one such company. Note the poor performance of The Monument Builders. Prices are as of the last trading day of the year that building was completed.

The Monument Builders	Company	Dow
Average 1 year Performance	− 5.7%	3.3%
Average 2 year Performance	− 1.2%	18.3%
Average 3 year Performance	8.2%	30.3%

Courtesy Victor Niederhoffer & Patrick Boyle,
Inspired by William J. Mitchell, Scientific American, Dec. 1997

Investors and money managers also exhibit their share of hubris. They drive up prices, throw P/E ratios out the window, ignore basic valuation principles and tout the "new economy," all of which contributes to a false euphoria. They fail to realize, " 'We're No.1' usually means 'not much longer.' Call it the 'executive boast' indicator. When company leaders pause to say they're at the top of their industry they're about to get passed by the competition." (Victor Niederhoffer and Laurel Kenner in *MSN Money*.) Here is what happened to some of their examples:

- "From the World's leading Energy Company... To the World's leading company!" (Enron, down 98%)
- "Priceline will reinvent the environmental DNA of global business." (Down 92%)
- "We're the best wireless phone service available." (Sprint, down 71%)
- "Gateway's goal is to become No. 1 on the Web, not because we are the biggest, but because we are the best." (Down 80%)

By contrast, we recall Microsoft president Steve Ballmer telling us a couple of years ago that tech stocks, including Microsoft, were overvalued. (They were.) Bill Gates has said that he expects economic and technical developments to continually challenge Microsoft's viability in years to come.

Intel co-founder and chairman Andrew Grove is famous for running scared, calling one of his books *Only the Paranoid Survive*. It's no coincidence that these companies are among the most successful. Their lack of excessive confidence makes us pretty sure that these two companies will indeed survive.

Look for managements who are building a business, not a monument. And look for determination and a bit of humility in their comments rather than hubris.

MARCH

MONDAY 17
St. Patrick's Day
Six of last Seven Mondays before Triple Witching were up

Innovation can't depend on trying to please the customer or the client. It is an elitist act by the inventor who acts alone and breaks rules.
— Dean Kamen (Inventor, President of DEKA R&D, *Business Week*, Feb. 12, 2001)

TUESDAY 18
FOMC Meeting

There is nothing as invigorating as the ego boost that comes from having others sign on when your company is just a dream. What they are saying when they agree to service customers, suppliers, employers or distributors is that they believe in you.
— Joshua Hyatt (*Inc. Magazine, Mapping the Entrepreneurial Mind*, August 1991)

WEDNESDAY 19

You have powers you never dreamed of. You can do things you never thought you could do. There are no limitations in what you can do except the limitations in your own mind.
— Darwin P. Kingsley (President New York Life, 1857-1932)

THURSDAY 20

We are like tenant farmers chopping down the fence around our house for fuel when we should be using Nature's inexhaustible sources of energy—sun, wind and tide. I'd put my money on the sun and solar energy. What a source of power! I hope we don't have to wait until oil and coal run out before we tackle that.
— Thomas Alva Edison (1847-1931)

FRIDAY 21
Triple Witching Day
down 5 of last 7

Awareness of competition and ability to react to it is a fundamental competence every business must have if it is to be long lived.
— Paul Allen (Microsoft co-founder)

SATURDAY 22

SUNDAY 23

EIGHT DAYS A MONTHS NOW OUTPERFORM REST OF MONTH EIGHT TO ONE

Years ago we demonstrated that the first halves of all months outperform the second halves about two to one. Since the greatest gains come at the ends, beginnings and now middles of months (see pages 88, 92, 136 & 137), we divided the months into different segments.

Percent changes in the S&P 500 for the last three trading days of the previous month through the second trading day of the next, plus the middle three trading days (nine through eleven) are compared with rest of the month versus the first half compared to the second half.

The 40-year time span is separated into two periods as the Dow basically traded between 500 and 1000 from 1962-1981 whereas 1982 to 2001 witnessed the Dow's meteoric 10,000+ point rise and the flood of regular mid-month 401(k) cash inflows. The shift in patterns is rather dramatic.

During the first 20 years first halves of months averaged 0.6% gain while second halves posted a loss. Since 1982 first halves and second halves now run neck and neck with second halves ahead by a nose. But, the top eight days of the month beat the rest by a better than an eight to one margin! This paradigm pattern shift is difficult to ignore.

FIRST & SECOND HALF OF MONTH VS. BEST EIGHT DAYS

1962-1981	Prime 5 Days	Super 3 Days	P5+S3 Days	Rest of Month	1st Half of Month	2nd Half of Month
Jan	0.9%	0.4%	1.3%	0.4%	0.8%	0.7%
Feb	0.02	−0.2	−0.2	−0.2	0.2	−0.7
Mar	0.3	0.04	0.4	0.05	1.0	−0.1
Apr	0.1	0.3	0.4	0.8	0.9	0.01
May	0.1	−0.2	−0.03	−1.2	−0.2	−1.3
Jun	0.3	−0.2	0.1	−0.01	0.7	−1.0
Jul	0.1	0.3	0.4	0.01	0.8	−0.4
Aug	−0.04	0.2	0.2	−0.6	0.5	−0.7
Sep	0.5	0.03	0.5	−0.01	0.5	−0.4
Oct	−0.4	−0.04	−0.4	0.2	1.1	−0.4
Nov	0.5	−0.3	0.2	0.6	1.0	0.1
Dec	0.5	−0.2	0.2	0.9	−0.05	0.8
Total	2.9%	0.2%	3.1%	1.0%	7.2%	−3.5%
Avg	0.24%	0.01%	0.26%	0.08%	0.60%	−0.29%

1982-2001	Prime 5 Days	Super 3 Days	P5+S3 Days	Rest of Month	1st Half of Month	2nd Half of Month
Jan	0.8%	0.9%	1.7%	−0.3%	−0.2%	1.8%
Feb	1.5	0.4	1.9	−0.8	1.1	−0.1
Mar	0.6	0.2	0.8	1.0	0.6	0.5
Apr	−0.3	0.1	−0.2	1.8	0.6	0.9
May	0.6	0.1	0.7	0.04	0.7	0.5
Jun	1.0	0.2	1.2	−0.4	0.5	0.7
Jul	0.9	0.4	1.3	−0.6	0.6	−0.2
Aug	0.3	0.2	0.5	0.8	−0.05	0.7
Sep	−0.7	0.1	−0.6	−1.5	−0.6	−0.2
Oct	0.4	0.4	0.9	−1.1	0.4	−0.1
Nov	1.9	0.2	2.1	0.4	1.4	0.6
Dec	0.3	−0.4	−0.1	1.9	0.7	1.6
Total	7.2%	2.8%	10.0%	1.3%	5.7%	6.7%
Avg	0.60%	0.23%	0.84%	0.11%	0.48%	0.56%

Based on S&P 500
Prime 5 – Last 3 of previous month + first 2 of next month; Super 3 – 9th, 10th, and 11th trading days

MARCH

End of March terrible lately

MONDAY
24

*If you are not willing to study, if you are not sufficiently interested
to investigate and analyze the stock market yourself
then I beg of you to become an outright long-pull investor,
to buy good stocks, and hold on to them; for otherwise your
chances of success as a trader will be nil.*
— Humphey B. Neill (*Tape Reading and Market Tactics*, 1931)

TUESDAY
25

*One determined person can make a significant difference; a small
group of determined people can change the course of history.*
— Sonia Johnson (author, lecturer)

WEDNESDAY
26

Genius is the ability to put into effect what is in your mind.
— F. Scott Fitzgerald (author, 1896-1940)

THURSDAY
27

The years teach much which the days never know.
— Ralph Waldo Emerson

FRIDAY
28

To know values is to know the meaning of the market.
— Charles Dow

SATURDAY
29

*April Sector Seasonalities: Bullish: UTY
(page 118)*

SUNDAY
30

APRIL ALMANAC

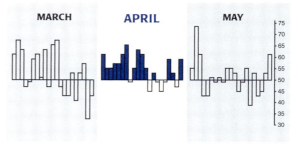

Market Probability Chart above is a graphic representation of the Market Probability Calendar on page 122.

◆ April has been the best Dow month (average 1.8%) since 1950 (page 48) ◆ April 1999 first month ever to gain 1000 Dow points, 856 in 2001, knocked off its high horse in 2002 down 458 ◆ First half of month still tends to do better than second half despite April 15th tax day ◆ Stocks anticipate great first quarter earnings by rising sharply before earnings are reported, rather than after ◆ Rarely a dangerous month except in big bear markets (like 2002) ◆ "Best six months" of the year end with April (page 50)

APRIL DAILY POINT CHANGES DOW JONES INDUSTRIALS

Previous Month Close	1993	1994	1995	1996	1997	1998	1999	2000	2001	2002
	3435.11	3635.96	4157.69	5587.14	6583.48	8799.81	9786.16	10921.92	9878.78	10403.94
1	4.33	H	—	50.58	27.57	68.51	46.35	—	—	– 41.24
2	– 68.63	—	—	33.96	– 94.04	118.32	H	—	– 100.85	– 48.99
3	—	—	10.72	18.06	– 39.66	– 3.23	—	300.01	– 292.22	– 115.42
4	—	– 42.61	33.20	– 6.86	48.72	—	—	– 57.09	29.71	36.88
5	8.38	82.06	– 1.04	H	—	—	174.82	– 130.92	402.63	36.47
6	– 1.62	4.32	4.84	—	—	49.82	– 43.84	80.35	– 126.96	—
7	19.45	13.53	– 12.79	—	29.84	– 76.73	121.82	– 2.79	—	—
8	– 0.54	– 19.00	—	– 88.51	53.25	– 65.02	112.39	—	—	– 22.56
9	H	—	—	– 33.96	– 45.32	103.38	– 23.86	—	54.06	– 40.41
10	—	—	5.53	– 74.43	– 23.79	H	—	75.08	257.59	173.06
11	—	14.57	– 11.07	1.09	–148.36	—	—	100.52	– 89.27	– 205.65
12	31.61	– 7.14	10.73	45.52	—	—	165.67	– 161.95	113.47	14.74
13	15.94	– 20.22	10.37	—	—	17.44	55.50	– 201.58	H	—
14	11.61	1.78	H	—	60.21	97.90	16.65	– 617.78	—	—
15	0.28	– 1.78	—	60.33	135.26	52.07	51.06	—	—	– 97.15
16	22.69	—	—	27.10	92.71	– 85.70	31.17	—	31.62	207.65
17	—	—	– 12.80	– 70.09	– 21.27	90.93	—	276.74	58.17	– 80.54
18	—	– 41.05	– 16.25	1.81	44.95	—	—	184.91	399.10	– 15.50
19	– 11.62	– 0.60	28.36	– 16.26	—	—	– 53.36	– 92.46	77.88	51.83
20	– 23.50	– 21.11	23.17	—	—	– 25.66	8.02	169.09	– 113.86	—
21	– 4.05	53.83	39.43	—	– 43.34	43.10	132.87	H	—	—
22	– 10.27	– 3.86	—	29.26	173.38	– 8.22	145.76	—	—	– 120.68
23	– 15.40	—	—	23.85	– 20.87	– 33.39	– 37.51	—	– 47.62	47.19
24	—	—	33.89	– 34.69	– 20.47	– 78.71	—	62.05	– 77.89	– 58.81
25	—	57.10	– 3.81	13.01	– 53.38	—	—	218.72	170.86	4.63
26	– 15.40	– 6.24	– 0.34	1.08	—	—	28.92	– 179.32	67.15	– 124.34
27	17.56	H*	14.87	—	—	–146.98	113.12	– 57.40	117.70	—
28	– 2.43	– 31.23	6.57	—	44.15	– 18.68	13.74	– 154.19	—	—
29	11.62	13.38	—	5.42	179.01	52.56	32.93	—	—	– 90.85
30	2.43	—	—	– 4.33	46.96	111.85	– 89.34	—	– 75.08	126.35
Close	3427.55	3681.69	4321.27	5569.08	7008.99	9063.37	10789.04	10733.91	10734.97	9946.22
Change	– 7.56	45.73	163.58	– 18.06	425.51	263.56	1002.88	– 188.01	856.19	– 457.72

*Nixon Memorial

April "Best Month" for Dow since 1950
Day-before-Good Friday gains are nifty

MARCH/APRIL

MONDAY
31

*I keep hearing "Should I buy? Should I buy?"
When I start hearing "Should I sell?" that's the bottom.*
— Nick Moore (portfolio manager, Jurika & Voyles,
TheStreet.com Mar. 12, 2001)

April first trading day Dow up 6 of last 8

TUESDAY
1

*If you can ever buy with a P/E equivalent to growth,
that's a good starting point.*
— Alan Lowenstein (co-portfolio manager, John Hancock
Technology Fund, *TheStreet.com*, Mar. 12, 2001)

WEDNESDAY
2

*What technology does is make people more productive.
It doesn't replace them.*
— Michael Bloomberg

THURSDAY
3

*Corporate guidance has become something of an art. The CFO
has refined and perfected his art, gracefully leading on the bulls
with the calculating grace and cunning of a great matador.*
— Joe Kalinowski (I/B/E/S)

FRIDAY
4

*If a man has no talents, he is unhappy enough; but if he has, envy
pursues him in proportion to his ability.*
— Leopold Mozart (to his son Wolfgang Amadeus, 1768)

SATURDAY
5

Daylight Savings Time begins

SUNDAY
6

ADD THE DECEMBER LOW INDICATOR TO YOUR PROGNOSTICATING ARSENAL

Jeffrey Saut, chief equity strategist at Raymond James, recently brought a forgotten but very interesting indicator to our attention. The original analysis is credited to Lucien Hooper, a *Forbes* columnist and Wall Street analyst back in the 70's. Hooper dismissed the importance of January and January's first week as reliable indicators. He noted that the trend could be random or even manipulated during a holiday-shortened week. Instead, said Hooper, "pay much more attention to the December low. If that low is violated during the first quarter of the New Year, watch out!"

The December Low Indicator is compared here to the January Barometer in years when the Dow closed below its previous December's closing low in the first quarter. Since 1950, though Hooper's indicator was wrong 11 of the 24 times on a full-year basis, he was absolutely correct in his "Watch Out" warning, as the Dow fell an additional 10.7% on average when December's low was breached in Q1. Only three significant drops occurred (not shown) when December's low was not breached in Q1 (1974, 1981 and 1987) and both indicators were wrong only four times. If we do not cross the December low, turn to our January Barometer for guidance. It has been virtually perfect, right nearly 100% of these times. (Email *service@hirschorg.com* for a copy of the complete results that appeared in our February 2002 *Almanac Investor* newsletter.)

YEARS THE DOW FELL BELOW ITS DECEMBER LOW IN THE FIRST QUARTER

Year	Previous Dec Low	Crossing Price	Date Crossed	Subseq. Low	% Change Cross-Low	Rest of Year % Change	Full Year % Change	Jan Bar
1952	262.29	261.37	2/19/52	256.35	— 1.9%	11.7%	8.4%	1.6%[2]
1953	281.63	281.57	2/11/53	255.49	— 9.3	— 0.2	— 3.8	— 0.7
1956	480.72	479.74	1/9/56	462.35	— 3.6	4.1	2.3	— 3.6 [1,2]
1957	480.61	477.46	1/18/57	419.79	— 12.1	— 8.7	— 12.8	— 4.2
1960	661.29	660.43	1/12/60	566.05	— 14.3	— 6.7	— 9.3	— 7.1
1962	720.10	714.84	1/5/62	535.76	— 25.1	— 8.8	— 10.8	— 3.8
1966	939.53	938.19	3/1/66	744.32	— 20.7	— 16.3	— 18.9	0.5 [1]
1968	879.16	871.71	1/22/68	825.13	— 5.3	8.3	4.3	— 4.4 [1,2]
1969	943.75	936.66	1/6/69	769.93	— 17.8	— 14.6	— 15.2	— 0.8
1970	769.93	768.88	1/26/70	631.16	— 17.9	9.1	4.8	— 7.6 [1,2]
1973	1000.00	996.46	1/29/73	788.31	— 20.9	— 14.6	— 16.6	— 1.7
1977	946.64	946.31	2/7/77	800.85	— 15.4	— 12.2	— 17.3	— 5.1
1978	806.22	804.92	1/5/78	742.12	— 7.8	0.0	— 3.1	— 6.2
1980	819.62	818.94	3/10/80	759.13	— 7.3	17.7	14.9	5.8 [2]
1982	868.25	865.30	1/5/82	776.92	— 10.2	20.9	19.6	— 1.8 [1,2]
1984	1236.79	1231.89	1/25/84	1086.57	— 11.8	— 1.6	— 3.7	— 0.9
1990	2687.93	2669.37	1/15/90	2365.10	— 11.4	— 1.3	— 4.3	— 6.9
1991	2565.59	2522.77	1/7/91	2470.30	— 2.1	25.6	20.3	4.2 [2]
1993	3255.18	3251.67	1/8/93	3241.95	— 0.3	15.5	13.7	0.7 [2]
1994	3697.08	3626.75	3/30/94	3593.35	— 0.9	5.7	2.1	3.3 [2]
1996	5059.32	5032.94	1/10/96	5032.94	0.0	28.1	26.0	3.3 [2]
1998	7660.13	7580.42	1/9/98	7539.07	— 0.5	21.1	16.1	1.0 [2]
2000	10998.39	10997.93	1/4/00	9796.03	— 10.9	— 1.9	— 6.2	— 5.1
2001	10318.93	10208.25	3/12/01	8235.81	— 19.3	— 1.8	— 7.1	3.5 [1]
2002	9763.96	9712.27	1/16/02	7702.34	— 20.7	At Press-time		— 1.6
			Average Drop		**— 10.7%**			

[1] January Barometer wrong   [2] December Low Indicator wrong

APRIL

MONDAY 7

To find one man in a thousand who is your true friend from unselfish motives is to find one of the great wonders of the world.
— Leopold Mozart (Quoted by Maynard Solomon, *Mozart*)

TUESDAY 8

By the law of nature the father continues master of his child no longer than the child stands in need of his assistance; after that term they become equal, and then the son entirely independent of the father, owes him no obedience, but only respect.
— Jean-Jacques Rousseau (*The Social Contract*)

WEDNESDAY 9

Industrial capitalism has generated the greatest productive power in human history. To date, no other socioeconomic system has been able to generate comparable productive power.
— Peter L. Berger (*The Capitalist Revolution*)

THURSDAY 10

Of the S&P 500 companies in 1957, only 74 were still on the list in 1998 and only 12 outperformed the index itself over that period. By 2020, more than 375 companies in the S&P 500 will consist of companies we don't know today.
— Richard Foster and Sarah Kaplan (*Creative Destruction*)

FRIDAY 11

Buy when you are scared to death; sell when you are tickled to death.
— Market Maxim (*The Cabot Market Letter*, April 12, 2001)

SATURDAY 12

SUNDAY 13

PRE-PRESIDENTIAL ELECTION YEARS
NO LOSERS IN 64 YEARS

Investors should feel somewhat more secure going into 2003. There hasn't been a down year in the third year of a presidential term since war-torn 1939, Dow off 2.9%. The only severe loss in a pre-presidential election year going back 84 years occurred in 1931 during the Depression.

Electing a president every four years has set in motion a political stock market cycle. Most bear markets take place in the first or second years after elections (see page 127). Then, the market improves. What happens is that each administration usually does everything in its power to juice up the economy so that voters are in a positive mood at election time.

Quite an impressive record. Chances are the winning streak will continue and that the market in pre-presidential election 2003 will gain ground. Prospects improve considerably if the market works off more of the market excesses from the still lingering millennial hangover created during the "bubble" years and puts in a solid base and bottom in the latter part of 2002.

PRE-PRESIDENTIAL ELECTION YEAR RECORD SINCE 1915

1915	Wilson (D)	World War I in Europe, but U.S. stocks up 81.7%.
1919	Wilson (D)	Post-Armistice 45.5% gain through November 3rd top. Dow up 30.5% for year.
1923	Harding/Coolidge (R)	Teapot Dome scandal a depressant, Dow loses 3.3%.
1927	Coolidge (R)	Bull market rolls on, up 28.8%.
1931	Hoover (R)	Depression, stocks slashed in half, Dow – 52.7%, S&P – 47.1%.
1935	Roosevelt (D)	Almost a straight up year, S&P 500 up 41.2%, Dow 38.5%.
1939	Roosevelt (D)	War clouds, Dow off 2.9% but 23.7% April/December gain. S&P – 5.5%.
1943	Roosevelt (D)	U.S. at war, prospects brighter, S&P +19.4%, Dow +13.8%.
1947	Truman (D)	S&P unchanged, Dow up 2.2%.
1951	Truman (D)	Dow +14.4%, S&P +16.5%.
1955	Eisenhower (R)	Dow +20.8%, S&P +26.4%.
1959	Eisenhower (R)	Dow +16.4%, S&P +8.5%.
1963	Kennedy/Johnson (D)	Dow +17.0%, S&P +18.9%.
1967	Johnson (D)	Dow +15.2%, S&P +20.1%.
1971	Nixon (R)	Dow +6.1%, S&P +10.8%, NASDAQ +27.4%.
1975	Ford (R)	Dow +38.3%, S&P +31.5%, NASDAQ +29.8%.
1979	Carter (D)	Dow +4.2%, S&P +12.3%, NASDAQ +28.1%.
1983	Reagan (R)	Dow +20.3%, S&P +17.3%, NASDAQ +19.9%.
1987	Reagan (R)	Dow +2.3%, S&P +2.0% despite October meltdown. NASDAQ – 5.4%.
1991	Bush (R)	Dow +20.3%, S&P +26.3%, NASDAQ +56.8%.
1995	Clinton (D)	Dow +33.5%, S&P +34.1%, NASDAQ +39.9%.
1999	Clinton (D)	Millennial fever crescendo: Dow +25.2%, S&P +19.5%, NASDAQ +85.6%.

Graph shows pre-presidential election years screened.
Based on Dow Jones industrials monthly ranges.

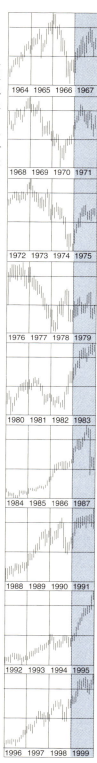

APRIL

Monday before Expiration Dow up 6 of last 8

MONDAY 14

Half the people alive today are already living in what we would consider intolerable conditions. One-sixth don't have access to clean drinking water; one-fifth live on less than a dollar a day; half the women in the world don't have equal rights with men; the forests are shrinking; the temperature's rising, and the oceans are rising because of the melting of the ice cap.
— Ted Turner (Billionaire, *New Yorker Magazine*, April 23, 2001)

Income Tax Deadline

TUESDAY 15

A leader has the ability to create infectious enthusiasm.
— Ted Turner (Billionaire, *New Yorker Magazine*, April 23, 2001)

WEDNESDAY 16

The average man desires to be told specifically which particular stock to buy or sell. He wants to get something for nothing. He does not wish to work.
— William Lefevre (Reminiscences of a Stock Operator)

Passover

Expiration Day Dow Up 8 of last 12
Day before April Good Fridays Dow up 7 of last 9

THURSDAY 17

The most dangerous thing that takes place [in companies] is that success breeds arrogance, and arrogance seems to make people stop listening to their customers and to their employees. And that is the beginning of the end. The challenge is not to be a great company; the challenge is to remain a great company.
— George Fisher (Motorola)

Good Friday
(Market Closed)

FRIDAY 18

People who can take a risk, who believe in themselves enough to walk away [from a company] are generally people who bring about change.
— Cynthia Danaher (Exiting GM of Hewlett-Packard's Medical Products Group, *Newsweek*)

SATURDAY 19

Easter Sunday

SUNDAY 20

DOWN JANUARYS: A REMARKABLE RECORD

In the first third of the 20th Century there was no correlation between January markets and the year as a whole (page 24). Then in 1972 we discovered that the 1933 "Lame Duck" Amendment to the Constitution changed the political calendar and the January Barometer was born. And its record has been magnificent. But to those who would like bull and bear markets to begin on January First and end on the last day of December, sorry we can't oblige. Critics look at the record of down Januarys and see a mixed bag. We look at it and always see the "pony."

Down Januarys are harbingers of trouble ahead, in the economic, political, or military arenas. Eisenhower's heart attack in 1955 cast doubt on whether he could run in 1956, a flat year. Two other election years were also flat. Eleven bear markets began with poor Januarys and four of them continued into second years. 1968 started down as we were mired in Vietnam, but Johnson's "bombing halt" changed the climate. Down Januarys were followed by substantial declines averaging *minus* 13.3%, providing excellent buying opportunities later in most years.

DOWN JANUARY S&P CLOSES TO LOW AND NEXT 11 MONTHS

Year	January Close	% Change	11-Month Low	Date of Low	Jan Close to low %	% Feb to Dec	Year % Change	
1953	26.38	− 0.7	22.71	14-Sep	− 13.9%	− 6.0%	− 6.6	bear
1956	43.82	− 3.6	44.10	28-May	0.9	6.5	2.6	FLAT
1957	44.72	− 4.2	38.98	22-Oct	− 12.8	− 10.6	− 14.3	bear
1960	55.61	− 7.1	52.30	25-Oct	− 6.0	4.5	− 3.0	bear
1962	68.84	− 3.8	52.32	26-Jun	− 24.0	− 8.3	− 11.8	bear
1968	92.24	− 4.4	87.72	5-Mar	− 4.9	12.6	7.7	Cont. bear
1969	103.01	− 0.8	89.20	17-Dec	− 13.4	− 10.6	− 11.4	bear
1970	85.02	− 7.6	69.20	26-May	− 18.6	8.4	0.1	Cont. bear
1973	116.03	− 1.7	92.16	5-Dec	− 20.6	− 15.9	− 17.4	bear
1974	96.57	− 1.0	62.28	3-Oct	− 35.5	− 29.0	− 29.7	bear
1977	102.03	− 5.1	90.71	2-Nov	− 11.1	− 6.8	− 11.5	bear
1978	89.25	− 6.2	86.90	6-Mar	− 2.6	7.7	1.1	Cont. bear
1981	129.55	− 4.6	112.77	25-Sep	− 13.0	− 5.4	− 9.7	bear
1982	120.40	− 1.8	102.42	12-Aug	− 14.9	16.8	14.8	Cont. bear
1984	163.42	− 0.9	147.82	24-Jul	− 9.5	2.3	1.4	FLAT
1990	329.07	− 6.9	295.46	11-Oct	− 10.2	0.4	− 6.6	bear
1992	408.79	− 2.0	394.50	8-Apr	− 3.5	6.6	4.5	FLAT
2000	1394.46	− 5.1	1264.74	20-Dec	− 9.3	− 5.3	− 10.1	bear
2002	1130.20	− 1.6	797.70	23-Jul	− 29.4	*At Press-time*		Cont. bear
				Totals	− 252.3%	− 32.1%		
				Average	− 13.3%	− 1.8%		

APRIL

MONDAY

21

Around the world, red tape is being cut. Whether it's telecom in Europe, water in South America, or power in Illinois, governments are stepping back, and competition is thriving where regulated monopolies once dominated.
— (*Fortune*, 12/20/99)

TUESDAY

22

IGNORANCE is not knowing something; STUPIDITY is not admitting your ignorance.
— Daniel Turov (*Turov on Timing*)

WEDNESDAY

23

When someone told me "We're going with you guys because no one ever got fired for buying Cisco (products)." That's what they used to say in IBM's golden age.
— Mark Dickey (Formerly of Cisco, now at SmartPipes, *Fortune*).

THURSDAY

24

Those who cannot remember the past are condemned to repeat it.
— George Santayana (American philosopher, poet)

FRIDAY

25

In the stock market those who expect history to repeat itself exactly are doomed to failure.
— Yale Hirsch

SATURDAY
26

May Sector Seasonalities: Bearish: FPP, SOX
(page 118)

SUNDAY

27

MAY ALMANAC

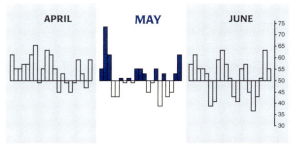

Market Probability Chart above is a graphic representation of the Market Probability Calendar on page 122.

◆ "May/June disaster area" between 1964 and 1984 with 15 out of 20 down Mays ◆ Between 1985 and 1997 May was the best month, gaining 3.3% per year on average ◆ Recent record four of last five Mays down after 13 straight gains in S&P ◆ Still sports a 1.7% average in last 15 years ◆ Worst six months of the year begin with May (page 50) ◆ A $10,000 investment compounded to $457,103 for November-April in 52 years compared to $77 loss for May-October ◆ Memorial Day week record: up 12 years in a row (1984-1995), down five of the last seven years with a 240-point Dow gain in 1999, and 495 points in 2000

MAY DAILY POINT CHANGES DOW JONES INDUSTRIALS

Previous Month Close	1993 3427.55	1994 3681.69	1995 4321.27	1996 5569.08	1997 7008.99	1998 9063.37	1999 10789.04	2000 10733.91	2001 10734.97	2002 9946.22
1	—	—	− 5.19	6.14	− 32.51	83.70	—	77.87	163.37	113.41
2	—	19.33	12.80	− 76.95	94.72	—	—	− 80.66	− 21.66	32.24
3	18.91	13.39	44.27	− 20.24	—	—	225.65	− 250.99	− 80.03	− 85.24
4	− 0.27	− 16.66	− 13.49	—	—	45.59	− 128.58	− 67.64	154.59	—
5	2.91	− 1.78	− 16.26	—	143.29	− 45.09	69.30	165.37	—	—
6	− 7.20	− 26.47	—	− 13.72	10.83	− 92.92	− 8.59	—	—	− 198.59
7	− 4.71	—	—	− 43.36	−139.67	− 77.97	84.77	—	− 16.07	28.51
8	—	—	40.47	53.11	50.97	78.47	—	25.77	− 51.66	305.28
9	—	− 40.46	6.91	1.08	32.91	—	—	− 66.88	− 16.53	− 104.41
10	6.09	27.37	13.84	43.00	—	—	− 24.34	− 168.97	43.46	97.50
11	25.47	− 27.37	6.57	—	—	36.37	18.90	178.19	− 89.13	—
12	13.56	23.80	19.37	—	123.22	70.25	− 25.78	63.40	—	—
13	− 34.32	6.84	—	64.46	− 18.54	50.07	106.82	—	—	169.74
14	− 4.98	—	—	42.11	11.95	− 39.61	− 193.87	—	56.02	188.48
15	—	—	6.91	0.73	47.39	− 76.23	—	198.41	− 4.36	− 54.46
16	—	11.82	− 2.42	9.61	−138.88	—	—	126.79	342.95	45.53
17	6.92	49.11	− 12.45	52.45	—	—	− 59.85	− 164.83	32.66	63.87
18	− 5.54	12.28	− 81.96	—	—	− 45.09	− 16.52	7.54	53.16	—
19	55.64	26.09	0.69	—	34.21	3.74	50.44	− 150.43	—	—
20	23.25	7.37	—	61.32	74.58	116.83	− 20.65	—	—	− 123.58
21	− 30.45	—	—	− 12.56	− 12.77	− 39.11	− 37.46	—	36.18	− 123.79
22	—	—	54.30	41.74	− 32.56	− 17.93	—	− 84.30	− 80.68	52.17
23	—	− 23.94	40.81	− 15.88	87.78	—	—	− 120.28	− 151.73	58.20
24	14.95	2.76	1.72	0.74	—	—	− 174.61	113.08	16.91	− 111.82
25	8.85	10.13	− 25.93	—	—	H	− 123.58	− 211.43	− 117.05	—
26	23.53	− 1.84	− 43.23	—	H	−150.71	171.07	− 24.68	—	—
27	14.67	3.68	—	H	37.50	− 27.16	− 235.23	—	—	H
28	− 27.40	—	—	− 53.19	− 26.18	33.63	92.81	—	H	− 122.68
29	—	—	H	− 35.84	− 27.05	− 70.25	—	H	33.77	− 58.54
30	—	H	9.68	19.58	0.86	—	—	227.89	− 166.50	− 11.35
31	H	1.23	86.46	− 50.23	—	—	H	− 4.80	39.30	13.56
Close	3527.43	3758.37	4465.14	5643.18	7331.04	8899.95	10559.74	10522.33	10911.94	9925.25
Change	99.88	76.68	143.87	74.10	322.05	−163.42	− 229.30	− 211.58	176.97	− 20.97

Was Number One month for nine straight years
But four of the last five have caused May tears

APRIL/MAY

MONDAY
28

Resentment is like taking poison and waiting for the other person to die.
— Malachy McCourt (*A Monk Swimming: A Memoir*)

TUESDAY
29

If we hire people bigger than ourselves, we will become a company of giants—smaller than ourselves, a company of midgets.
— David Ogilvy (*Forbes ASAP*)

End of "Best Six Months" of the Year (page 50)   ### WEDNESDAY

30

The single best predictor of overall excellence is a company's ability to attract, motivate, and retain talented people.
— Bruce Pfau (*Fortune*)

May first trading day Dow Up 8 of Last 10   ### THURSDAY
1

In most admired companies, key priorities are teamwork, customer focus, fair treatment of employees, initiative, and innovation. In average companies the top priorities are minimizing risk, respecting the chain of command, supporting the boss, and making budget.
— Bruce Pfau (*Fortune*)

FRIDAY

2

Some people say we can't compete with Intel. I say, like hell you can't...Dominant companies usually don't change unless they're forced to do so.
— David Patterson (Designing force behind R.I.S.C. and R.A.I.D., *WSJ* 8/28/98)

SATURDAY
3

SUNDAY
4

TOP PERFORMING MONTHS PAST 52½ YEARS
STANDARD & POOR'S 500 AND DOW JONES INDUSTRIAL

Monthly performance of the S&P and the Dow are ranked over the past 52½ years. Ranking the Dow by points gained no longer appears appropriate as most points were gained in the last ten years. NASDAQ monthly performance is shown on page 56.

January, April, November and December still hold the top four positions in both the Dow and S&P. This led to our discovery in 1986 of the market's best-kept secret. You can divide the year into two sections and have practically all the gains in one six-month section and very little in the other. September has been the worst month on both lists. (See "Best Six Months" on page 50.)

MONTHLY % CHANGES (JANUARY 1950 – JUNE 2002)

Standard & Poor's 500

Month	Total % Change	Avg.% Change	# Up	# Down
Jan	81.0%	1.5%	34	19
Feb	– 2.4	– 0.04	28	25
Mar	57.9	1.1	35	18
Apr	67.5	1.3	36	17
May	7.9	0.1	29	24
Jun	10.5	0.2	28	25
Jul	55.4	1.1	28	24
Aug	– 1.4	– 0.03	27	25
Sep*	– 27.0	– 0.5	21	30
Oct	35.3	0.7	30	22
Nov	85.1	1.6	34	18
Dec	93.5	1.8	40	12

% Rank				
Dec	93.5%	1.8%	40	12
Nov	85.1	1.6	34	18
Jan	81.0	1.5	34	19
Apr	67.5	1.3	36	17
Mar	57.9	1.1	35	18
Jul	55.4	1.1	28	24
Oct	35.3	0.7	30	22
Jun	10.5	0.2	28	25
May	7.9	0.1	29	24
Aug	– 1.4	– 0.03	27	25
Feb	– 2.4	– 0.04	28	25
Sep*	– 27.0	– 0.5	21	30
Total	463.3%	8.8%		
Average		0.74%		

Dow Jones Industrials

Month	Total % Change	Avg. % Change	# Up	# Down
Jan	80.6%	1.5%	36	17
Feb	9.8	0.2	30	23
Mar	53.6	1.0	34	19
Apr	97.3	1.8	33	20
May	– 1.1	– 0.02	27	26
Jun	– 7.4	– 0.1	26	27
Jul	61.5	1.2	32	20
Aug	– 4.2	– 0.1	29	23
Sep	– 43.6	– 0.8	19	33
Oct	15.7	0.3	30	22
Nov	81.9	1.6	35	17
Dec	94.9	1.8	38	14

% Rank				
Apr	97.3%	1.8%	33	20
Dec	94.9	1.8	38	14
Nov	81.9	1.6	35	17
Jan	80.6	1.5	36	17
Jul	61.5	1.2	32	20
Mar	53.6	1.0	34	19
Oct	15.7	0.3	30	22
Feb	9.8	0.2	30	23
May	– 1.1	– 0.02	27	26
Aug	– 4.2	– 0.1	29	23
Jun	– 7.4	– 0.1	26	27
Sep	– 43.6	– 0.8	19	33
Total	438.9%	8.4%		
Average		0.70%		

*No change 1979

The greatest bull cycle in history has altered the normal seasonality. Here is how the months ranked over the past 15 years (180 months) using total percentage gains on the Dow: December 39.2%, April 35.7%, July 32.0%, May 26.5%, January 23.3%, November 21.0%, February 13.8%, March 11.7%, June 6.3%, October –3.7%, September –15.0%, August –24.6%. Notice how July and May have edged out January and November during the last 15 years. Big losses in the period were: October 1987(crash), off 23.2%; August 1998 (SE Asia crisis), off 15.1%; August 1990 (Kuwait), off 10.0%; September 2001 (9/11 Attack), off 11.1%.

MAY

MONDAY

*Show me a good phone receptionist and
I'll show you a good company.*
— Harvey Mackay (*Pushing the Envelope*, 1999)

FOMC Meeting

TUESDAY

*Anytime there is change there is opportunity. So it is paramount
that an organization get energized rather than paralyzed.*
— Jack Welch (GE CEO, *Fortune*)

WEDNESDAY

*It's not the strongest of the species (think "traders") that survive,
nor the most intelligent, but the one most responsive to change.*
— Charles Darwin

THURSDAY

*There are no secrets to success. Don't waste your time looking for
them. Success is the result of perfection, hard work, learning from
failure, loyalty to those for whom you work, and persistence.*
— General Colin Powell

Day before Mother's Day Dow up 9 of last 14

FRIDAY

*Investors operate with limited funds and limited intelligence, they
don't need to know everything. As long as they understand
something better than others, they have an edge.*
— George Soros (Quoted in *Beating the Dow*)

SATURDAY
10

Mother's Day

SUNDAY

OUR "BEST SIX MONTHS" DISCOVERY (IN 1986) CONTINUES TO RACK UP PHENOMENAL GAINS

Since 1950 an excellent strategy has been to invest in the market between November 1st and April 30th each year and then switch into fixed income securities for the other six months. A glance at the chart on page 138 shows that November, December, January, March and April have been outstanding months since 1950. Add February, and voilà, an eye-opening strategy! These six consecutive months gained 10106.89 Dow points in 52 years, while the remaining May through October months *lost* 360.80 points.

As tech stocks have made the staid S&P 500 more volatile, we switched to the Dow last year. Percentage changes for each six-month period since 1950 are shown along with a compounding $10,000 investment.

The November-April $457,103 gain overshadows the May-October $77 loss. (S&P results were $319,241 to $8,154.) Just two November-April losses were double-digit and were due to our April 1970 Cambodian invasion and the fall 1973 OPEC oil embargo.

When we discovered this strategy in 1986, November-April outperformed May-October by $88,163 to minus $1,522. Results got even better these past 16 years $368,940 to $1,445 (or over 250 to 1).

As sensational as these results are, they can be more than doubled with a simple timing indicator, see page 52.

"Random walkers" eat your hearts out!

SIX-MONTH SWITCHING STRATEGY

	DJIA % Change May 1-Oct 31	Investing $10,000	DJIA % Change Nov 1-Apr 30	Investing $10,000
1950	5.0%	$10,500	15.2%	$11,520
1951	1.2	10,626	− 1.8	11,313
1952	4.5	11,104	2.1	11,551
1953	0.4	11,148	15.8	13,376
1954	10.3	12,296	20.9	16,172
1955	6.9	13,144	13.5	18,355
1956	− 7.0	12,224	3.0	18,906
1957	− 10.8	10,904	3.4	19,549
1958	19.2	12,998	14.8	22,442
1959	3.7	13,479	− 6.9	20,894
1960	− 3.5	13,007	16.9	24,425
1961	3.7	13,488	− 5.5	23,082
1962	− 11.4	11,950	21.7	28,091
1963	5.2	12,571	7.4	30,170
1964	7.7	13,539	5.6	31,860
1965	4.2	14,108	− 2.8	30,968
1966	− 13.6	12,189	11.1	34,405
1967	− 1.9	11,957	3.7	35,678
1968	4.4	12,483	− 0.2	35,607
1969	− 9.9	11,247	− 14.0	30,622
1970	2.7	11,551	24.6	38,155
1971	− 10.9	10,292	13.7	43,382
1972	0.1	10,302	− 3.6	41,820
1973	3.8	10,693	− 12.5	36,593
1974	− 20.5	8,501	23.4	45,156
1975	1.8	8,654	19.2	53,826
1976	− 3.2	8,377	− 3.9	51,727
1977	− 11.7	7,397	2.3	52,917
1978	− 5.4	6,998	7.9	57,097
1979	− 4.6	6,676	0.2	57,211
1980	13.1	7,551	7.9	61,731
1981	− 14.6	6,449	− 0.5	61,422
1982	16.9	7,539	23.6	75,918
1983	− 0.1	7,531	− 4.4	72,578
1984	3.1	7,764	4.2	75,626
1985	9.2	8,478	29.8	98,163
1986	5.3	8,927	21.8	119,563
1987	− 12.8	7,784	1.9	121,835
1988	5.7	8,228	12.6	137,186
1989	9.4	9,001	0.4	137,735
1990	− 8.1	8,272	18.2	162,803
1991	6.3	8,793	9.4	178,106
1992	− 4.0	8,441	6.2	189,149
1993	7.4	9,066	0.03	189,149
1994	6.2	9,628	10.6	209,199
1995	10.0	10,591	17.1	244,972
1996	8.3	11,470	16.2	284,657
1997	6.2	12,181	21.8	346,712
1998	− 5.2	11,548	25.6	435,470
1999	− 0.5	11,490	0.04	435,470
2000	2.2	11,743	− 2.2	425,890
2001	− 15.5	9,923	9.6	467,103
52-Year Gain (Loss)		**($77)**		**$457,103**

MAY

Day after Mother's Day Dow up 12 of last 15
Monday before expiration Dow up 11 of last 12

MONDAY
12

> From very early on, I understood that you can touch a piece of
> paper once…if you touch it twice, you're dead. Therefore, paper
> only touches my hand once. After that, it's either thrown away,
> acted on or given to somebody else.
> — Manuel Fernandez (Businessman, *Investor's Business Daily*)

TUESDAY

13

> The thing always happens that you really believe in.
> The belief in a thing makes it happen.
> — Frank Lloyd Wright (American architect)

WEDNESDAY

14

> If there's anything duller than being on a board in
> Corporate America, I haven't found it.
> — Ross Perot (*NY Times*, 10/28/92)

THURSDAY
15

> Never doubt that a small group of thoughtful, committed citizens can change
> the world: indeed it's the only thing that ever has.
> — Margaret Mead (American anthropologist)

Expiration Day Dow Down 7 of last 12

FRIDAY

16

> I had an unshakable faith. I had it in my head that if I had to, I'd
> crawl over broken glass. I'd live in a tent—it was gonna happen.
> And I think when you have that kind of steely
> determination…people get out of the way.
> — Rick Newcombe (Syndicator, *Investor's Business Daily*)

SATURDAY
17

SUNDAY
18

"BEST SIX MONTHS" RECORD SKYROCKETS WITH A SIMPLE MARKET-TIMING INDICATOR

Two years ago *Street Smart Report* writer Sy Harding, in his book, *Riding The Bear*, took our November-through-April strategy (page 50), enhanced it, and termed it the "Best mechanical system ever." He simply used the MACD (Moving Average Convergence Divergence) indicator developed by our friend Gerald Appel to enter the Best Six Months period up to a month earlier, if the market was in an uptrend. Conversely, Harding would exit up to a month later as long as the market kept moving up. But, if the market was trending down, you could delay a month getting in and even exit a month earlier. Thus, our "Best Six Months" could be lengthened or shortened a month or so.

Other services, online and printed, have also been picking up on the outstanding performance of the "Best Six Months" strategy but usually neglect to mention it was our discovery in 1986. Well, as they say, plagiarism is the sincerest form of flattery.

The results are astounding applying the simple MACD signals. Instead of $10,000 gaining $457,103 over the 52 recent years when invested only during the best six months (page 50), the gain more than doubled to $1,199,247. Ironically, the minor $77 loss during the worst six months deepened dramatically and that $10,000 investment lost $5,977 for the 52 years.

Impressive results for being invested during only 6½ months of the year on average! For the rest of the year you could park in a money market fund, or if a long-term holder, you could write options on your stocks (sell call options).

Updated signals are emailed to our monthly newsletter subscribers as soon as they are triggered. For further information on how the MACD indicator is calculated and the dates when signals were given or for a FREE newsletter sample, please email your name and address to *service@hirschorg.com* or call 201-767-4100.

SIX-MONTH SWITCHING STRATEGY+TIMING

	DJIA % Change May 1-Oct 31*	Investing $10,000	DJIA % Change Nov 1-Apr 30*	Investing $10,000
1950	7.3%	$10,730	13.3%	$11,330
1951	0.1	10,741	1.9	11,545
1952	1.4	10,891	2.1	11,787
1953	0.2	10,913	17.1	13,803
1954	13.5	12,386	16.3	16,053
1955	7.7	13,340	13.1	18,156
1956	− 6.8	12,433	2.8	18,664
1957	− 12.3	10,904	2.0	19,037
1958	20.7	13,161	16.7	22,216
1959	1.6	13,372	− 3.1	21,527
1960	− 4.9	12,717	16.9	25,165
1961	2.9	13,086	− 1.5	24,788
1962	− 15.3	11,084	22.4	30,341
1963	4.3	11,561	9.6	33,254
1964	6.7	12,336	6.2	35,316
1965	2.6	12,657	− 2.5	34,433
1966	− 16.4	10,581	14.3	39,357
1967	− 2.1	10,359	5.5	41,522
1968	3.4	10,711	0.2	41,605
1969	− 11.9	9,436	− 6.7	38,817
1970	− 1.4	9,304	20.8	46,891
1971	− 11.0	8,281	15.4	54,112
1972	− 0.6	8,231	− 1.4	53,354
1973	− 11.0	7,326	0.1	53,407
1974	− 22.4	5,685	28.2	68,468
1975	0.1	5,691	18.5	81,135
1976	− 3.4	5,498	− 3.0	78,701
1977	− 11.4	4,871	0.5	79,095
1978	− 4.5	4,652	9.3	86,451
1979	− 5.3	4,405	7.0	92,503
1980	9.3	4,815	4.7	96,851
1981	− 14.6	4,112	0.4	97,238
1982	15.5	4,749	23.5	120,089
1983	2.5	4,868	− 7.3	111,323
1984	3.3	5,029	3.9	115,665
1985	7.0	5,381	38.1	159,733
1986	− 2.8	5,230	28.2	204,778
1987	− 14.9	4,451	3.0	210,921
1988	6.1	4,723	11.8	235,810
1989	9.8	5,186	3.3	243,592
1990	− 6.7	4,839	15.8	282,080
1991	4.8	5,071	11.3	313,955
1992	− 6.2	4,757	6.6	334,676
1993	5.5	5,019	5.6	353,418
1994	3.7	5,205	13.1	399,716
1995	7.2	5,580	16.7	466,469
1996	9.2	6,093	21.9	568,626
1997	3.6	6,312	18.5	673,822
1998	− 12.4	5,529	39.9	942,677
1999	− 6.4	5,175	5.1	990,754
2000	− 6.0	4,865	5.4	1,044,255
2001	− 17.3	4,023	15.8	1,209,247
52-Year Gain (Loss)		**(5,977)**		**$1,199,247**

*MACD generated entry and exit points (earlier or later) can lengthen or shorten six month periods

MAY

MONDAY
19

The secret to business is to know something that nobody else knows.
— Aristotle Onassis (Greek shipping billionaire)

TUESDAY
20

Excellent firms don't believe in excellence—only in constant improvement and constant change.
— Tom Peters (*In Search Of Excellence*)

WEDNESDAY
21

A good manager is a man who isn't worried about his own career but rather the careers of those who work for him…Don't worry about yourself! Take care of those who work for you and you'll float to greatness on their achievements.
— H.S.M. Burns

THURSDAY
22

Setting a goal is not the main thing. It is deciding how you will go about achieving it and staying with that plan.
— Tom Landry (Head Coach Dallas Cowboys, 1960-1988)

Happy Bull indicates S&P up 71.4% of the time 17th trading day of May last 21 years (page 123) but, Friday before Memorial Day Dow down 6 of last 10

FRIDAY
23

Technology will gradually strengthen democracies in every country and at every level.
— Bill Gates

SATURDAY
24

SUNDAY
25

JUNE ALMANAC

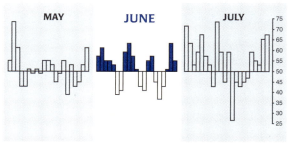

Market Probability Chart above is a graphic representation of the Market Probability Calendar on page 122.

◆ The "summer rally" in most years is the weakest rally of all four seasons (page 70) ◆ Week after June triple-witching day in last 12 years was up in 1995 and 1998 and down all other ten times (page 76) ◆ In 53 years June has been up 28 down 25 on the S&P, and up 26 down 27 on the Dow ◆ Average gain has been a mere 0.2% on the S&P, –0.1% on the Dow but a surprisingly strong 1.2% for NASDAQ ◆ Last 9 pre-election year Junes have fared well, except 1971 (off 1.8%) and 1991 (off 4.0%) ◆ June ranks near the bottom on the Dow since 1950 (see page 48), but has performed better in past 15 years ◆ NASDAQ weakening in June, off 9.4% in 2002, S&P down 7.2% and the Dow off 6.7%, creating worst 2nd Q since 1970

JUNE DAILY POINT CHANGES DOW JONES INDUSTRIALS

Previous Month Close	1993 3527.43	1994 3758.37	1995 4465.14	1996 5643.18	1997 7331.04	1998 8899.95	1999 10559.74	2000 10522.33	2001 10911.94	2002 9925.25
1	24.91	2.46	7.61	—	—	22.42	36.52	129.87	78.47	—
2	1.11	– 1.84	– 28.36	—	– 41.64	– 31.13	– 18.37	142.56	—	—
3	– 8.58	13.23	—	– 18.47	22.75	– 87.44	85.80	—	—	– 215.46
4	0.27	—	—	41.00	– 42.49	66.76	136.15	—	71.11	– 21.95
5	—	—	32.16	31.77	35.63	167.15	—	20.54	114.32	108.96
6	—	– 3.70	8.65	– 30.29	130.49	—	—	– 79.73	– 105.60	– 172.16
7	– 13.01	– 12.61	– 23.17	29.92	—	—	109.54	77.29	20.50	– 34.97
8	– 21.59	– 6.46	– 3.46	—	—	31.89	– 143.74	– 144.14	– 113.74	—
9	1.39	3.69	– 34.58	—	42.72	– 19.68	– 75.35	– 54.66	—	—
10	– 20.21	20.31	—	– 9.24	60.77	– 78.22	– 69.02	—	—	55.73
11	13.29	—	—	– 19.21	36.56	– 159.93	– 130.76	—	– 54.91	– 128.14
12	—	—	22.47	– 0.37	135.64	23.17	—	– 49.85	26.29	100.45
13	—	9.67	38.05	– 10.34	70.57	—	—	57.63	– 76.76	– 114.91
14	9.68	31.71	6.57	– 8.50	—	—	72.82	66.11	– 181.49	– 28.59
15	– 22.69	– 24.42	5.19	—	—	– 207.01	31.66	26.87	– 66.49	—
16	19.65	20.93	14.52	—	– 9.95	37.36	189.96	– 265.52	—	—
17	10.24	– 34.56	—	3.33	– 11.31	164.17	56.68	—	—	213.21
18	– 27.12	—	—	– 24.75	– 42.07	– 16.45	13.93	—	21.74	18.70
19	—	—	42.89	20.32	58.35	– 100.14	—	108.54	– 48.71	– 144.55
20	—	– 34.88	– 3.12	11.08	19.45	—	—	– 122.68	50.66	– 129.80
21	16.05	– 33.93	– 3.46	45.80	—	—	– 39.58	62.58	68.10	– 177.98
22	– 13.29	16.80	42.54	—	—	– 1.74	– 94.35	– 121.62	– 110.84	—
23	– 30.72	– 25.68	– 3.80	—	– 192.25	117.33	– 54.77	28.63	—	—
24	23.80	– 62.15	—	12.56	153.80	95.41	– 132.03	—	—	28.03
25	0.28	—	—	1.48	– 68.08	11.71	17.73	—	– 100.37	– 155.00
26	—	—	– 34.59	– 36.57	– 35.73	8.96	—	138.24	– 31.74	– 6.71
27	—	48.56	– 8.64	– 5.17	33.47	—	—	– 38.53	– 37.64	149.81
28	39.31	– 15.86	14.18	– 22.90	—	—	102.59	23.33	131.37	– 26.66
29	– 11.35	– 2.59	– 6.23	—	—	52.82	160.20	– 129.75	– 63.81	—
30	– 2.77	– 42.09	5.54	—	– 14.93	– 45.34	155.45	49.85	—	—
Close	3516.08	3624.96	4556.10	5654.63	7672.79	8952.02	10970.80	10447.89	10502.40	9243.26
Change	– 11.35	– 133.41	90.96	11.45	341.75	52.07	411.06	– 74.44	– 409.54	– 681.99

*May-June disaster had been in restrain
But lately May and June have caused much pain*

MAY/JUNE

Memorial Day
(Market Closed)

MONDAY

The way a young man spends his evenings is a part of that thin area between success and failure.
— Robert R. Young

Memorial Day Week Dow up 14 of last 19

TUESDAY

I sold enough papers last year of high school to pay cash for a BMW.
— Michael Dell (Founder Dell Computer, Forbes)

WEDNESDAY

Every time everyone's talking about something, that's the time to sell.
— George Lindemann (Billionaire, Forbes)

THURSDAY

A.I. (artificial intelligence) is the science of how to get machines to do the things they do in the movies.
— Professor Astro Teller (Carnegie Mellon University)

FRIDAY

A day will come when all nations on our continent will form a European brotherhood…A day will come when we shall see… the United States of Europe…reaching out for each other across the seas.
— Victor Hugo (French novelist, playwright, Hunchback of Notre Dame and Les Misérables, 1802-1885)

SATURDAY
31

June Sector Seasonalities: Bearish: XNG
(page 118)

SUNDAY

TOP PERFORMING NASDAQ MONTHS PAST 31½ YEARS

Prior to its recent 71.8% drop, the worst bear market in its history, NASDAQ stocks ran away during four consecutive months, November, December, January and February, with an average gain of 11.1%. This was equal to a compounded annual rate of 37.2%. These months were also the best months to own high-tech stocks. Then came the slaughter of November 2000, down 22.9%, the massacre of February 2001, down 22.4%, December 2001, up only 1.0%, January 2002, –0.8%, and February 2002 –10.5%.

You can see the months graphically on page 139. January by itself is awesome, up 4.1% on average. What appears as a Death Valley abyss occurs during NASDAQ's bleakest four months: July, August, September and October.

MONTHLY CHANGES (JANUARY 1971 – JUNE 2002)

	NASDAQ Composite*					Dow Jones Industrials			
Month	Total % Change	Avg.% Change	# Up	# Down	Month	Total % Change	Avg. % Change	# Up	# Down
Jan	131.9%	4.1%	23	9	Jan	70.8%	2.2%	22	10
Feb	22.2	0.7	18	14	Feb	15.4	0.5	18	14
Mar	13.4	0.4	20	12	Mar	32.5	1.0	21	11
Apr	35.3	1.1	21	11	Apr	66.3	2.1	18	14
May	22.3	0.7	18	14	May	12.3	0.4	17	15
Jun	39.0	1.2	20	12	Jun	9.7	0.3	18	14
Jul	– 4.9	– 0.2	15	16	Jul	18.1	0.6	16	15
Aug	6.7	0.2	17	14	Aug	– 6.8	– 0.2	17	14
Sep	– 25.8	– 0.8	17	14	Sep	– 39.7	– 1.3	9	22
Oct	– 5.9	– 0.2	15	16	Oct	4.5	0.1	18	13
Nov	51.1	1.6	20	11	Nov	37.9	1.2	21	10
Dec	75.5	2.4	19	12	Dec	58.4	1.9	23	8
% Rank					% Rank				
Jan	131.9%	4.1%	23	9	Jan	70.8%	2.2%	22	10
Dec	75.5	2.4	19	12	Apr	66.3	2.1	18	14
Nov	51.1	1.6	20	11	Dec	58.4	1.9	23	8
Jun	39.0	1.2	20	12	Nov	37.9	1.2	21	10
Apr	35.3	1.1	21	11	Mar	32.5	1.0	21	11
May	22.3	0.7	18	14	Jul	18.1	0.6	16	15
Feb	22.2	0.7	18	14	Feb	15.4	0.5	18	14
Mar	13.4	0.4	20	12	May	12.3	0.4	17	15
Aug	6.7	0.2	17	14	Jun	9.7	0.3	18	14
Jul	– 4.9	– 0.2	15	16	Oct	4.5	0.1	18	13
Oct	– 5.9	– 0.2	15	16	Aug	– 6.8	– 0.2	17	14
Sep	– 25.8	– 0.8	17	14	Sep	– 39.7	– 1.3	9	22
Totals	360.8%	11.2%			Totals	279.4%	8.8%		
Average		0.94%			Average		0.73%		

For comparison, Dow figures are shown. During the period NASDAQ averaged a 0.94% gain per month, nearly 30 percent more than the Dow's 0.73% per month. Between January 1971 and January 1982 NASDAQ's composite index doubled in the twelve years, while the Dow stayed flat. Different NASDAQ seasonal strategies are displayed on Page 58.

*Based on NASDAQ composite, prior to Feb. 5, 1971 based on National Quotation Bureau indices

JUNE

June first trading day Dow up 9 of last 12

MONDAY

2

Let me tell you the secret that has led me to my goal.
My strength lies solely in my tenacity.
— Louis Pasteur (French chemist,
founder of microbiology, 1822-1895)

TUESDAY

3

Success is going from failure to failure without loss of enthusiasm.
— Winston Churchill (British statesman, 1874-1965)

WEDNESDAY

4

The game is lost only when we stop trying.
— Mario Cuomo (Former NY Governor, *C-Span*)

THURSDAY

5

Ideas are easy; it's execution that's hard.
— Jeff Bezos (Amazon.com)

FRIDAY

6

Buy when others are despondently selling and
sell when others are greedily buying.
— Mark Mobius (On investing in foreign countries)

SATURDAY

7

SUNDAY

8

NASDAQ "BEST SIX MONTHS" STRATEGY BEATS DOW "BEST EIGHT" EVEN BETTER, "WORST FOUR" A BUST

Even though the new economy stocks have come back to earth (with NASDAQ dropping 71.7% from March 2000 to September 2001) and are now judged by the same fundamental benchmarks as the old economy stocks, NASDAQ stocks still beat the Dow over the "Best Six Months" period (page 50). As NASDAQ figures date back to 1971, there are only 31 years of results.

A hypothetical $10,000 investment in the NASDAQ Composite during the November through April months gained $130,066, which is about 177 times the measly $734 earned in the remaining six-month period. May/October months only got into the plus column starting in 1995 but are fading fast the last two years.

Seasonal trading strategies using the NASDAQ, Dow and S&P averages for different monthly periods are in the table below. Most outstanding is the eight-month period for NASDAQ. Here you have a gain of $237,477 in 31 years versus a loss for the remaining four months. In all the "Best-Months" periods NASDAQ trounces the S&P about two or more to one. In sharp contrast, NASDAQ's best four months outperform S&P's best four months nearly three to one.

EIGHT-MONTH SWITCHING STRATEGY

	NASDAQ % Change Jul 1-Oct 31	NASDAQ Investing $10,000	NASDAQ % Change Nov 1-Jun 30	NASDAQ Investing $10,000
1971	−2.5%	9,750	23.8%	12,377
1972	0.1	9,762	−22.5	9,596
1973	9.1	10,650	−31.1	6,616
1974	−14.1	9,146	33.4	8,826
1975	−11.5	8,092	17.3	10,354
1976	0.03	8,095	10.4	11,429
1977	−2.2	7,916	23.4	14,099
1978	−7.6	7,312	24.3	17,526
1979	−1.9	7,174	16.4	20,403
1980	22.2	8,765	11.9	22,834
1981	−9.5	7,932	−12.3	20,034
1982	24.1	9,846	49.9	30,028
1983	−13.9	8,482	−12.7	26,211
1984	3.1	8,743	19.9	31,428
1985	−1.2	8,635	38.6	43,565
1986	−11.0	7,682	17.7	51,281
1987	−23.9	5,848	22.1	62,600
1988	−3.1	5,667	13.8	71,247
1989	4.7	5,932	1.5	72,288
1990	−28.7	4,232	44.3	104,303
1991	14.1	4,828	3.8	108,264
1992	7.4	5,184	16.3	125,936
1993	10.7	5,739	−9.4	114,090
1994	10.1	6,320	20.1	136,976
1995	11.0	7,015	14.4	156,670
1996	3.1	7,231	18.1	184,959
1997	10.5	7,991	18.9	219,909
1998	−6.5	7,471	51.6	333,468
1999	10.4	8,251	33.7	445,846
2000	−15.0	7,010	−35.9	285,868
2001	−21.8	5,484	−13.4	247,477
	31-Year Loss	**($4,516)**	**31-Year Gain**	**$237,477**

$10,000 INVESTED IN NASDAQ, S&P & DOW (1971-2002) BEST/WORST MONTHS

Mos.	Best Mos.	NASDAQ	S&P	Dow	Mos.	Worst Mos.	NASDAQ	S&P	Dow
8	Nov 1-Jun 30	$237,477	$113,266	$146,593	4	Jul 1-Oct 31	−$4,516	−$1,948	−$3,377
6	Nov 1-Apr 30	130,066	67,304	112,634	6	May 1-Oct 31	734	3,400	−1,386
4	Nov 1-Feb 28	96,398	33,708	41,631	8	Mar 1-Oct 31	6,056	16,171	12,268
3	Nov 1-Jan 31	85,419	33,479	35,914	9	Feb 1-Oct 31	10,523	17,111	14,878

Based on NASDAQ composite, prior to Feb. 5, 1971 based on National Quotation Bureau indices

JUNE

MONDAY 9

The finest thought runs the risk of being irrevocably forgotten if we do not write it down.
— Arthur Schopenhauer (German philosopher)

TUESDAY 10

Nothing gives one person so much advantage over another as to remain always cool and unruffled under all circumstances.
— Thomas Jefferson

WEDNESDAY 11

All you need to succeed is a yellow pad and a pencil.
— Andre Meyer (Top deal maker at Lazard Freres)

THURSDAY 12

Give me a stock clerk with a goal and I will give you a man who will make history. Give me a man without a goal, and I will give you a stock clerk.
— James Cash Penney (J.C. Penney founder)

FRIDAY 13

It is tact that is golden, not silence.
— Samuel Butler (English writer, 1600-1680)

SATURDAY 14

Father's Day **SUNDAY 15**

NASDAQ'S "BEST EIGHT MONTHS" SHOOT THE MOON WITH A SIMPLE MACD TIMING INDICATOR

We never thought we could find a system that could top the "Best Six Months" with MACD timing (page 52) but we did. Look at NASDAQ's monthly performance (page 56 and 139) and you'll see NASDAQ's amazing eight-month run from November through June. A $10,000 investment in these eight months since 1971 gained $237,477 versus a loss of $4,516 during the void that is the four-month period July-October (page 58).

Using the same MACD timing indicators on the NASDAQ as is done for the Dow (page 52) sends NASDAQ's results to the moon. Over the 31 years since NASDAQ began, the gain on the same $10,000 nearly doubles to $434,944 and the loss during the four-month void increases to -$6,798. Only four sizeable losses occur during the favorable period and the bulk of NASDAQ's bear markets were avoided including 2000-2001 bear.

BEST EIGHT MONTHS STRATEGY + TIMING

MACD Signal Date	Worst 4 Months July 1-Oct 31* NASDAQ	% Change	Investing 10,000	MACD Signal Date	Best 8 Months Nov 1-June 30* NASDAQ	% Change	Investing 10,000
22-Jul-71	109.54	− 3.6%	9,640	4-Nov-71	105.56	24.1%	12,410
7-Jun-72	131.00	− 1.8	9,466	23-Oct-72	128.66	− 22.7	9,593
25-Jun-73	99.43	− 7.2	8,784	7-Dec-73	92.32	− 20.2	7,655
3-Jul-74	73.66	− 23.2	6,746	7-Oct-74	56.57	47.8	11,314
11-Jun-75	83.60	− 9.2	6,125	7-Oct-75	75.88	20.8	13,667
22-Jul-76	91.66	− 2.4	5,978	19-Oct-76	89.45	13.2	15,471
27-Jul-77	101.25	− 4.0	5,739	4-Nov-77	97.21	26.6	19,586
7-Jun-78	123.10	− 6.5	5,366	6-Nov-78	115.08	19.1	23,327
3-Jul-79	137.03	− 1.1	5,307	30-Oct-79	135.48	15.5	26,943
20-Jun-80	156.51	26.2	6,697	9-Oct-80	197.53	11.2	29,961
4-Jun-81	219.68	− 17.6	5,518	1-Oct-81	181.09	− 4.0	28,763
7-Jun-82	173.84	12.5	6,208	7-Oct-82	195.59	57.4	45,273
1-Jun-83	307.95	− 10.7	5,544	3-Nov-83	274.86	− 14.2	38,844
1-Jun-84	235.90	5.0	5,821	15-Oct-84	247.67	17.3	45,564
3-Jun-85	290.59	− 3.0	5,646	1-Oct-85	281.77	39.4	63,516
10-Jun-86	392.83	− 10.3	5,064	1-Oct-86	352.34	20.5	76,537
30-Jun-87	424.67	− 22.7	3,914	2-Nov-87	328.33	20.1	91,921
8-Jul-88	394.33	− 6.6	3,656	29-Nov-88	368.15	22.4	112,511
13-Jun-89	450.73	0.7	3,682	9-Nov-89	454.07	1.9	114,649
11-Jun-90	462.79	− 23.0	2,835	2-Oct-90	356.39	39.3	159,706
11-Jun-91	496.62	6.4	3,016	1-Oct-91	528.51	7.4	171,524
11-Jun-92	567.68	1.5	3,061	14-Oct-92	576.22	20.5	206,686
7-Jun-93	694.61	9.9	3,364	1-Oct-93	763.23	− 4.4	197,592
17-Jun-94	729.35	5.0	3,532	11-Oct-94	765.57	13.5	224,267
1-Jun-95	868.82	17.2	4,140	13-Oct-95	1018.38	21.6	272,709
3-Jun-96	1238.73	1.0	4,181	7-Oct-96	1250.87	10.3	300,798
4-Jun-97	1379.67	24.4	5,201	3-Oct-97	1715.87	1.8	306,212
1-Jun-98	1746.82	− 7.8	4,795	15-Oct-98	1611.01	49.7	458,399
1-Jun-99	2412.03	18.5	5,682	6-Oct-99	2857.21	35.7	622,047
29-Jun-00	3877.23	− 18.2	4,648	18-Oct-00	3171.56	− 32.2	421,748
1-Jun-01	2149.44	− 31.1	3,202	1-Oct-01	1480.46	5.5	444,944
3-Jun-02	1562.56						
	31-Year Loss		**($6,798)**		**31-Year Gain**		**$434,944**

*MACD generated entry and exit points (earlier or later) can lengthen or shorten eight month periods

JUNE

Monday before Triple Witching Dow up 8 of last 12

MONDAY

16

*There has never been a commercial technology like this (Internet)
in the history of the world, whereby the minute you adopt it,
it forces you to think and act globally.*
— Robert Hormats (Goldman, Sachs)

TUESDAY

17

*The difference between great people and others
is largely a habit —a controlled habit of doing
every task better, faster and more efficiently.*
— William Danforth (Ralston Purina founder)

WEDNESDAY

18

The man who can master his time can master nearly anything.
— Winston Churchill

THURSDAY
19

Eighty percent of success is showing up.
— Woody Allen

June Triple Witching Dow up 7 of last 13

FRIDAY

20

*At the age of 24, I began setting clear, written goals for
each area of my life. I accomplished more in the following year
than I had in the previous 24.*
— Brian Tracy (Motivational speaker)

SATURDAY
21

SUNDAY

22

FIRST-TRADING-DAY-OF-THE-MONTH PHENOMENON

For 38 months the sun shined regularly on first trading days of the month, except for seven occasions. But since October 2000, when the current major bear trend really started to bare its teeth, frightened investors switched from pouring money into the market on that day to pulling it out, eleven months out of twenty. Even so, first trading days retain an eye-popping history.

The Dow gained 2087.37 points in the last 58 months between September 2, 1997 (7622.42) and June 3, 2002 (9709.79). It is incredible that 2943.65 points were gained on 58 first trading days of the month. The remaining 1136 trading days combined saw the Dow lose 856.28 points during the period.

This averages out to gains of 50.75 points on first days, in contrast to a fractional point loss on all others. Converting to annual rates of return, at today's Dow levels, gives you about 249% versus a negative rate of return.

Interestingly, the first days of January, August and October fared the worst. In rising market trends first days perform much better so when national and world economies improve, corporate debacles no longer appear on the front page and geopolitical events cool down, perhaps first days of the month will again lead the market higher, though its current performance is nothing to complain about.

DOW POINTS GAINED ON FIRST DAY OF MONTH
FROM SEPTEMBER 1997 TO JUNE 3, 2002

	1997	1998	1999	2000	2001	2002	Totals
Jan		56.79	2.84	– 139.61	– 140.70	51.90	– 168.78
Feb		201.28	– 13.13	100.52	96.27	– 12.74	372.20
Mar		4.73	18.20	9.62	– 45.14	262.73	250.14
Apr		68.51	46.35	300.01	– 100.85	– 41.24	272.78
May		83.70	225.65	77.87	163.37	113.41	664.00
Jun		22.42	36.52	129.87	78.47	– 215.46	51.82
Jul		96.65	95.62	112.78	91.32		396.37
Aug		– 96.55	– 9.19	84.97	– 12.80		– 33.57
Sep	257.36	288.36	108.60	23.68	47.74		725.74
Oct	70.24	– 210.09	– 63.95	49.21	– 11.49		– 166.08
Nov	232.31	114.05	– 81.35	– 71.67	188.76		382.10
Dec	189.98	16.99	120.58	– 40.95	– 89.67		196.93
						Total	2943.65

FIRST DAYS VS. OTHER DAYS OF MONTH

	# of Days	Total Points Gained	Average Daily Point Gain	Annual Return
First days	58	2943.65	50.75	249%
Other days	1136	– 856.28	– 0.75	– 1.6%

JUNE

MONDAY 23

Anyone who has achieved excellence knows that it comes as a result of ceaseless concentration.
— Louise Brooks (Writer)

TUESDAY 24

FOMC Meeting (2 days)

People become attached to their burdens sometimes more than the burdens are attached to them.
— George Bernard Shaw

WEDNESDAY 25

Don't fritter away your time. Create, act, take a place wherever you are and be somebody.
— Theodore Roosevelt

THURSDAY 26

Some people are so boring they make you waste an entire day in five minutes.
— Jules Renard (French author, 1864-1910)

FRIDAY 27

Great spirits have always encountered violent opposition from mediocre minds.
— Albert Einstein

SATURDAY 28

July Sector Seasonalities: Bearish: RUT (page 118)

SUNDAY 29

JULY ALMANAC

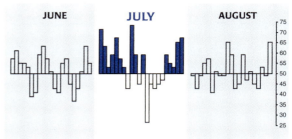

Market Probability Chart above is a graphic representation of the Market Probability Calendar on page 122.

◆ July is the best month of the third quarter (page 74) ◆ Start of second half brings an inflow of retirement funds ◆ First trading day up eleven out of thirteen times 1989-2001 ◆ July Dow down only three times in last 12 years but weak last four, NASDAQ down last four with big hits in 2000 and 2001 ◆ Average move of 1.1% on S&P, 1.2% on Dow, –0.2% on NASDAQ ◆ Dow up 1.4% in Pre-Election Julys ◆ RECORD: Up 32 times down 20 on the Dow ◆ Can be unpleasant in a bear market. ◆ Huge gain in July usually provides better buying opportunity over next four months ◆ Start of NASDAQ's worst four months of the year (page 56)

JULY DAILY POINT CHANGES DOW JONES INDUSTRIALS

Previous Month Close	1992	1993	1994	1995	1996	1997	1998	1999	2000	2001
	3318.52	3516.08	3624.96	4556.10	5654.63	7672.79	8952.02	10970.80	10447.89	10502.40
1	35.58	– 5.54	21.69	—	75.35	49.54	96.65	95.62	—	—
2	– 23.81	– 26.57	—	—	– 9.60	73.05	– 23.41	72.82	—	91.32
3	Closed	—	—	29.05	– 17.36	100.43	Closed	—	112.78*	– 22.61*
4	H	H	H	H	H	H	H	H	H	H
5	—	Closed	5.83	30.08	–114.88	—	—	Closed	– 77.07	– 91.25
6	8.91	– 34.04	22.02	48.77	—	—	66.51	– 4.12	– 2.13	– 227.18
7	– 44.03	25.74	13.92	38.73	—	– 37.32	– 6.73	52.24	154.51	—
8	– 1.89	38.75	20.72	—	– 37.31	103.82	89.93	– 60.47	—	—
9	30.80	6.64	—	—	31.03	–119.88	– 85.19	66.81	—	46.72
10	6.48	—	—	– 0.34	21.79	44.33	15.96	—	10.60	– 123.76
11	—	—	– 6.15	– 21.79	– 83.11	35.06	—	—	80.61	65.38
12	—	3.32	– 0.33	46.69	– 9.98	—	—	7.28	56.22	237.97
13	6.75	– 8.94	1.62	0.19	—	—	– 9.53	– 25.96	5.30	60.07
14	21.08	27.11	34.97	– 18.66	—	1.16	149.33	– 26.92	24.04	—
15	– 12.97	8.38	14.56	—	–161.05	52.73	– 11.07	38.31	—	—
16	16.21	– 22.64	—	—	9.25	63.17	93.72	23.43	—	– 66.94
17	– 29.99	—	—	27.47	18.12	– 18.11	9.78	—	– 8.48	134.27
18	—	—	1.62	– 50.01	87.30	–130.31	—	—	– 64.35	– 36.56
19	—	6.99	– 7.12	– 57.41	– 37.36	—	—	– 22.16	– 43.84	40.17
20	– 28.64	9.50	– 21.04	12.68	—	—	– 42.22	– 191.55	147.79	– 33.35
21	5.41	10.62	5.18	N/C	—	16.26	– 105.56	6.65	– 110.31	—
22	– 30.80	– 30.18	2.59	—	– 35.88	154.93	– 61.28	33.56	—	—
23	12.43	21.52	—	—	– 44.39	26.71	– 195.93	– 58.26	—	– 152.23
24	– 4.33	—	—	27.12	8.14	28.57	4.38	—	– 48.44	– 183.30
25	—	—	6.80	45.78	67.32	– 3.49	—	—	14.85	164.55
26	—	20.96	– 6.16	– 7.39	51.05	—	—	– 47.80	– 183.49	49.96
27	– 3.51	– 2.24	– 15.21	25.71	—	—	90.88	115.88	69.65	– 38.96
28	51.87	– 12.01	10.36	– 17.26	—	7.67	– 93.46	– 6.97	– 74.96	—
29	45.12	13.97	33.67	—	– 38.47	53.42	– 19.82	– 180.78	—	—
30	12.70	– 27.95	—	—	47.34	80.36	111.99	– 136.14	—	– 14.95
31	1.89	—	—	– 7.04	46.98	– 32.28	– 143.66	—	10.81	121.09
Close	3393.78	3539.47	3764.50	4708.47	5528.91	8222.61	8883.29	10655.15	10521.98	10522.81
Change	75.26	23.39	139.54	152.37	–125.72	549.82	– 68.73	– 315.65	74.09	20.41

Shortened trading day

When Dow and S&P in July are inferior
NASDAQ days tend to be even drearier

JUNE/JULY

MONDAY

Last day of second quarter Dow down 8 of last 11. June ends NASDAQ's "Best Eight Months" (page 58)

30

Most people can stay excited for two or three months. A few people can stay excited for two or three years. But a winner will stay excited for 20 to 30 years—or as long as it takes to win.
— A.L. Williams (Motivational speaker)

July Begins NASDAQ's Worst 4 months of the Year
July first trading day Dow up 12 of last 13

TUESDAY

1

I have learned as a composer chiefly through my mistakes and pursuits of false assumptions, not by my exposure to founts of wisdom and knowledge.
— Igor Stravinsky (Russian composer)

WEDNESDAY

2

It's not that I am so smart; it's just that I stay with problems longer.
— Albert Einstein

THURSDAY

3

What counts more than luck, is determination and perseverance. If the talent is there, it will come through. Don't be too impatient.
— Fred Astaire (The report from his first screen test stated, "Can't act. Can't sing. Balding. Can dance a little.")

Independence Day
(Market Closed)

FRIDAY

4

Love your enemies, for they tell you your faults.
— Benjamin Franklin

SATURDAY

5

SUNDAY

6

2001 DAILY DOW POINT CHANGES (DOW JONES INDUSTRIAL AVERAGE)

Week #		Monday**	Tuesday	Wednesday	Thursday	Friday**	Weekly Dow Close	Net Point Change
						2000 Close	10786.85	
1	J	H	−140.70	299.60	− 33.34	−250.40	10662.01	− 124.84
2	A	− 40.66	− 48.80	31.72	5.28	− 84.17	10525.38	− 136.63
3	N	H	127.28	− 68.32	93.94	− 90.69	10587.59	62.21
4		− 9.35	71.57	− 2.84	82.55	− 69.54	10659.98	72.39
5	F	42.21	179.01	6.16	96.27	−119.53	10864.10	204.12
6	E	101.75	− 8.43	− 10.70	− 66.17	− 99.10	10781.45	− 82.65
7	B	165.32	− 43.45	−107.91	95.61	− 91.20	10799.82	18.37
8		H	− 68.94	−204.30	0.23	− 84.91	10441.90	− 357.92
9		200.63	− 5.65	−141.60	− 45.14	16.17	10466.31	24.41
10	M	95.99	28.92	138.38	128.65	−213.63	10644.62	178.31
11	A	− 436.37	82.55	−317.34	57.82	−207.87	9823.41	− 821.21
12	R	135.70	−238.35	−233.76	− 97.52	115.30	9504.78	− 318.63
13		182.75	260.01	−162.19	13.71	79.72	9878.78	374.00
14	A	− 100.85	−292.22	29.71	402.63	−126.96	9791.09	− 87.69
15	P	54.06	257.59	− 89.27	113.47	H	10126.94	335.85
16	R	31.62	58.17	399.10	77.88	−113.86	10579.85	452.91
17		− 47.62	− 77.89	170.86	67.15	117.70	10810.05	230.20
18		− 75.08	163.37	− 21.66	− 80.03	154.59	10951.24	141.19
19	M	− 16.07	− 51.66	− 16.53	43.46	− 89.13	10821.31	− 129.93
20	A	56.02	− 4.36	342.95	32.66	53.16	11301.74	480.43
21	Y	36.18	− 80.68	−151.73	16.91	−117.05	11005.37	− 296.37
22		H	33.77	−166.50	39.30	78.47	10990.41	− 14.96
23	J	71.11	114.32	−105.60	20.50	−113.74	10977.00	− 13.41
24	U	− 54.91	26.29	− 76.76	−181.49	− 66.49	10623.64	− 353.36
25	N	21.74	− 48.71	50.66	68.10	−110.84	10604.59	− 19.05
26		−100.37	− 31.74	− 37.64	131.37	− 63.81	10502.40	− 102.19
27		91.32	− 22.61*	H	− 91.25	−227.18	10252.68	− 249.72
28	J	46.72	−123.76	65.38	237.97	60.07	10539.06	286.38
29	U	− 66.94	134.27	− 36.56	40.17	− 33.35	10576.65	37.59
30	L	− 152.23	− 83.30	164.55	49.96	− 38.96	10416.67	− 159.98
31		− 14.95	121.09	− 12.80	41.17	− 38.40	10512.78	96.11
32	A	− 111.47	57.43	−165.24	5.06	117.69	10416.25	− 96.53
33	U	− 0.34	− 3.74	− 66.22	46.57	−151.74	10240.78	− 175.47
34	G	79.29	−145.93	102.76	− 47.75	194.02	10423.17	182.39
35		− 40.82	−160.32	−131.13	−171.32	30.17	9949.75	− 473.42
36		H	47.74	35.78	−192.43	−234.99	9605.85	− 343.90
37	S	− 0.34	Closed	Closed	Closed	Closed	9605.51	− 0.34
38	E	− 684.81	− 17.30	−144.27	−382.92	−140.40	8235.81	−1369.70
39	P	368.05	56.11	− 92.58	114.03	166.14	8847.56	611.75
40		− 10.73	113.76	173.19	− 62.90	58.89	9119.77	272.21
41	O	− 51.83	− 15.50	188.42	169.59	− 66.29	9344.16	224.39
42	C	3.46	36.61	−151.26	− 69.75	40.89	9204.11	− 140.05
43	T	172.92	− 36.95	5.54	117.28	82.27	9545.17	341.06
44		− 275.67	−147.52	− 46.84	188.76	59.64	9323.54	− 221.63
45		117.49	150.09	− 36.75	33.15	20.48	9608.00	284.46
46	N	− 53.63	196.58	72.66	48.78	− 5.40	9866.99	258.99
47	O	109.47	− 75.08	− 66.70	H	125.03*	9959.71	92.72
48	V	23.04	−110.15	−160.74	117.56	22.14	9851.56	− 108.15
49		− 87.60	129.88	220.45	− 15.15	− 49.68	10049.46	197.90
50	D	− 128.01	− 33.08	6.44	−128.36	44.70	9811.15	− 238.31
51	E	80.82	106.42	72.10	− 85.31	50.16	10035.34	224.19
52	C	N/C*	H	52.80	43.17	5.68	10136.99	101.65
53		− 115.49				Year's Close	10021.50	− 115.49†
Totals		− 389.33**	336.86	−396.53	976.41	−1292.76**		− 765.35

Bold Color: Down Friday, Down Monday   *Shortened trading days: Jul 3, Nov 23, Dec 24   †Partial week

Market closed for four days following 9/11 attack
** On Monday holidays, the following Tuesday is included in the Monday total
** On Friday holidays, the preceding Thursday is included in the Friday total

JULY

MONDAY 7

*The highest reward for a person's toil is not what they get for it,
but what they become by it.*
— John Ruskin (English writer)

TUESDAY 8

*Moses Shapiro (of General Instrument) told me, "Son, this is
Talmudic wisdom. Always ask the question 'If not?' Few people
have good strategies for when their assumptions are wrong."
That's the best business advice I ever got.*
— John Malone (CEO of cable giant TCI, Fortune, 2/16/98)

WEDNESDAY 9

*The universal line of distinction between the strong and the weak
is that one persists, while the other hesitates, falters, trifles and at
last collapses or caves in.*
— Edwin Percy Whipple (American essayist, 1819-1886)

THURSDAY 10

*The task of leadership is not to put greatness into humanity, but to
elicit it, for the greatness is already there.*
— Sir John Buchan (Former Governor-General of Canada)

FRIDAY 11

*The greatest lie ever told: Build a better mousetrap and the world
will beat a path to your door.*
— Yale Hirsch

SATURDAY 12

SUNDAY 13

TAKE ADVANTAGE OF DOWN FRIDAY/ DOWN MONDAY WARNING

For market professionals and serious traders, Fridays and Mondays are the most important days of the week. Friday is the day for squaring positions—trimming longs or covering shorts before taking off for the weekend. Pros want to limit their exposure (particularly to stocks that are not acting well) since there could be unfavorable developments before trading resumes two or more days later.

Monday is important because the market then has the chance to reflect any weekend news, plus what traders think after digesting the previous week's action and the many Monday morning research and strategy comments.

We've been watching Friday-Monday market behavior for 30 years. It has varied in that time, with Monday going from being a bad day to a good day on balance.

But one consistent pattern is the negative implication when a down Monday (or first trading day of the week) follows a down Friday (or last trading day of the week):
1. Two out of three times, stocks extend Monday's drop within two days.
2. An overwhelming five out of six times, stocks are lower within five days including two Monday selling climaxes (down 554.26 Dow points Oct. 27, 1997; off 512.61 Aug. 31, 1998).
3. In the last five and a half years, the Dow failed to drop quickly just eight times after a DF/DM combination. In each of these cases, the market was only two to three weeks from a mostly good-sized drop.

Another fascinating phenomenon involves clusters of DFs/DMs, which are important danger signals. The second table shows fourteen such clusters over the recent five and a half-year period and the subsequent market action. Usually a significant market drop soon follows a DF/DM cluster.

Also observe 2001 Daily Dow Point Changes on page 66. Notice the market topped after the first cluster on February 1 at 10983.63 and bottomed on March 22 at 9389.48. Following a cluster of three consecutive DF/DMs in the summer, the Dow had already dropped 800 points prior to the 9/11 Attack On America.

DOWN FRIDAYS/DOWN MONDAYS

Year	Total	Day 1	Day 2	Day 3	Day 4	Day 5	Mon. 500 pt. Sell Climax	Errors
1997	6	2	3				1	0
1998	9	3	1			1	1	3
1999	9	7		1				1
2000	12	4	4	1	2	1		0
2001	12	7	3			1		1
2002**	12	5	2			2		3
Totals	**60**	**28**	**13**	**2**	**2**	**5**	**2**	**8**

(Day Dow Closed Lower Than Monday: Day 1 – Day 5)

DF/DM CLUSTERS* Year	# of Weeks	Ending Wk #	Top Wk #	Approx. Point Lost	Weeks it took
1997	2 Consecutive	6	10	600	5
1998	2 Consecutive	22	29	1800	6
1999	2 Consecutive	22	24	400	1
	3 Consecutive	33	35	1200	5
2000	2 out of 3	6	6	1100	3
	2 Consecutive	38	38	800	3
	2 Consecutive	47	47	200	2
2001	2 out of 3	4	5	1600	7
	2 out of 3	26	26	300	2
	3 Consecutive	32	32	2400	6
2002**	2 Consecutive	3	5	200	1
	2 out of 3	8	11	800	6
	2 Consecutive	14	14	400	5
	2 Consecutive	19	20	2600	10

*Excluding those ending with Selling Climax **Partial year through July 26, 2002

JULY

MONDAY
14

*Mid July shows strength 9th trading day
Happy Bull indicates S&P up 90.5% of the time (page 123)
Monday before expiration day up Dow up 7 of last 13*

*In order to be great writer (or "investor") a person must have a
built-in, shockproof crap detector.*
— Ernest Hemingway

TUESDAY
15

*You have to find something that you love enough to be able to take
risks, jump over the hurdles and break through the brick walls that
are always going to be placed in front of you. If you don't have
that kind of feeling for what it is you're doing, you'll stop at the
first giant hurdle.*
— George Lucas (Star Wars director)

WEDNESDAY
16

*You may not have started out life in the best of circumstances. But
if you can find a mission in life worth working for and believe in
yourself, nothing can stop you from achieving success.*
— Kemmons Wilson (Holiday Inn founder)

THURSDAY
 17

*The average bottom-of-the-ladder person is potentially as creative
as the top executive who sits in the big office. The problem is that
the person on the bottom of the ladder doesn't trust his own
brilliance and doesn't, therefore, believe in his own ideas.*
— Robert Schuller (Minister)

FRIDAY
18

*Expiration day Dow down 7 of last 12
Historically one of two (October 9) worst trading days
of the year S&P up only 23.8% of the time (page 123)*

*Towering genius disdains a beaten path.
It scorns to tread in the footsteps of any predecessor,
however illustrious. It thirsts for distinction.*
— Abraham Lincoln

SATURDAY
19

SUNDAY
20

A RALLY FOR ALL SEASONS

In any year when the market is a disappointment, you hear talk of a summer rally. Parameters for this "rally" were defined by the late Ralph Rotnem as the lowest close in the Dow industrial average in May or June to the highest close in July, August, or September. Such a big deal is made of the "summer rally" that one might get the impression the market puts on its best razzle-dazzle performance in the summertime. Nothing could be further from the truth! Not only does the market "rally" in every season of the year, but it does so with more gusto in the winter, spring, and fall than in the summer.

Winters in 39 years averaged a 13.7% gain as measured from the low in November or December to the first quarter closing high. Spring was up 10.8% followed by fall with 10.6%. Last and least was the average 9.4% "summer rally." Nevertheless, no matter how thick the gloom or grim the outlook, don't despair! There's always a rally for all seasons, statistically.

SEASONAL GAINS IN DOW JONES INDUSTRIALS

	WINTER RALLY Nov/Dec Low to 1 Q. High	SPRING RALLY Feb/Mar Low to 2 Q. High	SUMMER RALLY May/Jun Low to 3 Q. High	FALL RALLY Aug/Sep Low to 4 Q. High
1964	15.3%	6.2%	9.4%	8.3%
1965	5.7	6.6	11.6	10.3
1966	5.9	4.8	3.5	7.0
1967	11.6	8.7	11.2	4.4
1968	7.0	11.5	5.2	13.3
1969	0.9	7.7	1.9	6.7
1970	5.4	6.2	22.5	19.0
1971	21.6	9.4	5.5	7.4
1972	19.1	7.7	5.2	11.4
1973	8.6	4.8	9.7	15.9
1974	13.1	8.2	1.4	11.0
1975	36.2	24.2	8.2	8.7
1976	23.3	6.4	5.9	4.6
1977	8.2	3.1	2.8	2.1
1978	2.1	16.8	11.8	5.2
1979	11.0	8.9	8.9	6.1
1980	13.5	16.8	21.0	8.5
1981	11.8	9.9	0.4	8.3
1982	4.6	9.3	18.5	37.8
1983	15.7	17.8	6.3	10.7
1984	5.9	4.6	14.1	9.7
1985	11.7	7.1	9.5	19.7
1986	31.1	18.8	9.2	11.4
1987	30.6	13.6	22.9	5.9
1988	18.1	13.5	11.2	9.8
1989	15.1	12.9	16.1	5.7
1990	8.8	14.5	12.4	8.6
1991	21.8	11.2	6.6	9.3
1992	14.9	6.4	3.7	3.3
1993	8.9	7.7	6.3	7.3
1994	9.7	5.2	9.1	5.0
1995	13.6	19.3	11.3	13.9
1996	19.2	7.5	8.7	17.3
1997	17.6	6.5	18.4	7.3
1998	20.3	13.6	7.2	23.1
1999	15.1	21.6	8.2	12.6
2000	10.8	14.4	9.8	3.4
2001	5.9	20.8	1.7	23.1
2002	14.8	7.9		
Totals	534.5%	421.8%	357.3%	403.1%
Average	13.7%	10.8%	9.4%	10.6%

JULY

End of July closes well, EXCEPT if bear market in progress

MONDAY 21

> *The mind is not a vessel to be filled but a fire to be kindled.*
> — Plutarch (Greek biographer and philosopher, *Parallel Lives*, 46-120 AD)

TUESDAY 22

> *The greatest good you can do for another is not just to share your riches, but to reveal to him his own.*
> — Benjamin Disraeli (British prime minister, 1804-1881)

WEDNESDAY 23

> *In this game, the market has to keep pitching, but you don't have to swing. You can stand there with the bat on your shoulder for six months until you get a fat pitch.*
> — Warren Buffett

THURSDAY 24

> *Follow the course opposite to custom and you will almost always do well.*
> — Jean Jacques Rousseau

FRIDAY 25

> *In an uptrend, if a higher high is made but fails to carry through, and prices dip below the previous high, the trend is apt to reverse. The converse is true for downtrends.*
> — Victor Sperandeo (*Trader Vic—Methods of a Wall Street Master*)

SATURDAY 26

August Sector Seasonalities: Bullish: BTK; Bearish: XAL, CYC (page 118)

SUNDAY 27

AUGUST ALMANAC

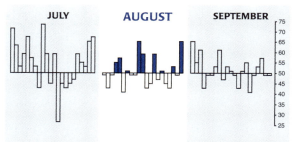

Market Probability Chart above is a graphic representation of the Market Probability Calendar on page 122.

◆ Money flow from harvesting made August a great stock market month in 1900 when 37.5% of the population was farming ◆ Now a little more than 2% farm and August is one of the worst months for the S&P and Dow ◆ Has become the worst month in the past 15 years on Dow and S&P, third worst on NASDAQ (though up 11.7% in 2000 but down 10.9% in 2001 ◆ Dow up 1.8% in Pre-Election Augusts ◆ Shortest bear in history (45 days) caused by turmoil in Russia ended here in 1998, with a record 1344.22 point drop in the Dow, off 15.1% ◆ Saddam Hussein triggered a 10.0% slide in 1990 ◆ Best Dow gains: 1982 (11.5%) and 1984 (9.8%) as bear markets ended

AUGUST DAILY POINT CHANGES DOW JONES INDUSTRIALS

Previous Month Close	1992 3393.78	1993 3539.47	1994 3764.50	1995 4708.47	1996 5528.91	1997 8222.61	1998 8883.29	1999 10655.15	2000 10521.98	2001 10522.81
1	—	—	33.67	− 8.10	65.84	− 28.57	—	—	84.97	− 12.80
2	—	21.52	− 1.95	− 10.22	85.08	—	—	9.19	80.58	41.17
3	1.62	0.28	− 3.56	11.27	—	—	− 96.55	31.35	19.05	− 38.40
4	− 11.08	− 9.22	− 26.87	− 17.96	—	4.41	− 299.43	− 2.54	61.17	—
5	− 19.18	− 3.08	− 18.77	—	− 5.55	− 10.91	59.47	119.05	—	—
6	− 24.58	11.46	—	—	21.83	71.77	30.90	− 79.79	—	− 111.47
7	− 8.38	—	—	9.86	22.56	− 71.31	20.34	—	99.26	57.43
8	—	—	6.79	0.00	− 5.18	−156.78	—	—	109.88	− 165.24
9	—	15.65	1.95	− 21.83	− 32.18	—	—	− 6.33	− 71.06	5.06
10	5.40	− 3.35	11.00	− 27.83	—	—	− 23.17	− 52.55	2.93	117.69
11	− 6.48	10.62	− 15.86	− 25.36	—	30.89	− 112.00	132.65	119.04	—
12	− 10.27	− 14.26	17.81	—	23.67	−101.27	90.11	1.59	—	—
13	− 7.56	0.56	—	—	− 57.70	− 32.52	− 93.46	184.26	—	0.34
14	15.67	—	—	41.56	19.60	13.71	− 34.50	—	148.34	− 3.74
15	—	—	− 8.42	− 19.02	− 1.10	−247.37	—	—	− 109.14	− 66.22
16	—	9.50	24.28	− 1.76	23.67	—	—	73.14	− 58.61	46.57
17	− 4.05	7.83	− 8.09	− 8.45	—	—	149.85	70.29	47.25	− 151.74
18	4.59	17.88	− 21.05	− 13.03	—	108.70	139.80	− 125.70	− 9.16	—
19	− 22.42	7.27	− 0.32	—	9.99	114.74	− 21.37	− 27.54	—	—
20	− 2.17	3.35	—	—	21.82	103.13	− 81.87	136.77	—	79.29
21	− 50.79	—	—	− 2.82	− 31.44	−127.28	− 77.76	—	33.33	− 145.93
22	—	—	− 3.89	5.64	43.65	− 6.04	—	—	59.34	102.76
23	—	− 9.50	24.61	− 35.57	− 10.73	—	—	199.15	5.50	− 47.75
24	− 25.93	32.98	70.90	− 4.23	—	—	32.96	− 16.46	38.09	194.02
25	4.05	13.13	− 16.84	20.78	—	− 28.34	36.04	42.74	9.89	—
26	14.59	− 3.91	51.16	—	− 28.85	− 77.35	− 79.30	− 127.59	—	—
27	7.83	− 7.55	—	—	17.38	5.11	− 357.36	− 108.28	—	40.82
28	12.97	—	—	− 7.40	1.11	− 92.90	− 114.31	—	60.21	− 160.32
29	—	—	17.80	14.44	− 64.73	− 72.01	—	—	− 37.74	− 131.13
30	—	3.36	18.45	− 3.87	− 31.44	—	—	− 176.04	− 112.09	− 171.32
31	− 10.26	7.26	− 3.88	5.99	—	—	− 512.61	− 84.85	112.09	30.17
Close	3257.35	3651.25	3913.42	4610.56	5616.21	7622.42	7539.07	10829.28	11215.10	9949.75
Change	−136.43	111.78	148.92	− 97.91	87.30	−600.19	−1344.22	174.13	693.12	− 573.06

*August's a good month to go on vacation
Trading stocks will likely lead to frustration*

JULY/AUGUST

MONDAY
28

It's a buy when the 10-week moving average crosses the 30-week moving average and the slope of both averages is up.
— Victor Sperandeo (*Trader Vic—Methods of a Wall Street Master*)

TUESDAY
29

Pullbacks near the 30-week moving average are often good times to take action.
— Michael Burke (*Investors Intelligence*)

WEDNESDAY
 30

News on stocks is not important. How the stock reacts to it is important.
— Michael Burke (*Investors Intelligence*)

THURSDAY
 31

The first stocks to double in a bull market will usually double again.
— Michael Burke (*Investors Intelligence*)

August worst month last 15 years on Dow (−1.6%) and S&P (−1.4%), third worst on NASDAQ (−0.2%)

FRIDAY
1

Keep away from people who try to belittle your ambitions. Small people always do that, but the really great make you feel that you, too, can become great.
— Mark Twain

SATURDAY
2

SUNDAY
3

FIRST MONTH OF FIRST THREE QUARTERS IS THE MOST BULLISH

Looking at monthly percent changes over the years, one can't help noticing that the market is the strongest in the opening month of the first three quarters. The investment calendar reflects the annual, semi-annual and quarterly operations of institutions during January, April and July. The fourth quarter behaves differently since it is affected by year-end portfolio adjustments and presidential and congressional elections in even-numbered years.

The average month-to-month change between 1950 and 1990 shows the S&P 500 gaining 1.3% on average in first months of the first three quarters. Second months barely eked out any gain, while third months, thanks to March, moved up 0.3% on average.

After experiencing the most powerful bull market of all time during the 1990s, followed by the down cycle of a generation (perhaps two), we separated all the figures for the Dow Industrial average beginning with 1991. First months averaged gains of 1.71%. Results for the second and third months were 0.19% and 0.07%, respectfully. The last two years have realigned the results closer with the past. Still the first month of the first three quarters out gains the other months many fold.

We tallied figures for NASDAQ (page 150) and first months results in the same period were 1.81%. Second months averaged 0.23% and third months 0.85%. The continuing fall from grace of technology shares and the major 2000-2002 bear trend have brought the new economy NASDAQ in line with the old economy Dow and now bullishness in the first month of the first three quarters is evident across the board.

AVERAGE S&P 500 % CHANGE FIRST THREE QUARTERS 1950-1990

	1st month	2nd month	3rd month
First Q	1.5%	−0.1%	1.1%
Second Q	1.3	−0.3	0.3
Third Q	1.1	0.5	−0.5
Total	**3.9%**	**0.1%**	**0.9%**
Average	**1.30%**	**0.03%**	**0.30%**

DJI % CHANGES FOR MOST RECENT YEARS

First Quarter

	Jan	Feb	Mar
1991	3.9%	5.3%	1.1%
1992	1.7	1.4	−1.0
1993	0.3	1.8	1.9
1994	6.0	−3.7	−5.1
1995	0.2	4.3	3.7
1996	5.4	1.7	1.9
1997	5.7	0.9	−4.3
1998	−0.02	8.1	3.0
1999	4.1	−3.2	3.9
2000	−4.8	−7.4	7.8
2001	0.9	−3.6	−8.7
2002	−1.0	1.9	2.9

Second Quarter

	Apr	May	Jun
1991	−0.9%	4.8%	−4.0%
1992	3.8	1.1	−2.3
1993	−0.2	2.9	−0.3
1994	1.3	2.1	−3.5
1995	3.9	3.3	2.0
1996	−0.3	1.3	0.2
1997	6.5	4.6	4.7
1998	0.9	−1.9	3.9
1999	3.8	−2.5	5.4
2000	−1.7	−2.0	−0.7
2001	8.7	1.6	−3.8
2002	−4.4	−0.2	−6.9

Third Quarter

	Jul	Aug	Sep
1991	4.1%	0.6%	−0.9%
1992	2.3	−4.0	0.4
1993	0.7	3.2	−2.6
1994	3.8	4.0	−1.8
1995	3.3	−2.1	3.9
1996	−2.2	1.6	4.7
1997	7.2	−7.3	4.2
1998	−1.2	−14.6	6.2
1999	−2.9	1.6	−4.5
2000	0.7	6.6	−5.0
2001	0.2	−5.4	−11.1
Total	**59.8%**	**6.8%**	**−4.7%**
Average	**1.71%**	**0.19%**	**−0.13%**

AUGUST

MONDAY 4

The heights by great men reached and kept
Were not attained by sudden flight,
But they, while their companions slept,
Were toiling upward in the night.
— Henry Wadsworth Longfellow

TUESDAY 5

In democracies, nothing is more great or brilliant than commerce;
it attracts the attention of the public and fills the imagination of
the multitude; all passions of energy are directed towards it.
— Alexis de Tocqueville (*Democracy in America*, 1840)

WEDNESDAY 6

I was in search of a one-armed economist so that the guy could
never make a statement and then say: "on the other hand."
— Harry S. Truman

THURSDAY 7

As far as paying off debt is concerned, there are very few instances
in history when any government has ever paid off debt.
— Walter Wriston (Retired CEO of Citicorp and Citibank)

FRIDAY 8

A committee is a cul de sac down which ideas are
lured and then quietly strangled.
— Sir Barnett Cocks (Member of Parliament)

SATURDAY 9

SUNDAY 10

DOWN TRIPLE-WITCHING WEEKS TRIGGER MORE WEAKNESS WEEK AFTER

DOWN TRIPLE-WITCHING TEND TO BE DOWN WEEK AFTER

	Dow Point Changes	
	Expiration Week	Week After
1991	— 6.93	— 89.36
	— 34.98	— 58.81
	33.54	— 13.19
	20.12	167.04
1992	40.48	— 44.95
	— 69.01	— 2.94
	21.35	— 76.73
	9.19	12.97
1993	43.76	— 31.60
	— 10.24	— 3.88
	— 8.38	— 70.14
	10.90	6.15
1994	32.95	—120.92
	3.33	—139.84
	58.54	—101.60
	116.08	26.24
1995	38.04	65.02
	86.80	75.05
	96.85	— 33.42
	19.87	— 78.76
1996	114.52	51.67
	55.78	— 50.60
	49.94	— 15.54
	179.53	76.51
1997	— 130.67	— 64.20
	14.47	—108.79
	174.30	4.91
	— 82.01	— 76.98
1998	303.91	—110.35
	— 102.07	231.67
	100.16	133.11
	81.87	314.36
1999	27.20	— 81.31
	365.05	—303.00
	— 224.80	—524.30
	32.73	148.33
2000	666.41	517.49
	— 164.76	— 44.55
	— 293.65	— 79.63
	— 277.95	200.60
2001	— 821.21	—318.63
	— 353.36	— 19.05
	—1369.70	611.75
	224.19	101.65
2002	34.74	—179.56
	— 220.42	— 10.53
Up	30	17
Down	16	29

Since the S&P index futures began trading in June 1982, traders have analyzed what the market does prior, during and following their expirations in hopes of finding the "Holy Grail." Locating a consistent trading pattern is never easy. For as soon as a pattern becomes obvious, the market almost always tends to "move the goal posts."

• Triple-witching week (TWW) refers to expirations in all three categories: S&P futures; put and call options on other indices; and options on stocks. Here are some TWW patterns:

• TWWs became more bullish in the last decade, except in the second quarter.

• Following weeks became more bearish, except in the fourth quarter.

• TWWs have tended to be down in flat periods and dramatically so during the recent bubble-bursting bear.

• "DOWN WEEKS TEND TO FOLLOW DOWN TRIPLE-WITCHING WEEKS" is the most interesting pattern. Since 1991, of 16 down TWWs, 13 following weeks were also down. This is surprising inasmuch as the previous decade had an exactly opposite pattern: There were also 13 down TWWs then, but 12 UP WEEKS followed them.

Jan. 1991 to 2Q 2002 (42 Qs)
Dow 2633.66 to 9243.26 up 251.0%

	Triple Witching		Following Week	
	Up	Down	Up	Down
1Q	9	3	3	9
2Q	5	7	2	10
3Q	7	4	3	8
4Q	9	2	9	2
Totals	30	16	17	29

June 1982 to 1990 (35 Qs)
Dow 819.54 to 2633.66 up 221.4%

	Triple Witching		Following Week	
	Up	Down	Up	Down
1Q	5	2	4	4
2Q	6	3	7	2
3Q	4	5	7	2
4Q	6	3	7	1
Totals	21	13	25	9

AUGUST

Monday before expiration day Dow up 9 of last 12
Mid-August stronger than beginning

MONDAY
11

> *A good new chairman of the Federal Reserve Bank*
> *is worth a $10 billion tax cut.*
> — Paul H. Douglas (U.S. Senator: 1949-1967)

FOMC Meeting

TUESDAY
12

> *An entrepreneur tends to lie some of the time.*
> *An entrepreneur in trouble tends to lie most of the time.*
> — Anonymous

WEDNESDAY
13

> *There is always plenty of capital for those who can*
> *create practical plans for using it.*
> — Napoleon Hill (Author, *Think and Grow Rich*, 1883-1970)

THURSDAY

14

> *In business, the competition will bite you if you keep running;*
> *if you stand still, they will swallow you.*
> — William Knudsen (Former President of GM)

Expiration day Dow Down 9 of last 12

FRIDAY

15

> *All the features and achievements of modern civilization are,*
> *directly or indirectly, the products of the capitalist process.*
> — Joseph A. Schumpeter (Austrian-American economist,
> *Theory of Economic Development*, 1883-1950)

SATURDAY
16

SUNDAY
17

WHY A 50.2% GAIN IN THE DOW IS POSSIBLE FROM ITS 2002 LOW TO ITS 2003 HIGH

Normally, major corrections occur sometime in the first or second years following presidential elections. In the last ten midterm election years, bear markets began or were in progress six times in a row before the onset in 1982 of the biggest bull cycle in Wall Street history. Since then, we experienced a bull year in 1986, a Saddam Hussein-induced bear in 1990, a flat year in 1994, and the shortest bear market on record (down 19.3% in 45 days) in 1998.

The puniest midterm advance, 14.5% from the 1946 low, was during the industrial contraction after World War II. The next four smallest advances, with the major depressant in parentheses, were: 1978 (OPEC–Iran) 21.0%, 1930 (economic collapse) 23.4%, 1966 (Vietnam) 26.7%, and 1990 (Persian Gulf War) 34.0%.

A hypothetical portfolio of stocks bought at midterm election-year lows since 1914 has gained 50.2% on average when the stock market reached its subsequent highs in the following pre-election years. A swing of such magnitude is equivalent to a move from 7000 to 10500 or from 7700 to 11550. From the bottom of 1994 a Dow gain of 1000 points was intimated; it rose 1623.12 points. The suggestion of a 2000-point gain from the 1998 low turned out to be 3958.05 points.

Pretty impressive seasonality! There is no reason to think the quadrennial Presidential Election/Stock Market Cycle will not continue. Page 127 shows how effectively presidents "managed" to have much stronger economies in the third and fourth years of their terms than in their first two.

At press-time the Dow (7702.34) is down about 23.1% for the year and off 27.6% from the March 19, 2002 high. A solid midterm election year bottom is likely to occur later in the year and at substantially lower prices. Considering the parabolic nature of the market's rise during the "bubble," the current 2000-? decline may last longer than any in the last 70 years. But, however muted, the rally off the 2002 midterm low will provide a reliable opportunity. Even at the outset of the depression the Dow rallied 23.4% from December 1930 to February 1931.

% CHANGE IN DOW JONES INDUSTRIALS BETWEEN THE MIDTERM YEAR LOW AND THE HIGH IN THE FOLLOWING YEAR

	Midterm Year Low		Pre-Election Year High		
	Date of Low	Dow	Date of High	Dow	% Gain
1	Jul 30 1914*	52.32	Dec 8 1915	98.45	88.2%
2	Jan 15 1918**	73.38	Nov 3 1919	119.62	63.0
3	Jan 10 1922**	78.59	Mar 20 1923	105.38	34.1
4	Mar 30 1926*	135.20	Dec 31 1927	202.40	49.7
5	Dec 31 1930	157.51	Feb 24 1931	194.36	23.4
6	Jul 26 1934*	85.51	Nov 19 1935	148.44	73.6
7	Mar 31 1938*	98.95	Sep 12 1939	155.92	57.6
8	Apr 28 1942*	92.92	Jul 14 1943	145.82	56.9
9	Oct 9 1946	163.12	Jul 24 1947	186.85	14.5
10	Jan 13 1950**	196.81	Sep 13 1951	276.37	40.4
11	Jan 11 1954**	279.87	Dec 30 1955	488.40	74.5
12	Feb 25 1958**	436.89	Dec 31 1959	679.36	55.5
13	Jun 26 1962*	535.74	Dec 18 1963	767.21	43.2
14	Oct 7 1966*	744.32	Sep 25 1967	943.08	26.7
15	May 26 1970*	631.16	Apr 28 1971	950.82	50.6
16	Dec 6 1974*	577.60	Jul 16 1975	881.81	52.7
17	Feb 28 1978*	742.12	Oct 5 1979	897.61	21.0
18	Aug 12 1982*	776.92	Nov 29 1983	1287.20	65.7
19	Jan 22 1986	1502.29	Aug 25 1987	2722.42	81.2
20	Oct 11 1990*	2365.10	Dec 31 1991	3168.84	34.0
21	Apr 4 1994	3593.35	Dec 13 1995	5216.47	45.2
22	Aug 31 1998*	7539.07	Dec 31 1999	11497.12	52.5
23	Jul 23 2002 ?	7702.34 *? at press time*	2003		
				Average	**50.2%**

* Bear Market ended   ** Bear previous year

AUGUST

Beware the "Summer Rally" hype historically the weakest rally of all seasons Averages 9.4% on the Dow (page 70), 2001 only 1.7%

MONDAY

18

The political problem of mankind is to combine three things: economic efficiency, social justice, and individual liberty.
— John Maynard Keynes

TUESDAY

19

The only thing that saves us from the bureaucracy is its inefficiency.
— Eugene McCarthy

WEDNESDAY

20

The most valuable executive is one who is training somebody to be a better man than he is.
— Robert G. Ingersoll (American lawyer and orator, "the Great Agnostic," 1833-1899)

THURSDAY

21

You know you're right when the other side starts to shout.
— I. A. O'Shaughnessy

FRIDAY

22

If you bet on a horse, that's gambling. If you bet you can make three spades, that's entertainment. If you bet cotton will go up three points, that's business. See the difference?
— Blackie Sherrod

SATURDAY
23

SUNDAY

24

DON'T-SELL-STOCKS-ON-MONDAY MANTRA MAY BE BACK

Mondays were on a dazzling eleven-year winning streak. From 1990 through 2000 Mondays gained 6067.37 Dow points, while all four other days gained a total of 1966.28 points. In 2001 and the first half of 2002 Mondays lost 783.85 Dow points versus –759.74 on the other days. In past flat years and bear market cycles Monday was the worst day of the week. See pages 66, 132-135.

ANNUAL DOW POINT CHANGES FOR DAYS OF THE WEEK SINCE 1953

Year	Monday	Tuesday	Wednesday	Thursday	Friday	Year's Closing DJIA	Year's Point Change
1953	— 37.39	— 6.70	19.63	7.25	6.21	280.90	— 11.00
1954	9.80	9.15	24.31	36.05	44.18	404.39	123.49
1955	— 56.09	34.31	45.83	0.78	59.18	488.40	84.01
1956	— 30.15	— 16.36	— 15.30	9.86	63.02	499.47	11.07
1957	—111.28	— 5.93	64.12	4.26	— 14.95	435.69	— 63.78
1958	14.36	26.73	29.10	24.25	53.52	583.65	147.96
1959	— 35.69	20.25	4.11	20.49	86.55	679.36	95.71
1960	—104.89	— 9.90	— 5.62	10.35	46.59	615.89	— 63.47
1961	— 17.66	4.29	87.51	— 5.74	46.85	731.14	115.25
1962	— 88.44	13.03	9.97	— 4.46	— 9.14	652.10	— 79.04
1963	— 43.61	81.85	16.23	26.07	30.31	762.95	110.85
1964	— 3.89	14.34	39.84	21.96	67.61	874.13	111.18
1965	— 70.23	36.65	57.03	2.75	68.93	969.26	95.13
1966	—126.73	— 54.24	56.13	— 45.69	— 13.04	785.69	— 183.57
1967	— 73.17	35.94	25.50	98.37	32.78	905.11	119.42
1968*	3.28	37.97	25.16	— 59.00	31.23	943.75	38.64
1969	—152.05	— 48.82	18.33	17.79	21.36	800.36	— 143.39
1970	— 99.00	— 47.14	116.07	1.81	66.82	838.92	38.56
1971	— 15.89	22.44	13.70	6.23	24.80	890.20	51.28
1972	— 85.08	— 3.55	65.24	6.14	147.07	1020.02	129.82
1973	—192.68	29.09	— 5.94	41.56	— 41.19	850.86	— 169.16
1974	—130.99	29.13	— 20.31	— 12.60	— 99.85	616.24	— 234.62
1975	59.80	— 129.96	56.93	129.48	119.92	852.41	236.17
1976	81.16	61.32	50.88	— 26.79	— 14.33	1004.65	152.24
1977	— 66.38	— 43.66	— 79.61	8.53	7.64	831.17	— 173.48
1978	— 31.79	— 70.34	71.33	— 65.71	70.35	805.01	— 26.16
1979	— 27.72	4.72	— 18.84	73.97	1.60	838.74	33.73
1980	— 89.40	137.92	137.77	— 112.78	51.74	963.99	125.25
1981	— 55.47	— 39.72	— 13.95	— 13.66	33.81	875.00	— 88.99
1982	21.69	70.22	28.37	14.65	36.61	1046.54	171.54
1983	39.34	— 39.75	149.28	48.30	14.93	1258.64	212.10
1984	— 40.48	44.70	— 129.24	84.36	— 6.41	1211.57	— 47.07
1985	86.96	43.97	56.19	49.45	98.53	1546.67	335.10
1986	— 56.03	113.72	178.65	32.17	80.77	1895.95	349.28
1987	—651.77	338.45	382.03	142.47	— 168.30	1938.83	42.88
1988	139.28	295.28	— 60.48	— 220.90	76.56	2168.57	229.74
1989	— 3.23	93.25	233.25	70.08	191.28	2753.20	584.63
Sub Total	—2041.51	1053.97	1713.20	422.10	1313.54		2461.30
1990	153.11	41.57	47.96	— 330.48	— 31.70	2633.66	— 119.54
1991	174.58	64.52	174.53	251.08	— 129.54	3168.83	535.17
1992	302.94	— 114.81	3.12	90.38	— 149.35	3301.11	132.28
1993	441.72	— 155.93	243.87	— 0.04	— 76.64	3754.09	452.98
1994	133.77	— 22.69	29.98	— 159.66	98.95	3834.44	80.35
1995	203.99	269.04	357.02	150.44	302.19	5117.12	1282.68
1996	631.88	150.08	— 34.24	261.66	321.77	6448.27	1331.15
1997	761.96	2362.53	— 590.17	— 989.48	— 84.86	7908.25	1459.98
1998	271.31	1057.74	591.63	—1576.71	929.21	9181.43	1273.18
1999	955.60	—1562.34	826.68	984.45	1111.30	11497.12	2315.69
2000	2035.79	536.13	—1978.34	407.30	—1711.15	10786.85	— 710.27
2001	—388.48	336.01	— 396.53	1089.88	—1406.23	10021.50	— 765.35
2002**	—395.37	— 651.95	530.20	— 215.93	— 45.19	9243.26	— 778.24
SubTotal	5283.52	2309.90	— 194.29	37.11	— 871.96		6490.06
Totals	3242.01	3363.87	1518.91	384.99	441.58		8951.36

*Most Wednesdays closed last 7 months of 1968   **Partial year through June 28, 2002

AUGUST

End of August Murderous 6 years in a row
Average loss for last week of August Dow:
−4.6%; S&P: −4.3%; NAS: −2.0%

MONDAY

25

Beware of inside information…all inside information.
— Jesse Livermore (*How to Trade In Stocks*)

TUESDAY

26

Life is an illusion. You are what you think you are.
— Yale Hirsch

WEDNESDAY

27

What the superior man seeks, is in himself.
What the inferior man seeks, is in others.
— Confucious

THURSDAY

28

During the first period of a man's life,
the greatest danger is: not to take the risk.
— Soren Kierkegaard

FRIDAY

29

In the realm of ideas, everything depends on enthusiasm;
in the real world, all rests on perseverance.
— Goethe

SATURDAY

30

September Sector Seasonalities: Bullish: CMR,
XTC, DRG; Bearish: SOX (page 118)

SUNDAY

31

SEPTEMBER ALMANAC

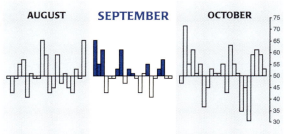

Market Probability Chart above is a graphic representation of the Market Probability Calendar on page 122.

◆ Start of business year, end of vacations, and back to school made September a leading barometer month in first 60 years of the century, now when portfolio managers get back from the Hamptons after Labor Day they tend to clean house ◆ Biggest % loser on the S&P and Dow in last 52 years (page 48) ◆ Streak of four great Septembers averaging 4.2% gains ended with three hefty losers in a row (see below) ◆ Day after Labor Day up 7 of last 8 ◆ Opened strong seven years in a row but tends to close weak due to end-of-quarter mutual fund portfolio restructuring

SEPTEMBER DAILY POINT CHANGES DOW JONES INDUSTRIALS

	1992	1993	1994	1995	1996	1997	1998	1999	2000	2001
Previous Month Close	3257.35	3651.25	3913.42	4610.56	5616.21	7622.42	7539.07	10829.28	11215.10	9949.75
1	8.91	− 6.15	− 11.98	36.98	—	H	288.36	108.60	23.68	—
2	24.05	− 19.00	− 15.86	—	H	257.36	− 45.06	− 94.67	—	—
3	1.89	7.83	—	—	32.18	14.86	− 100.15	235.24	—	H
4	− 10.27	—	—	H	8.51	− 27.40	− 41.97	—	H	47.74
5	—	—	H	22.54	− 49.94	− 44.83	—	—	21.83	35.78
6	—	H	13.12	13.73	52.90	—	—	H	50.03	− 192.43
7	H	− 26.83	− 12.45	− 14.09	—	—	H	− 44.32	− 50.77	− 234.99
8	− 21.34	− 18.17	22.21	31.00	—	12.77	380.53	2.21	− 39.22	—
9	10.80	0.56	− 33.65	—	73.98	16.73	− 155.76	43.06	—	—
10	33.77	32.14	—	—	− 6.66	−132.63	− 249.48	− 50.97	—	− 0.34
11	0.54	—	—	4.22	27.74	− 58.30	179.96	—	− 25.16	Closed*
12	—	—	− 14.47	42.27	17.02	81.99	—	—	37.74	Closed*
13	—	12.58	19.52	18.31	66.58	—	—	1.90	− 51.05	Closed*
14	70.52	− 18.45	15.47	36.28	—	—	149.85	− 120.00	− 94.71	Closed*
15	− 48.90	17.89	58.55	− 4.23	—	− 21.83	79.04	− 108.91	− 160.41	—
16	− 8.11	− 2.80	− 20.53	—	50.68	174.78	65.39	− 63.96	—	—
17	− 3.51	− 17.60	—	—	− 0.37	− 9.48	− 216.01	66.17	—	− 684.81
18	11.35	—	—	− 17.16	− 11.47	36.28	21.89	—	− 118.54	− 17.30
19	—	—	3.37	− 13.37	− 9.62	− 5.45	—	—	− 19.23	− 144.27
20	—	− 37.45	− 67.63	25.65	20.72	—	—	20.27	− 101.37	− 382.92
21	− 6.22	− 38.56	− 17.49	− 25.29	—	—	37.59	− 225.43	77.60	− 140.40
22	− 39.98	9.78	− 14.47	− 3.25	—	79.56	− 36.05	− 74.40	81.85	—
23	− 2.16	− 7.27	− 5.38	—	6.28	− 26.77	257.21	− 205.48	—	—
24	9.18	3.36	—	—	− 20.71	− 63.35	− 152.42	− 39.26	—	368.05
25	− 37.55	—	—	5.78	3.33	− 58.70	26.78	—	− 39.22	56.11
26	—	—	17.49	− 4.33	− 8.51	74.17	—	—	− 176.83	− 92.58
27	—	24.59	13.80	− 3.25	4.07	—	—	24.06	− 2.96	114.03
28	25.94	− 1.68	15.14	25.29	—	—	80.07	− 27.86	195.70	166.14
29	− 9.46	0.28	− 23.55	1.44	—	69.25	− 28.32	− 62.05	− 173.14	—
30	4.86	− 11.18	− 11.44	—	9.25	− 46.17	− 237.90	123.47	—	—
Close	3271.66	3555.12	3843.19	4789.08	5882.17	7945.26	7842.62	10336.95	10650.92	8847.56
Change	14.31	− 96.13	− 70.23	178.52	265.96	322.84	303.55	− 492.33	− 564.18	−1102.19

Market closed for four days after 9/11 terrorist attack

September is when leaves and stocks tend to fall
For blue chips it's the worst month of all

SEPTEMBER

MONDAY 1

Labor Day
(Market Closed)

September opens strong seven years in a row but tends to close weak, worst month for Dow, S&P and NASDAQ last 52 and 31 years (pages 48 and 56)

For a country, everything will be lost when the jobs of an economist and a banker become highly respected professions.
— Montesquieu

TUESDAY 2

Those heroes of finance are like beads on a string, when one slips off, the rest follow.
— Henrik Ibsen

WEDNESDAY 3

Every man is the architect of his own fortune.
— Appius Claudius

THURSDAY 4

All a parent can give a child is roots and wings.
— Chinese proverb

FRIDAY 5

The worse a situation becomes the less it takes to turn it around, the bigger the upside.
— George Soros

SATURDAY 6

SUNDAY 7

A CORRECTION FOR ALL SEASONS

While there's a rally for every season (page 70), almost always there's a decline or correction, too. Fortunately, corrections tend to be smaller than rallies, and that's what gives the stock market its long-term upward bias. In each season the average bounce outdoes the average setback. On average the net gain between the rally and the correction is smallest in summer and fall.

The summer setback tends to be slightly outdone by the average correction in the fall. Tax selling and portfolio cleaning are the usual explanations—individuals sell to register a tax loss and institutions like to get rid of their losers before preparing year-end statements. The October jinx also plays a major part. Since 1964, there have been 15 fall declines of over 10%, and in eight of them (1966, 1974, 1978, 1979, 1987, 1990, 1997 and 2000) the worst damage was done in October, where so many bear markets end. Important October lows were also seen in 1998 and 1999. Most often, it has paid to buy after fourth quarter or late third quarter "waterfall declines" for a rally that may continue into January or even beyond.

SEASONAL CORRECTIONS IN DOW JONES INDUSTRIALS

	WINTER Nov/Dec High to 1 Q. Low	SPRING Feb/Mar High to 2 Q. Low	SUMMER May/Jun High to 3 Q. Low	FALL Aug/Sep High to 4 Q. Low
1964	− 0.2%	− 2.4%	− 1.0%	− 2.1
1965	− 2.5	− 7.3	− 8.3	− 0.9
1966	− 6.0	− 13.2	− 17.7	− 12.7
1967	− 4.2	− 3.9	− 5.5	− 9.9
1968	− 8.8	− 0.3	− 5.5	+ 0.4
1969	− 8.7	− 8.7	− 17.2	− 8.1
1970	− 13.8	− 20.2	− 8.8	− 2.5
1971	− 1.4	− 4.8	− 10.7	− 13.4
1972	− 0.5	− 2.6	− 6.3	− 5.3
1973	− 11.0	− 12.8	− 10.9	− 17.3
1974	− 15.3	− 10.8	− 29.8	− 27.6
1975	− 6.3	− 5.6	− 9.9	− 6.7
1976	− 0.2	− 5.1	− 4.7	− 8.9
1977	− 8.5	− 7.2	− 11.5	− 10.2
1978	− 12.3	− 4.0	− 7.0	− 13.5
1979	− 2.5	− 5.8	− 3.7	− 10.9
1980	− 10.0	− 16.0	− 1.7	− 6.8
1981	− 6.9	− 5.1	− 18.6	− 12.9
1982	− 10.9	− 7.5	− 10.6	− 3.3
1983	− 4.1	− 2.8	− 6.8	− 3.6
1984	− 11.9	− 10.5	− 8.4	− 6.2
1985	− 4.8	− 4.4	− 2.8	− 2.3
1986	− 3.3	− 4.7	− 7.3	− 7.6
1987	− 1.5	− 6.6	− 1.7	− 36.1
1988	− 6.7	− 7.0	− 7.6	− 4.5
1989	− 1.7	− 2.4	− 3.1	− 6.6
1990	− 7.9	− 4.0	− 17.3	− 18.4
1991	− 6.3	− 3.6	− 4.5	− 6.3
1992	+ 0.1	− 3.3	− 5.4	− 7.6
1993	− 2.7	− 3.1	− 3.0	− 2.0
1994	− 4.4	− 9.6	− 4.4	− 7.1
1995	− 0.8	− 0.1	− 0.2	− 2.0
1996	− 3.5	− 4.6	− 7.5	+ 0.2
1997	− 1.8	− 9.8	− 2.2	− 13.3
1998	− 7.0	− 0.4	− 18.2	− 13.1
1999	− 2.7	− 1.7	− 8.1	− 11.5
2000	− 14.8	− 7.4	− 4.1	− 11.8
2001	− 14.5	− 13.6	− 27.4	− 16.2
2002	− 5.1	− 14.2		
Totals	− 235.1%	− 257.1%	− 329.3%	− 348.7%
Average	− 6.0%	− 6.6%	− 8.7%	− 9.2%

SEPTEMBER

MONDAY

8

*There is only one side of the market and it is not the bull side
or the bear side, but the right side.*
— Jesse Livermore

TUESDAY

9

*It isn't as important to buy as cheap as possible
as it is to buy at the right time.*
— Jesse Livermore

WEDNESDAY
10

*Patriotism is when love of your own people comes first. Nationalism
is when hate for people other that your own comes first.*
— Charles De Gaulle
(French president and WWII General, 1890-1970, May 1969)

In Memory of our comrades and colleagues
lost on September 11, 2001

"In Memory"

THURSDAY
11

Let's roll!
— Todd Beamer (Passenger on United Airlines Flight 93
just before foiling the hijackers, September 11, 2001)

FRIDAY

12

Interviewer: *How is it possible to fight an enemy
willing and ready to die for his cause?
Accommodate him!*
— General Norman Schwartzkof (Ret. Commander of Allied
Forces in 1990-1991 Gulf War, December 2001)

SATURDAY

13

SUNDAY

14

MARKET BEHAVIOR THREE DAYS BEFORE AND THREE DAYS AFTER HOLIDAYS

Many years ago investors became aware that the market tended to go up on the day before holidays and sell off the day after. We have kept track of this tendency in the *Stock Trader's Almanac* since the first edition in 1968. Recently, we began to notice that a transformation was taking place. Some holidays seemed to be favored by the bulls, while others weren't.

To see what has been taking place more clearly, we have separated eight holidays into three groups: those positive the day after, those negative the day after, and the sole holiday negative both the day before and after. Notice that we are showing average percent changes for the Dow Jones industrial average, Standard & Poor's 500, and the Zweig Unweighted Price Index.

Bear in mind that the Dow and S&P are both blue chip indices, whereas the Zweig (ZUPI) would be more representative of smaller cap stocks. This is evident on the last day of the year with ZUPI smaller stocks having a field day, while their larger brethren in the Dow and S&P are showing losses on average. The best six-day span can be seen for ZUPI stocks on the three days before and three days after New Year's Day, a gain of about 1.8 percent on average.

The worst day after a holiday, for which we have no explanation, is the day after Easter. Surprisingly, the following day is the best second day after a holiday.

Presidents' Day is the least bullish of all the holidays, bearish the day before and two days after. Eleven dogs in a row on the Dow the day before Presidents' Day.

HOLIDAYS: 3 DAYS BEFORE, 3 DAYS AFTER (Average % Change 1980 - May 31, 2002)

	−3	−2	−1	Positive Day After	+1	+2	+3
S&P 500	0.03	0.36	−0.17	**New Year's**	−0.12	0.47	−0.06
DJIA	−0.01	0.30	−0.24	**Day**	0.13	0.47	0.14
ZUPI	0.13	0.36	0.51		0.13	0.43	0.25
S&P 500	0.14	−0.12	0.04	**Memorial**	0.33	0.16	0.25
DJIA	0.14	−0.18	−0.03	**Day**	0.42	0.19	0.20
ZUPI	−0.10	0.03	0.16		0.11	0.10	0.23
S&P 500	−0.002	−0.47	0.25	**Labor**	0.11	−0.01	−0.07
DJIA	−0.002	−0.52	0.24	**Day**	0.22	0.04	−0.12
ZUPI	0.14	−0.15	0.25		−0.09	−0.03	0.19
S&P 500	−0.11	0.09	0.12	**Thanksgiving**	0.26	−0.29	0.28
DJIA	0.01	0.11	0.20		0.20	−0.27	0.34
ZUPI	−0.22	−0.13	0.12		0.33	−0.25	0.17
S&P 500	0.12	0.17	0.29	**Christmas**	0.24	0.08	0.36
DJIA	0.17	0.28	0.37		0.29	0.06	0.32
ZUPI	0.01	0.16	0.39		0.11	0.12	0.39
				Negative Day After			
S&P 500	0.25	0.02	0.19	**Good**	−0.50	0.54	0.07
DJIA	0.18	0.003	0.20	**Friday**	−0.35	0.55	0.07
ZUPI	0.07	0.11	0.16		−0.43	0.29	0.09
S&P 500	0.05	0.23	0.10	**Independence**	−0.44	0.01	0.30
DJIA	0.02	0.17	0.08	**Day**	−0.36	0.07	0.24
ZUPI	0.15	0.14	0.15		−0.20	−0.06	0.11
				Negative Before & After			
S&P 500	0.28	0.01	−0.47	**Presidents'**	−0.28	−0.08	−0.003
DJIA	0.27	0.04	−0.40	**Day**	−0.18	−0.15	−0.03
ZUPI	0.19	0.004	−0.09		−0.32	−0.13	−0.05

Data courtesy of Martin Zweig/Catherine Nolan

SEPTEMBER

Monday before Triple Witching Dow up 8 of last 12

MONDAY

15

I don't know where speculation got such a bad name, since I know of no forward leap which was not fathered by speculation.
— John Steinbeck

FOMC Meeting

TUESDAY

16

To affect the quality of the day, that is the highest of the arts.
— Henry David Thoreau

WEDNESDAY

17

Imagination is more important than knowledge.
— Albert Einstein

THURSDAY

18

He who knows nothing is confident of everything.
— Anonymous

*September Triple Witching day
Dow down 8 of last 12*

FRIDAY

19

I just wait until the fourth year, when the business cycle bottoms, and buy whatever I think will have the biggest bounce.
— Larry Tisch's investment style

SATURDAY
20

SUNDAY

21

END-OF-MONTH BULLISH SEASONALITY SHIFTING

Trading patterns are changing dramatically. For many years the last day plus the first four days were the best days of the month. Thousands took advantage of this anomaly and thrived. The market currently exhibits greater bullish bias from the last three trading days of the previous month through the first two days of the current month and now shows dramatic bullishness during the middle three trading days nine to eleven, due to 401(k) cash inflows (see pages 36, 92, 136 and 137). 1995-2000 "bubble" mania overrode this pattern with market strength all month long. Some big hits came on Super Eight Days during the ensuing 2½-year decline yet as the stock market has returned to earth monthly bullishness at the ends, beginnings and middles of months appears to be resuming.

SUPER EIGHT DAYS DOW % CHANGES VS. REST-OF MONTH

	Super 8 Days	Rest of Month	Super 8 Days	Rest of Month	Super 8 Days	Rest of Month
	1994		1995		1996	
Jan	0.30%	2.69%	1.75%	−1.50%	2.10%	1.12%
Feb	2.57	−2.95	1.20	2.19	1.07	4.46
Mar	−1.04	−2.30	−0.52	4.21	0.65	1.24
Apr	−3.43	1.98	0.75	2.81	2.44	−4.20
May	1.40	−0.02	1.41	1.18	0.71	1.86
Jun	0.55	−2.38	1.85	1.08	−1.04	1.22
Jul	0.48	0.89	0.73	2.88	−2.91	−1.36
Aug	1.45	2.44	−0.42	−2.00	3.09	1.25
Sep	1.50	−1.93	1.97	1.73	1.07	1.84
Oct	−0.34	0.02	0.70	−1.99	2.37	−0.74
Nov	−0.17	−3.48	3.30	4.29	2.46	6.86
Dec	2.27	1.83	1.39	−0.60	−3.70	3.82
Totals	**5.53%**	**−3.22%**	**14.13%**	**14.29%**	**8.31%**	**17.36%**
Average	**0.46%**	**−0.27%**	**1.18%**	**1.19%**	**0.69%**	**1.45%**
	1997		1998		1999	
Jan	0.80%	0.91%	4.18%	−2.30%	0.98%	0.08%
Feb	4.19	1.46	5.43	1.55	0.76	1.62
Mar	−3.83	1.58	3.06	2.53	−0.68	3.74
Apr	−4.50	2.66	2.29	−1.47	2.84	7.09
May	5.49	3.81	2.37	−1.79	−0.83	−1.92
Jun	1.63	2.55	−4.64	4.47	0.20	0.01
Jul	2.85	2.64	3.55	−3.43	5.87	−1.74
Aug	−2.39	−1.76	−4.75	0.17	−0.35	2.41
Sep	4.51	−3.57	−4.92	−0.59	−5.83	−2.32
Oct	2.45	−6.73	0.68	3.59	−2.86	2.97
Nov	6.56	−2.84	6.19	4.57	4.25	2.45
Dec	2.53	−3.57	−2.75	2.11	0.29	3.92
Totals	**20.27%**	**−2.84%**	**10.69%**	**9.42%**	**4.63%**	**18.32%**
Average	**1.69%**	**−0.24%**	**0.89%**	**0.78%**	**0.39%**	**1.53%**
	2000		2001		2002	
Jan	−4.09%	0.46%	2.13%	−2.36%	−1.92%	−0.23%
Feb	0.43	−9.10	1.41	−3.36	−1.41	4.27
Mar	2.76	5.62	−1.50	−3.30	4.11	−2.64
Apr	−2.79	4.77	−2.61	9.56	−2.46	0.08
May	0.70	−7.86	2.02	1.53	3.62	−4.06
Jun	5.99	−4.10	−2.46	−2.45		
Jul	−0.65	0.83	2.16	−2.29		
Aug	3.08	3.75	0.24	−2.48		
Sep	−3.27	−2.34	−3.62	−12.05		
Oct	−0.85	−1.47	4.51	5.36		
Nov	5.81	−4.06	1.01	2.48		
Dec	−2.96	4.44	0.19	1.99		
Totals	**4.15%**	**−9.06%**	**3.47%**	**−7.37%**	**1.93%**	**−2.59%**
Average	**0.35%**	**−0.76%**	**0.29%**	**−0.61%**	**0.39%**	**−0.52%**

		Super 8 Days		Rest of Month (15 Days)	
101		Net % Changes	73.12%	Net % Changes	34.31%
Month		Average Period	0.63%	Average Period	0.26%
Totals		Average Day	0.08%	Average Day	0.02%

SEPTEMBER

Septembers close weak (page 82 and 123)

MONDAY

22

*Spend at least as much time researching a stock
as you would choosing a refrigerator.*
— Peter Lynch

TUESDAY

23

*The first rule is not to lose.
The second rule is not to forget the first rule.*
— Warren Buffett

WEDNESDAY

24

*Press on. Nothing in the world can take the place of persistence.
Talent will not: nothing is more common than unrewarded talent.
Education alone will not: the world is full of educated failures.
Persistence alone is omnipotent.*
— Calvin Coolidge

THURSDAY

25

*Companies already dominant in a field rarely produce the
breakthroughs that transform it.*
— George Gilder

FRIDAY

26

*With enough inside information and a million dollars,
you can go broke in a year.*
— Warren Buffett

Rosh Hashanah

SATURDAY

27

October Sector Seasonalities: Bullish: XAL,
MSH, BKX, FPP, XAU, SOX, XBD (page 118)

SUNDAY

28

OCTOBER ALMANAC

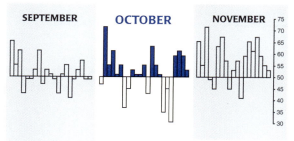

Market Probability Chart above is a graphic representation of the Market Probability Calendar on page 122.

◆ Known as the jinx month because of crashes in 1929, 1987, the 554-point drop on October 27, 1997, back-to-back massacres in 1978 and 1979 and Friday the 13th in 1989 ◆ Yet October is a "bear killer" and turned the tide in nine post-WWII bear markets: 1946, 1957, 1960, 1962, 1966, 1974, 1987, 1990, and 1998 ◆ Worst six months of the year ends with October (page 48) ◆ One of the worst months on NASDAQ (page 56) ◆ October is a great time to buy stocks, especially high-tech stocks ◆ Can get into Best Six Months earlier using MACD (page 52)

OCTOBER DAILY POINT CHANGES DOW JONES INDUSTRIALS

Previous Month Close	1992 3271.66	1993 3555.12	1994 3843.19	1995 4789.08	1996 5882.17	1997 7945.26	1998 7842.62	1999 10336.95	2000 10650.92	2001 8847.56
1	− 17.29	25.99	—	—	22.73	70.24	− 210.09	− 63.95	—	− 10.73
2	− 53.76	—	—	− 27.82	29.07	12.03	152.16	—	49.21	113.76
3	—	—	3.70	− 11.56	− 1.12	11.05	—	—	19.61	173.19
4	—	− 3.35	− 45.76	− 9.03	60.01	—	—	128.23	64.74	− 62.90
5	− 21.61	9.50	− 13.79	22.04	—	—	− 58.45	− 0.64	− 59.56	58.89
6	− 0.81	11.73	− 11.78	6.50	—	61.64	16.74	187.75	− 128.38	—
7	− 25.94	− 15.36	21.87	—	− 13.05	78.09	− 1.29	− 51.29	—	—
8	23.78	1.11	—	—	− 13.04	− 83.25	9.78	112.71	—	− 51.83
9	− 39.45	—	—	− 42.99	− 36.15	− 33.64	167.61	—	− 28.11	− 15.50
10	—	—	23.89	− 5.42	− 8.95	− 16.21	—	—	− 44.03	188.42
11	—	8.67	55.51	14.45	47.71	—	—	− 1.58	− 110.61	169.59
12	37.83	− 0.28	− 1.68	29.63	—	—	101.95	− 231.12	− 379.21	− 66.29
13	27.01	10.06	14.80	28.90	—	27.01	− 63.33	− 184.90	157.60	—
14	− 5.94	18.44	20.52	—	40.62	24.07	30.64	54.45	—	—
15	− 20.80	8.10	—	—	− 5.22	− 38.31	330.58	− 266.90	—	3.46
16	− 0.27	—	—	− 9.40	16.03	− 119.10	117.40	—	46.62	36.61
17	—	—	13.46	11.56	38.39	− 91.85	—	—	− 149.09	− 151.26
18	—	12.58	− 6.39	− 18.42	35.03	—	—	96.57	− 114.69	− 69.75
19	14.04	− 6.99	18.50	24.93	—	—	49.69	88.65	167.96	40.89
20	− 2.43	9.78	− 24.89	− 7.59	—	74.41	39.40	187.43	83.61	—
21	1.08	− 8.94	− 19.85	—	− 3.36	139.00	13.38	− 94.67	—	—
22	13.78	13.14	—	—	− 29.07	− 25.79	13.91	172.56	—	172.92
23	6.76	—	—	− 39.38	− 25.34	− 186.88	− 80.85	—	45.13	− 36.95
24	—	—	− 36.00	28.18	− 43.98	− 132.36	—	—	121.35	5.54
25	—	24.31	− 4.71	− 29.98	14.54	—	—	− 120.32	− 66.59	117.28
26	36.47	− 1.12	− 2.36	− 49.86	—	—	− 20.08	− 47.80	53.64	82.27
27	− 8.38	− 7.83	26.92	37.93	—	− 554.26	− 66.17	92.76	210.50	—
28	15.67	23.20	55.51	—	− 34.29	337.17	5.93	227.64	—	—
29	− 5.13	− 7.27	—	—	34.29	8.35	123.06	107.33	—	− 275.67
30	− 19.99	—	—	14.82	− 13.79	− 125.00	97.07	—	245.15	− 147.52
31	—	—	− 22.54	− 1.09	36.15	61.13	—	—	135.37	− 46.84
Close	3226.28	3680.59	3908.12	4755.48	6029.38	7442.80	8592.10	10729.86	10971.14	9075.14
Change	− 45.38	125.47	64.93	− 33.60	147.21	− 502.46	749.48	392.91	320.22	227.58

Though October is NASDAQ's "Worst month of the year"
Buy tech stocks and you'll soon wear a grin ear to ear

SEPTEMBER/OCTOBER

MONDAY
29

The greatest discovery of my generation is that human beings can alter their lives by altering their attitudes.
— William James

Start looking for MACD seasonal BUY Signal (pages 52 and 60)
Newsletter subscribers will be emailed the alert when it triggers
Email service@hirschorg.com for details

TUESDAY
30

If all the economists in the world were laid end to end, they still wouldn't reach a conclusion.
— George Bernard Shaw

October no longer worst month, but still weak performer (pages 48 and 56)
End of "Worst Six Months" and "Worst Eight Months" (pages 50 and 58)
Known as "bear-killer" (page 90)

WEDNESDAY
1

Early in March (1960), Dr. Arthur F. Burns called on me...Burns' conclusion was that unless some decisive action was taken, and taken soon, we were heading for another economic dip which would hit its low point in October, just before the elections.
— Richard M. Nixon (*Six Crises*)

THURSDAY

2

The best minds are not in government. If any were, business would hire them away.
— Ronald Reagan

FRIDAY
3

It is a funny thing about life; if you refuse to accept anything but the best, you very often get it.
— W. Somerset Maugham

SATURDAY
4

SUNDAY
5

FIRST CAME THE PRIME FIVE DAYS; NOW END, BEGINNING AND MID-MONTH ARE STRONGEST

Dow % changes in the first table are for the last trading day of the previous month plus the first four of the current month between 1967 and 1983. During this 17-year period, spent mostly in the Dow 750-1000 range, these prime five days gained 793.27 points while the rest of the month's 16 (on average) trading days lost 319.46. So many investors taking advantage of this seasonality by switching between no-load equity and money market funds, along with the start of the biggest bull cycle in history, altered the pattern (see pages 36, 88, 136-137).

NET DOW % CHANGE OF PRIME FIVE DAYS (1967-1983)

	Jan	Feb	Mar	Apr	May	Jun	Jul	Aug	Sep	Oct	Nov	Dec
1967	2.85	0.83	0.66	−1.00	0.80	−0.26	0.82	2.47	1.62	−0.24	−3.53	1.03
1968	0.38	0.20	−0.89	4.48	0.68	1.67	1.54	−0.73	3.01	2.45	−0.05	0.20
1969	−2.05	0.48	1.16	−1.30	2.99	−0.66	1.55	2.78	−1.08	−1.06	0.55	−1.73
1970	0.90	0.26	3.02	0.83	−2.58	3.27	−1.98	−1.62	0.70	2.83	2.39	4.44
1971	−0.41	1.12	1.06	1.03	−1.13	1.81	1.54	−1.39	1.67	1.89	0.66	3.13
1972	2.18	0.03	2.80	2.83	−0.92	−2.03	1.28	2.70	0.48	−1.45	4.06	0.86
1973	3.95	−1.31	3.28	−3.72	3.44	−1.18	−2.74	−2.25	1.82	0.28	−5.73	−2.51
1974	3.40	−4.37	1.90	0.53	1.13	5.20	−1.48	1.07	3.20	−6.01	−0.58	−5.20
1975	6.29	2.55	4.19	−2.99	3.95	3.33	−1.38	−2.16	0.78	1.79	0.18	−3.43
1976	5.43	−0.41	−0.84	0.96	−1.26	−0.17	−0.95	0.75	2.86	−3.18	−1.00	1.23
1977	−1.92	−1.01	2.15	−0.70	1.74	0.47	−0.42	−0.20	2.04	0.24	−1.55	−2.46
1978	−4.44	−0.49	−0.75	0.57	−0.30	3.87	−1.12	3.75	1.47	1.76	0.37	4.02
1979	3.07	−3.40	2.43	1.25	−1.06	1.62	0.37	1.17	−1.38	0.30	−2.10	0.40
1980	−0.82	−0.01	−3.09	−1.20	0.61	1.47	1.86	0.22	1.14	4.75	1.60	−1.94
1981	1.96	−0.22	−0.23	0.21	−3.08	−0.76	−3.09	0.83	−3.42	0.99	3.14	0.76
1982	−1.30	−1.99	−2.21	1.80	2.16	−2.42	−1.55	−2.01	2.35	4.19	5.98	5.26
1983	2.25	1.24	1.79	−2.24	0.02	−0.16	−0.28	−2.73	4.02	2.31	−0.42	−1.39
Totals	21.71	−6.52	16.44	1.34	7.18	15.07	−6.03	2.64	21.58	11.84	3.96	2.68
Up	11	8	11	10	10	9	7	9	14	12	9	10
Down	6	9	6	7	7	8	10	8	3	5	8	7

The second table shows that the new seasonality shifted to the last three trading days of the previous month through the first two of the current month and the middle three trading days nine-eleven, when 401(k) deductions seem to be invested, in the 1984-2002 period. These super eight days did 72.5% better than the prime five did in these years. In the earlier period the prime five outperformed the super eight by nearly two and a half to one. We've had some nasty drops the last five years during the super eight days with September down four in a row posting a losing record overall.

NET DOW % CHANGE OF SUPER EIGHT DAYS (1984-2002)

	Jan	Feb	Mar	Apr	May	Jun	Jul	Aug	Sep	Oct	Nov	Dec
1984	−0.19	−1.46	1.59	2.11	0.58	0.08	2.68	3.72	−2.04	0.88	−0.10	−2.74
1985	−0.55	1.38	−0.98	0.94	−3.36	0.45	1.59	−0.03	−0.76	2.66	2.29	2.90
1986	2.88	5.36	1.43	1.80	−4.02	2.33	−1.32	0.87	−2.00	2.86	0.79	2.07
1987	5.28	3.85	−0.76	−4.58	0.34	0.75	1.21	2.24	−6.71	−1.95	8.97	−1.20
1988	6.59	3.92	2.59	−3.80	2.79	6.06	3.02	1.29	2.57	1.62	−2.16	0.54
1989	0.35	2.64	0.65	1.78	4.43	−0.32	−2.51	0.78	0.35	−0.78	0.95	1.72
1990	1.24	2.86	4.09	1.31	3.94	4.14	3.45	−0.76	0.07	1.14	2.43	0.31
1991	−2.12	6.52	1.79	4.80	−1.27	3.41	2.97	1.04	−0.41	1.90	−3.63	2.82
1992	5.85	−1.57	1.86	2.00	1.28	1.30	2.14	1.63	1.75	−1.52	−0.55	0.32
1993	−0.41	−2.12	1.29	−1.01	−0.04	1.06	0.17	−0.23	−0.70	1.30	1.07	−0.24
1994	0.30	2.57	−1.04	−3.43	1.40	0.55	0.48	1.45	1.50	−0.34	−0.17	2.27
1995	1.75	1.20	−0.52	0.75	1.41	1.85	0.73	−0.42	1.97	0.70	3.30	1.39
1996	2.10	1.07	0.65	2.44	0.71	−1.04	−2.91	3.09	1.07	2.37	2.46	−3.70
1997	0.80	4.19	−3.83	−4.50	5.49	1.63	2.85	−2.39	4.51	2.45	6.56	2.53
1998	4.18	5.43	3.06	2.29	2.37	−4.64	3.55	−4.75	−4.92	0.68	6.19	−2.75
1999	0.98	0.76	−0.68	2.84	−0.83	0.20	5.87	−0.35	−5.83	−2.86	4.25	0.29
2000	−4.09	0.43	2.76	−2.79	0.70	5.99	−0.65	3.08	−3.27	−0.85	5.81	−2.96
2001	2.13	1.41	−1.50	−2.61	2.02	−2.46	2.16	0.24	−3.62	4.51	1.01	0.19
2002	−1.92	−1.41	4.11	−2.46	3.62							
Totals	25.15	37.05	16.55	−2.13	21.56	21.32	25.47	10.49	−16.47	14.75	39.46	3.75
Up	13	15	12	11	14	14	14	11	8	12	13	12
Down	6	4	7	8	5	4	4	7	10	6	5	6

OCTOBER

Yom Kippur

MONDAY

6

Capitalism without bankruptcy is like Christianity without hell.
— Frank Borman (CEO Eastern Airlines, April 1986)

TUESDAY

7

*I'm always turned off by an overly optimistic letter from
the president in the annual report. If his letter is
mildly pessimistic to me that's a good sign.*
— Philip Carret
(Centenarian, Founded Pioneer Fund in 1928, 1896-1998)

WEDNESDAY

 8

*When I talk to a company that tells me the last analyst showed up
three years ago, I can hardly contain my enthusiasm.*
— Peter Lynch

**Historically one of two (July 18) worst
trading days of the year
S&P up only 23.8% of the time (page 123)**

THURSDAY

9

*Analysts are supposed to be critics of corporations.
They often end up being public relations spokesmen for them.*
— Ralph Wanger (Chief Investment Officer, Acorn Fund)

FRIDAY

10

*It's a lot of fun finding a country nobody knows about.
The only thing better is finding a country everybody's
bullish on and shorting it.*
— Jim Rogers

SATURDAY

11

SUNDAY

12

TRADING CLASSIC CHART PATTERNS
By Thomas N. Bulkowski
THE BEST INVESTMENT BOOK OF THE YEAR

Reviewed by Barbara Rockefeller
[First reviewed by Ms. Rockefeller in Active Trader *Magazine, September 2002]*

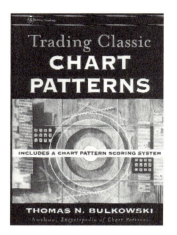

As in his earlier *Encyclopedia of Chart Patterns*, Tom Bulkowski's great contribution in his latest book, *Trading Classic Chart Patterns*, is practical trading advice based on what works and what doesn't. He provides statistical analysis of chart patterns backed by thorough research.

When Bulkowski uses the word "probability," he means it literally, unlike commentators who throw the word around casually. If you spend any time looking at charts, you can't avoid seeing some patterns, such as head-and-shoulder formations, triangles, or at least support and resistance. In *Encyclopedia*, Bulkowski described how to identify patterns, the range of likely outcomes, and how often the patterns delivered the different outcomes within the range. This was a stunning achievement in its own right.

In the new book, Bulkowski builds on his pattern-definition base to deliver the good stuff: a system for picking the best patterns on which to risk your money. The central theme is that identifying the pattern is not enough. We don't trade patterns, we trade stocks. It's a more complex process to pick the highest probability trade in a specific stock.

Bulkowski's focus in the latest book is establishing guidelines on how to weed the losers from the winners. Knowing how a pattern has performed in the past is helpful, but we all want to know how well a chart pattern will do this time. To that end, Bulkowski has developed a scoring system. Admittedly, it is not perfect, but it is quick and easy to use and it does improve results from pure pattern-recognition alone.

Even the best trading books, such as *Trader Vic – Methods of a Wall Street Master* (by Victor Sperandeo, John Wiley & Sons, 1991, Best Investment Book of the Year *1992 Stock Trader's Almanac*) and John Bollinger's *Bollinger on Bollinger Bands* (McGraw-Hill, 2002, one of the Top Investment Books this year; see page 98) discuss patterns, but refrain from offering probabilities or describe what else is going on in a given trade situation. Man does not live by bread alone, and top traders don't trade on pattern alone. Exactly when should you buy after a double bottom? How will you know when to sell and how much can you expect to make? Nobody but Bulkowski answers these questions.

In the first part of the book, Bulkowski reviews charting and trading basics, including support and resistance, trendlines, stops and common trading mistakes. The second part delves into the most common chart patterns and what to expect from them, including case studies that combine knowledge of the pattern with an understanding of the other factors affecting the situation, including concurrent patterns (such as gaps), market trend and volume, to name a few.

One case study stands out—a trade done in Medarex, a Nasdaq drug stock. First Bulkowski finds the start of a downtrend, which occurred at a level of a horizontal consolidation. The stock proceeded to fall 20 percent before estab-

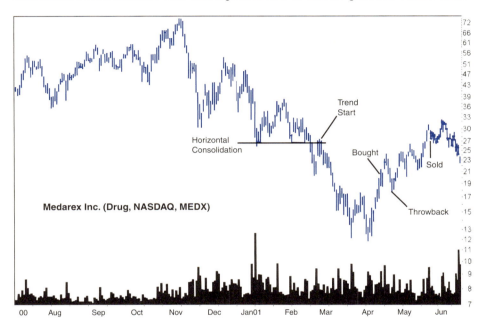

lishing a double bottom. We expect this to be a reversal area, but just as we think a long trade is about to be executed, various aspects of the move are measured and scored.

For example, the double bottom in question was a "tall" one, meaning the highest high minus the lowest low divided by the breakout price was 33 percent, against a median value for short-term double bottoms of 17.1 percent. It gets a score of +1, because tall double bottoms are more likely to deliver the pattern's probable median gain.

Volume got a score of –1 because it was only average, and we prefer above average volume on a breakout. However, some of the other scoring criteria get +1s, resulting in a final pattern score of +4. Any score over zero implies the stock will beat the median (26.2 percent) rise off the breakout at the confirmation line. In this case, the stock rose as it was supposed to (37 percent). The sale was executed near a round number marking resistance (about 22 percent of horizontal support and resistance levels are round numbers, more than chance would have). The actual gain was 45 percent in two months – fairly high among

(continued on page 96)

YEAR'S BEST BOOK *(continued from page 95)*

the cases in the book, but for results like that we will gladly plough through the process.

A virtue of Bulkowski's work is that he doesn't fall in love with particular patterns. He not only reveals the times they fail, he quantifies those failures (unlike some authors who show you only the perfect charts and neglect to mention the other times the pattern didn't work). Bulkowski arrived at his figures by analyzing 10 years of data (from 1991) for 700 stocks.

For those of us who thought that patterns are too subjective and judgmental, Bulkowski's work is a revelation. Just because analysis requires judgment doesn't mean there is an unlimited number of equally valid interpretations. Once you factor in the other pattern and non-pattern elements, using a scoring system, there is only one correct trading decision. It may still be too risky for your personal taste, but the forecast is clear.

Bulkowski's *Encyclopedia* was intended as a reference book for chart patterns. *Trading Classic Chart Patterns* is not a reference work; it's a useful tool. When you are sitting at your computer screen looking at a chart of your stock, it's a matter of minutes to use the book to score your possible trade. What could be more directly useful?

Bulkowski has a breezy, easy-to-read style and he writes in the first person, telling you how he tackled various projects, and revealing the outcomes. He is generous with stories about his own trading, including his mistakes (which, of course, lead to more research).

But the book is exhausting to read. You can only do one small section at a time, preferably while you have a chart in front of you of the issue under review. Even then you will have to revisit the section several times before all the material sinks in, including the warnings. *Trading Classic Chart Patterns*, along with *Encyclopedia of Chart Patterns*, is the first real advance on the basic chart pattern work done by Edwards and Magee more than 50 years ago.

Barbara Rockefeller, president of Rockefeller Treasury Services, an independent research firm, is an international economist with a focus on foreign exchange. She has worked as a forecaster, trader and consultant at Citibank and other financial institutions. She currently publishes two daily reports on international financial markets and foreign exchange and technical analysis-based reports on stocks and stock indices. She is the author of How to Trade Stocks Internationally, *published in Japan in 1999,* CNBC 24/7 Trading: Around the Clock, Around the World *(John Wiley & Sons, 2000) and* The Global Trader *(John Wiley & Sons, 2001, one of the Top Investment Books this year; see page 98). Ms. Rockefeller is also a contributing analyst to our monthly* Almanac Investor *newsletter. For a sample of her work in the newsletter or if you are interested in a custom analysis of your stocks from Barbara Rockefeller send one stock to* **service@hirschorg.com** *for a sample report or call 201-767-4100. Reports are delivered in Adobe Acrobat format.*

RESERVE YOUR 2004 ALMANAC

As a special service to Almanac readers, we offer you the opportunity to purchase the *2004 Stock Trader's Almanac* at a pre-publication discount. To order call Toll-Free 800-477-3400, ext. 2 and <u>Save 20%</u> off the regular price. You may also fax your order to 201-767-7337 or go to www.stocktradersalmanac.com.

RESERVE YOUR 2004 STOCK TRADER'S ALMANAC NOW!

❏ Please reserve _____ copies of your **37th Edition 2004 Stock Trader's Almanac**. $23.95 (regularly $29.95) for single copies plus $5.95 shipping *($10.95 to Canada, $16.95 to all other foreign countries).* Discount quantity prices available on request.

❏ $_____ payment enclosed
(US funds only, drawn on a US bank)

Charge Credit Card (check one)

❏ VISA ❏ MasterCard ❏ AmEx

Name _____

Address _____

City _____

State _____ Zip _____

Account # _____

Expiration Date _____

Signature _____

❏ Send _____ additional copies of the **2003 STOCK TRADER'S ALMANAC**. $29.95 for single copies plus $5.95 shipping *($10.95 to Canada, $16.95 to all other foreign countries).* Discount quantity prices available on request.

❏ $_____ payment enclosed
(US funds only, drawn on a US bank)

Charge Credit Card (check one)

❏ VISA ❏ MasterCard ❏ AmEx

Name _____

Address _____

City _____

State _____ Zip _____

Account # _____

Expiration Date _____

Signature _____

THE THIRTY-SEVENTH EDITION
of the Stock Trader's Almanac will be published in the Fall of 2003. Mail the postpaid card below to reserve your copy of the 2004 Edition.

BUSINESS REPLY MAIL
FIRST CLASS   PERMIT NO. 239   WESTWOOD, NJ

POSTAGE WILL BE PAID BY ADDRESSEE:

The Hirsch Organization Inc.
PO Box 2069
River Vale, NJ 07675-9988

BUSINESS REPLY MAIL
FIRST CLASS   PERMIT NO. 239   WESTWOOD, NJ

POSTAGE WILL BE PAID BY ADDRESSEE:

The Hirsch Organization Inc.
PO Box 2069
River Vale, NJ 07675-9988

OCTOBER

MONDAY 13

**Columbus Day
(Bond Market Closed)**

Monday before expiration up 10 of last 12

---

*Short-term volatility is greatest at turning points and
diminishes as a trend becomes established.*
— George Soros

TUESDAY 14

The bigger a man's head gets, the easier it is to fill his shoes.
— Anonymous

WEDNESDAY 15

---

*The test of success is not what you do when you are on top.
Success is how high you bounce when you hit bottom.*
— General George S. Patton

THURSDAY 16

When an old man dies, a library burns down.
— African proverb

FRIDAY 17

Options expiration day up 6 of last 12

---

*The usual bull market successfully weathers a number of tests until
it is considered invulnerable, whereupon it is ripe for a bust.*
— George Soros

SATURDAY 18

Crash October 19, 1987 Dow down 22.6% in one day

SUNDAY 19

YEAR'S TOP INVESTMENT BOOKS

Trading Classic Chart Patterns, Thomas N. Bulkowski, John Wiley & Sons, $69.95. Technical analysts seemed irrelevant during the recent roaring bull market when swarms of investors felt invincible. If they only had some knowledge about simple chart patterns they could have saved themselves fortunes and grief, instead of riding the down escalator of the 2000-2002 bear market. The Best Investment Book Of The Year. (See page 94.)

Encyclopedia of Chart Patterns, Thomas N. Bulkowski, John Wiley & Sons, $79.95. First-rate technical analyst Barbara Rockefeller calls Bulkowski's work the best since the classic *Technical Analysis Of Stock Trends* by Edwards & Magee back in 1948. Provides a statistical assessment of the results of the various chart formations. Invaluable!

The Global-Investor Book of Investing Rules: Invaluable Advice From 150 Master Investors, Philip Jenks & Stephen Eckett, Financial Times/Prentice Hall, $29.00. An unprecedented, up-to-the-minute portfolio of investment advice from 150 of the world's leading fund managers, traders, analysts, economists, and investment experts. Every expert has distilled his or her advice down to its very essence, presenting specific "dos and don'ts," techniques, and ideas you can use right now.

The Psychology Of Trading: Tools and Tactics for Minding the Markets, Brett N. Steenbarger, Ph.D., John Wiley & Sons, $39.95, due January. "Investigate, then invest" was for many years the slogan of the New York Stock Exchange. We always thought a better one would be, "Investigate YOURSELF, then invest." Brett Steenbarger's *The Psychology of Trading* should help you increase your annual investment rate of return. Mandatory reading for anyone intending to earn a livelihood through trading.

Bollinger On Bollinger Bands, John Bollinger, McGraw-Hill. $49.95. CNBC's Ron Insana best describes this unusual book: "Is a must read for all students of the markets. Bollinger bands [around price trends] set the boundaries for expectations, and allow traders to understand the degree and speed with which markets [and stocks] can move. When they are broken they contain some of the most important information an investor could want."

Profit With Options, Lawrence G. McMillan, John Wiley & Sons, $39.95. The top name in the options arena has written a hands-on manual that takes you on a complete course through the options process. We have always been fascinated by the fact that a number of investors make about 15 percent a year "writing" options. A friend of ours liked to keep writing options on quality companies until he worked his original purchase price down to zero.

Practical Speculation In an Uncertain World, Victor Niederhoffer and Laurel Kenner, John Wiley & Sons, $29.95. Last year's Almanac was dedicated to the author, "Master Speculator and Raconteur who inspired me 28 years ago, and continues to do so." His first book, *Education of a Speculator*, is a *tour de force* and unlike any other investment book ever written. Niederhoffer and Kenner examine the increasingly volatile and noisy market to see what works in trading. From politics and risk to surviving and science, *Practical Speculation* calls on science as its

(continued on page 100)

OCTOBER

Late October is time to buy depressed high tech stocks (page 90)

MONDAY

*You try to be greedy when others are fearful,
and fearful when others are greedy.*
— Warren Buffett

TUESDAY

I never hired anybody who wasn't smarter than me.
— Don Hewett (Producer, 60 Minutes)

WEDNESDAY

Chance favors the informed mind.
— Louis Pasteur

THURSDAY

Drawing on my fine command of language, I said nothing.
— Robert Benchley

FRIDAY

24

*I've never been poor, only broke. Being poor is a frame of mind.
Being broke is only a temporary situation.*
— Mike Todd (Movie Producer, 1903-1958)

SATURDAY

25

Daylight Saving Time ends

SUNDAY

YEAR'S TOP INVESTMENT BOOKS (continued from page 98)

guide to present a "periodic table of investing" and ultimately presents important approaches to risk, speculation, and investing in an uncertain world.

The Global Trader, Barbara Rockefeller, John Wiley & Sons, $59.95. Many new opportunities have opened up for traders with the advent of "globalization." Here are the best ways to participate in foreign markets, including the new iShares, which trade on the Amex. Just as we have seasonal tendencies in US markets, similar patterns do exist in other countries too. Author's firm specializes in foreign exchange forecasting and currency management.

Wall Street Secrets: 7 Things You Need to Know, Michael Scott Lawrie, Joyous Noise Publishing, $9.99. Here is a mini crash course in the last century's best thinking on and measurement of the stock market. Many interesting and provocative studies illustrated.

Paving Wall Street, Ross M. Miller, John Wiley & Sons, $34.95. In the movie, *A Beautiful Mind*, John Nash wrote a paper on "equilibrium" that got him a Nobel Prize. In a way, decisions by millions of individuals result in a continuous equilibrium with some degree of volatility depending on economic and exogenous events. This book is an excellent guide to the future of Wall Street.

How America Made A Fortune and Lost Its Shirt, Steve Gelsi and Thom Calalndra (Editor), Alpha Books, $21.95. CBS MarketWatch "Stories Behind the Numbers" series, to paraphrase John Kenneth Galbraith, shows that "financial genius is STILL a rising stock market."

Fooled By Randomness: The Hidden Role of Chance in the Markets and Life, Nassim Nicholas Taleb, Texere Publishing, $27.95. Captivating insight on how we perceive and deal with "luck." A Peter L. Bernstein testimonial states, "As a nonrandom consequence, your understanding of life and your money will expand exponentially."

Conquer The Crash, Robert R. Prechter Jr., John Wiley & Sons, $27.95. Following the biggest boom of all time, Elliott Wave guru Prechter tells how to survive and prosper in what's turning out to be the biggest bust since the 1930s. He believes we may be in for some deflation and tougher times.

Rich Shareowner, Poor Shareowner, Will Marshall, iUniverse Inc., $19.95. Charming business novel set in a Colorado dude ranch addresses what creates value for Shareowners and effective techniques investors need to know in order to avoid future Enrons, WorldComs, Global Crossings, and other bombs.

Alpha Books
201 West 103 Street
Indianapolis IN 46290

Joyous Noise Publishing
301 Chula Vista
Santa Fe NM 87501

iUniverse Inc.
5220 S. 16th Street
Lincoln NE 68512

John Wiley & Sons
605 Third Avenue
New York NY 10158

McGraw-Hill
Two Penn Plaza
New York NY 10121

Financial Times Prentice Hall
One Lake Street
Upper Saddle River NJ 07458

Texere Publishing
55 East 52 Street
New York NY 10055

OCTOBER/NOVEMBER

MONDAY

27

The measure of success is not whether you have a tough problem to deal with, but whether it's the same problem you had last year.
— John Foster Dulles
(Secretary of State under Eisenhower, 1888-1959)

FOMC Meeting

TUESDAY
28

Don't be scared to take big steps—you can't cross a chasm in two small jumps.
— David Lloyd George (British Prime Minister, 1916-1922)

1929 Crash October 28 and 29, Dow down 23.9% in two days

WEDNESDAY

29

Choose a job you love, and you will never have to work a day in your life.
— Confucius

THURSDAY

30

I cannot give you a formula for success but I can give you a formula for failure: Try to please everybody.
— Herbert Swope (American Journalist, 1882-1958)

Halloween

FRIDAY

31

Under capitalism, the seller chases after the buyer and that makes both of them work better; under socialism, the buyer chases the seller, and neither has time to work.
— Andrei Sakharov's Uncle Ivan

"Best Six Months" begin Dow and S&P
"Best Eight" on NASDAQ (pages 50 and 58)

SATURDAY

November Sector Seasonalities: Bullish:
XCI, CYC, NDX, COMP, PSE (page 118)

SUNDAY

NOVEMBER ALMANAC

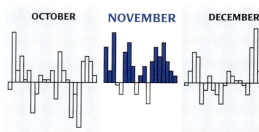

Market Probability Chart above is a graphic representation of the Market Probability Calendar on page 122.

◆ Among the top three S&P months of the year along with December and January (page 48) ◆ Also start of the "best six months" of the year (page 50) ◆ Simple timing indicator almost triples "best six months" strategy (page 52) ◆ Up 34 times, down 18 on S&P, 35/17 on Dow ◆ Day before and after Thanksgiving Day combined, only 9 losses in 50 years (page 108) ◆ Start of NASDAQ's best three months despite massacre in November 2000 following the first undecided presidential election since 1888

NOVEMBER DAILY POINT CHANGES DOW JONES INDUSTRIALS

Previous Month Close	1992 3226.28	1993 3680.59	1994 3908.12	1995 4755.48	1996 6029.38	1997 7442.80	1998 8592.10	1999 10729.86	2000 10971.14	2001 9075.14
1	—	12.02	– 44.75	11.20	– 7.45	—	—	– 81.35	– 71.67	188.76
2	35.93	5.03	– 26.24	41.91	—	—	114.05	– 66.67	– 18.96	59.64
3	– 9.73	– 35.77	8.75	16.98	—	231.59	N/C	27.22	– 62.56	—
4	– 29.44	– 36.89	– 38.36	—	19.75	14.74	76.99	30.58	—	—
5	20.80	18.45	—	—	39.50	3.44	132.33	64.84	—	117.49
6	– 3.78	—	—	– 11.56	96.53	– 9.33	59.99	—	159.26	150.09
7	—	—	1.35	– 16.98	28.33	–101.92	—	—	– 25.03	– 36.75
8	—	4.47	21.87	55.64	13.78	—	—	14.37	– 45.12	33.15
9	0.81	– 7.83	1.01	11.56	—	—	– 77.50	– 101.53	– 72.81	20.48
10	– 15.40	23.48	– 9.76	6.14	—	– 28.73	– 33.98	– 19.58	– 231.30	—
11	14.86	– 1.12	– 20.52	—	35.78	6.14	– 40.16	– 2.44	—	—
12	– 0.54	22.08	—	—	10.44	–157.41	5.92	174.02	—	– 53.63
13	– 6.76	—	—	2.53	8.20	86.44	89.85	—	– 85.70	196.58
14	—	—	28.26	– 1.09	38.76	84.72	—	—	163.81	72.66
15	—	– 6.99	– 3.37	50.94	35.03	—	—	– 8.57	26.54	48.78
16	– 27.29	33.25	18.84	46.61	—	—	91.66	171.58	– 51.57	– 5.40
17	– 12.42	– 6.42	– 17.15	20.59	—	125.74	– 24.97	– 49.24	– 26.16	—
18	14.05	– 19.01	– 12.79	—	– 1.12	– 47.40	54.83	152.61	—	—
19	2.16	8.67	—	—	50.69	73.92	14.94	– 31.81	—	109.47
20	17.83	—	—	– 6.86	32.42	101.87	103.50	—	– 167.22	– 75.08
21	—	—	– 45.75	40.46	– 11.55	54.46	—	—	31.85	– 66.70
22	—	– 23.76	– 91.52	18.06	53.29	—	—	85.63	– 95.18	H
23	– 4.32	3.92	– 3.36	H	—	—	214.72	– 93.89	H	125.03*
24	25.66	13.41	H	7.23*	—	–113.15	– 73.12	12.54	70.91*	—
25	17.56	H	33.64*	—	76.03	41.03	13.13	H	—	—
26	H	– 3.63*	—	—	– 19.38	– 14.17	H	– 19.26*	—	23.04
27	15.94*	—	—	22.04	– 29.07	H	18.80*	—	75.84	– 110.15
28	—	—	31.29	7.22	H	28.35*	—	—	– 38.49	– 160.74
29	—	– 6.15	– 1.01	27.46	22.36*	—	—	– 40.99	121.53	117.56
30	22.96	6.15	0.68	– 31.07	—	—	– 216.53	– 70.11	– 214.62	22.14
Close	3305.16	3683.95	3739.23	5074.49	6521.70	7823.13	9116.55	10877.81	10414.49	9851.56
Change	78.88	3.36	–168.89	319.01	492.32	380.33	524.45	147.95	– 556.65	776.42

* Shortened trading day

*Astute investors always smile and remember
When stocks seasonally start soaring, and salute November*

NOVEMBER

MONDAY 3

Get inside information from the president and you will probably lose half your money. If you get it from the chairman of the board, you will lose all your money.
— Jim Rogers

Election Day   ### TUESDAY 4

Things may come to those who wait, but only the things left by those who hustle.
— Abraham Lincoln

WEDNESDAY 5

There is one thing stronger than all the armies in the world, and this is an idea whose time has come.
— Victor Hugo

THURSDAY 6

He who wants to persuade should put his trust not in the right argument, but in the right word. The power of sound has always been greater than the power of sense.
— Joseph Conrad

FRIDAY 7

There have been three great inventions since the beginning of time: The fire, the wheel, and central banking.
— Will Rogers

SATURDAY 8

SUNDAY 9

BE CONTRARY!
GO AGAINST BULLISH/BEARISH FERVOR

One of life's greatest joys as a market professional is finding an indicator that enables you to predict the direction of the market or a stock. Paul Macrae Montgomery of Legg, Mason, Wood Walker originated the "Magazine Cover Theory" back in 1971. When Time, Newsweek, Business Week, or others have extremely bullish or bearish covers, especially featuring a picture of a bull or a bear, it pays to run in the opposite direction.

Marty Zweig used to count the number of bullish "Investment advisory ads in Barron's" to use as a bearish indicator when the number shot up. Also, when Barron's used to announce their biggest issue ever the market tended to be ripe for a correction. They stopped making such announcements after it was publicized. (We shoulda kept quiet!)

Be on guard when you see enormous publicity about the prognosticating prowess of any analyst or investment advisor. He or she is likely about to fall on his or her face. Constant media attention is very seductive and may cause the recipient to feel invincible. One even predicted an earthquake in Los Angeles back in 1981. We call it the "Walking on Water Indicator."

Here are a number of statements contrarians should write down on paper or post on a wall. Do that and it will save you or make you a fortune:

"Financial genius is a rising stock market." — John Kenneth Galbraith (*The Great Crash*)

"It is wise to remember that too much success (in the market) is in itself an excellent warning." — Gerald Loeb (*The Battle For Investment Survival*)

"Look for the market to turn down when market letter advertisements start carrying lists of their previous recommendations showing impressive gains." — Yale Hirsch

"When a company president is ready to buy you lunch it's time to sell the stock. When he has something really good, you can't get him on the phone." —Phil Stoller

"When everyone is bearish, a market must go up because no sellers are left; conversely, when everyone is bullish, a market must go down because no buyers are left." — Anonymous

"An overly optimistic letter from the president in the annual report always turns me off. If his letter is mildly pessimistic to me, that's a good sign."
— Philip L. Carret (Centenarian, Founded Pioneer Fund in 1928, 1896-1998)

"Analysts are supposed to be critics of corporations. They often end up being public relations spokesmen for them."
— Ralph Wanger (Chief Investment Officer, Acorn Fund)

"Get inside information from the president and you will probably lose half your money. If you get it from the chairman of the board, you will lose all your money."
— Jim Rogers

HOWEVER: *"The CROWD is always wrong at market turning points but often times right once a trend sets in. The reason many market fighters go broke is they believe the CROWD is always wrong. There is nothing further from the truth. Unless volatility is extremely low or very high one should think twice before betting against the CROWD."* — Shawn Andrew (Ricercar Fund/SA)

NOVEMBER

MONDAY

10

I measure what's going on, and I adapt to it. I try to get my ego out of the way. The market is smarter than I am so I bend.
— Martin Zweig

Veteran's Day

TUESDAY

11

The higher a people's intelligence and moral strength, the lower will be the prevailing rate of interest.
— Eugen von Bohm-Bawerk
(Austrian economist, *Capital and Interest*, 1851-1914)

WEDNESDAY
12

When everybody starts looking really smart, and not realizing that a lot of it was luck, I get scared.
— Raphael Yavneh (*Forbes*)

THURSDAY

13

Methodology is the last refuge of a sterile mind.
— Marianne L. Simmel

FRIDAY

14

Don't put all your eggs in one basket.
— (Market maxim)

SATURDAY

15

SUNDAY

16

MOST OF THE SO-CALLED "JANUARY EFFECT" TAKES PLACE IN DECEMBER'S LAST TWO WEEKS

Over the years we reported annually on the fascinating January Effect, showing that Standard and Poor's Low-Priced Stock Index during January handily outperformed the S&P 500 Index 40 out of 43 years between 1953 and 1995. Readers saw that "Cats and Dogs" on average quadrupled the returns of blue chips in this period. Then, the January Effect disappeared over the next four years.

In addition, S&P decided to discontinue their Low-Priced Index. S&P's SmallCap 600 index was launched October 17, 1994 not giving us an historically significant set of data. Looking at the graph on page 114, which shows small cap stocks beginning to outperform the blue chips in mid-December, made the decision simple; just compare the Russell 1000 index of large capitalization stocks to the Russell 2000 smaller capitalization stocks. Doing it in half-month segments was an inspiration and proved to be quite revealing, as you can see in the table.

15-YEAR AVERAGE RATES OF RETURN (1987-2002)

	Russell 1000		Russell 2000	
From 12/15	Change	Annualized	Change	Annualized
12/15-12/31	2.4%	85.8%	4.2%	189.9%
12/15-01/15	2.4	33.3	4.7	73.2
12/15-01/31	4.0	36.3	6.2	61.6
12/15-02/15	4.8	32.8	8.1	59.3
12/15-02/28	4.0	22.0	8.8	52.3
From 12/31				
12/31-01/15	−0.01	−0.2	0.4	12.2
12/31-01/31	1.5	19.8	1.9	25.6
12/31-02/15	2.4	21.0	3.7	34.2
12/31-02/28	1.7	10.9	4.3	28.6

23-YEAR AVERAGE RATES OF RETURN (1979-2002)

	Russell 1000		Russell 2000	
From 12/15	Change	Annualized	Change	Annualized
12/15-12/31	1.9%	64.4%	3.3%	133.2%
12/15-01/15	2.5	34.7	4.9	78.0
12/15-01/31	3.8	35.3	6.2	61.6
12/15-02/15	4.6	30.8	7.9	57.6
12/15-02/28	4.1	22.5	8.4	49.9
From 12/31				
12/31-01/15	0.6	16.0	1.6	49.4
12/31-01/31	1.9	25.6	2.8	39.2
12/31-02/15	2.6	23.2	4.5	41.7
12/31-02/28	2.3	14.6	4.9	33.1

Small-cap strength in December's last two weeks becomes even more magnified after the 1987 market crash. Note the dramatic shift in the gains the last two weeks of December during the 15-year period starting in 1987 versus the 23 years from 1979 to 2002. With all the beaten down small stocks being dumped for tax loss purposes it pays to get a head start on the January Effect in mid-December.

NOVEMBER

Week Before Thanksgiving week, S&P up 10 years in a row
Monday Before Expiration up 5 of last 8

MONDAY
17

Put your eggs in one basket and watch the basket.
— (An alternate strategy)

TUESDAY
18

*Buy a stock the way you would buy a house.
Understand and like it such that you'd be content to own it
in the absence of any market.*
— Warren Buffett

WEDNESDAY
19

*The market is a voting machine, whereon countless individuals
register choices which are the product partly of
reason and partly of emotion.*
— Graham & Dodd

THURSDAY
20

*Your emotions are often a reverse indicator of
what you ought to be doing.*
— John F. Hindelong (Dillon, Reed)

Options Expiration up 7 of last 12

FRIDAY
21

*When the S&P Index Future premium over "Cash" gets too high,
I sell the future and buy the stocks. If the premium disappears,
well, buy the future and sell the stocks.*
— Neil Elliott (Fahnestock)

SATURDAY
22

SUNDAY
23

TRADING THE THANKSGIVING MARKET

For 35 years the combination of the Wednesday before Thanksgiving and the Friday after had a great track record, except for two occasions. Attributing this phenomenon to the warm "holiday spirit" was a no-brainer. But, publishing it in the 1987 Almanac was the "kiss of death." It's been right only half the time since then. However, going long into weakness Wednesday and staying in through the following Monday improves the record immensely.

WHAT DOW JONES INDUSTRIALS DID ON
THE DAY BEFORE AND AFTER THANKSGIVING

	Tuesday Before	Wednesday Before		Friday After	Total Gain Dow Points	Dow Close	Next Monday
1952	— 0.18	1.54		1.22	2.76	283.66	0.04
1953	1.71	0.65		2.45	3.10	280.23	1.14
1954	3.27	1.89		3.16	5.05	387.79	0.72
1955	4.61	0.71		0.26	0.97	482.88	— 1.92
1956	— 4.49	— 2.16		4.65	2.49	472.56	— 2.27
1957	— 9.04	10.69		3.84	14.53	449.87	— 2.96
1958	— 4.37	8.63		8.31	16.94	557.46	2.61
1959	2.94	1.41		1.42	2.83	652.52	6.66
1960	— 3.44	1.37	T	4.00	5.37	606.47	— 1.04
1961	— 0.77	1.10		2.18	3.28	732.60	— 0.61
1962	6.73	4.31	H	7.62	11.93	644.87	— 2.81
1963	32.03	— 2.52		9.52	7.00	750.52	1.39
1964	— 1.68	— 5.21	A	— 0.28	— 5.49	882.12	— 6.69
1965	2.56	N/C		— 0.78	— 0.78	948.16	— 1.23
1966	— 3.18	1.84	N	6.52	8.36	803.34	— 2.18
1967	13.17	3.07		3.58	6.65	877.60	4.51
1968	8.14	— 3.17	K	8.76	5.59	985.08	— 1.74
1969	— 5.61	3.23		1.78	5.01	812.30	— 7.26
1970	5.21	1.98	S	6.64	8.62	781.35	12.74
1971	— 5.18	0.66		17.96	18.62	816.59	13.14
1972	8.21	7.29	G	4.67	11.96	1025.21	— 7.45
1973	—17.76	10.08		— 0.98	9.10	854.00	—29.05
1974	5.32	2.03	I	— 0.63	1.40	618.66	—15.64
1975	9.76	3.15		2.12	5.27	860.67	— 4.33
1976	— 6.57	1.66	V	5.66	7.32	956.62	— 6.57
1977	6.41	0.78		1.12	1.90	844.42	— 4.85
1978	— 1.56	2.95	I	3.12	6.07	810.12	3.72
1979	— 6.05	— 1.80		4.35	2.55	811.77	16.98
1980	3.93	7.00	N	3.66	10.66	993.34	—23.89
1981	18.45	7.90		7.80	15.70	885.94	3.04
1982	— 9.01	9.01	G	7.36	16.37	1007.36	— 4.51
1983	7.01	— 0.20		1.83	1.63	1277.44	— 7.62
1984	9.83	6.40		18.78	25.18	1220.30	— 7.95
1985	0.12	18.92		— 3.56	15.36	1472.13	—14.22
1986	6.05	4.64		— 2.53	2.11	1914.23	— 1.55
1987	40.45	—16.58	D	—36.47	—53.05	1910.48	—76.93
1988	11.73	14.58		—17.60	— 3.02	2074.68	6.76
1989	7.25	17.49	A	18.77	36.26	2675.55	19.42
1990	—35.15	9.16		—12.13	— 2.97	2527.23	5.94
1991	14.08	—16.10	Y	— 5.36	—21.46	2894.68	40.70
1992	25.66	17.56		15.94*	33.50	3282.20	22.96
1993	3.92	13.41		— 3.63*	9.78	3683.95	— 6.15
1994	—91.52	— 3.36		33.64*	30.28	3708.27	31.29
1995	40.46	18.06		7.23*	25.29	5048.84	22.04
1996	—19.38	—29.07		22.36*	— 6.71	6521.70	N/C
1997	41.03	—14.17		28.35*	14.18	7823.13	189.98
1998	—73.12	13.13		18.80*	31.93	9333.08	216.53
1999	—93.89	12.54		19.26*	— 6.72	10988.91	—40.99
2000	31.85	—95.18		70.91*	—24.27	10470.23	75.84
2001	—75.08	—66.70		125.03*	58.33	9959.71	23.04

*Shortened trading day

NOVEMBER

MONDAY
24

To me, the "tape" is the final arbiter of any investment decision.
I have a cardinal rule: Never fight the tape!
— Martin Zweig

TUESDAY
25

Stocks are super-attractive when the Fed is loosening and interest
rates are falling. In sum: Don't fight the Fed!
— Martin Zweig

(Bond Market Closes Early) **WEDNESDAY**
26

Every successful enterprise requires three people—
a dreamer, a businessman, and a son-of-a-bitch.
— Peter McArthur (1904)

Thanksgiving **THURSDAY**
(Market Closed) **27**

The public may boo me, but when I go home
and think of my money, I clap.
— Horace (Roman poet-critic, *Epistles*, c. 20 BC)

(Shortened Trading Day) **FRIDAY**
28

I always keep these seasonal patterns in the back of my mind.
My antennae start to purr at certain times of the year.
— Kenneth Ward

SATURDAY
29

December Sector Seasonalities: Bullish: **SUNDAY**
XOI, XAU, RUT, XBD (page 118) **30**

DECEMBER ALMANAC

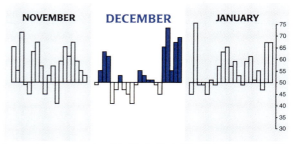

Market Probability Chart above is a graphic representation of the Market Probability Calendar on page 122.

◆ Average 1.8% gain on S&P since 1950 makes it Numero Uno (page 48) ◆ No large Dow loss since 1980, minus 3.0%, two others were 1957 and 1968 (page 145) ◆ Just one loss in last 15 years on S&P, in 1996, 15-year 2.4% average gain ◆ "Free lunch" served on Wall Street at month end (page 112) ◆ Small-caps start to outperform larger caps near middle of month (page 114) ◆ "Santa Claus Rally" visible in graph above and on page 116 ◆ In 1998 was part of best fourth quarter since 1928 ◆ Only two down Decembers on Dow in last 13 pre-presidential election years: 1975 (-1.0%), 1983 (-1.4%) ◆ Second best month on NASDAQ, 2.4% since 1971

DECEMBER DAILY POINT CHANGES DOW JONES INDUSTRIALS

Previous Month Close	1992	1993	1994	1995	1996	1997	1998	1999	2000	2001
	3305.16	3683.95	3739.23	5074.49	6521.70	7823.13	9116.55	10877.81	10414.49	9851.56
1	−10.80	13.13	−38.36	12.64	—	189.98	16.99	120.58	−40.95	—
2	−8.11	5.03	44.75	—	0.00	5.72	−69.00	40.67	—	—
3	−9.72	1.96	—	—	−79.01	13.18	−184.86	247.12	—	−87.60
4	12.15	—	—	52.39	−19.75	18.15	136.46	—	186.56	129.88
5	—	—	−3.70	37.93	14.16	98.97	—	—	338.62	220.45
6	—	6.14	4.03	21.68	−55.16	—	—	−61.17	−234.34	−15.15
7	18.65	8.67	−10.43	−39.74	—	—	54.33	−118.36	−47.02	−49.68
8	14.85	15.65	−49.79	−2.53	—	−38.29	−42.49	−38.53	95.55	—
9	1.63	−4.75	5.38	—	82.00	−61.18	−18.79	66.67	—	—
10	−11.62	10.89	—	—	9.31	−70.87	−167.61	89.91	—	−128.01
11	−8.11	—	—	27.46	−70.73	−129.80	−19.82	—	12.89	−33.08
12	—	—	27.26	−9.40	−98.81	−10.69	—	—	42.47	6.44
13	—	23.76	−3.03	41.55	1.16	—	—	−32.11	26.17	−128.36
14	−11.88	−21.80	30.95	−34.32	—	—	−126.16	−32.42	−119.45	44.70
15	−7.84	−25.71	19.18	−5.42	—	84.29	127.70	65.15	−240.04	—
16	−29.18	9.22	41.72	—	−36.52	53.72	−32.70	19.57	—	—
17	14.05	25.43	—	—	39.98	−18.90	85.22	12.54	—	80.82
18	44.04	—	—	−101.52	38.44	−110.91	27.81	—	210.47	106.42
19	—	—	−16.49	34.68	126.87	−90.21	—	—	−61.05	72.10
20	—	3.64	−23.55	−50.57	10.76	—	—	−113.16	−265.44	−85.31
21	−0.81	−10.06	34.65	37.21	—	—	85.22	56.27	168.36	50.16
22	8.64	17.04	13.12	1.44	—	63.02	55.61	3.06	148.27	—
23	−7.56	−4.47	18.51	—	4.62	−127.54	157.57	202.16	—	—
24	12.70*	Closed	—	—	33.83*	−31.64*	15.96*	Closed	—	N/C*
25	H	H	H	H	H	H	H	H	H	H
26	—	—	Closed	12.29	23.83	19.18*	—	—	56.88	52.80
27	—	35.21	28.26	−4.34	14.23	—	—	−14.68	110.72	43.17
28	7.02	0.84	−22.20	−10.12	—	—	8.76	85.63	65.60	5.68
29	−22.42	0.56	−6.06	21.32	—	113.10	94.23	7.95	−81.91	—
30	10.26	−18.45	1.01	—	−11.54	123.56	−46.34	−31.80	—	—
31	−19.99	−21.79	—	—	−101.10	−7.72	−93.21	44.26	—	−115.49
Close	3301.11	3754.09	3834.44	5117.12	6448.27	7908.25	9181.43	11497.12	10786.85	10021.50
Change	−4.05	70.14	95.21	42.63	−73.43	85.12	64.88	619.31	372.36	169.94

Shortened trading day

If Santa Claus should fail to call
Bears may come to Broad and Wall

DECEMBER

*Since 1950 December #1 S&P month,
#2 Dow; since 1971 #2 S&P and NASDAQ,
#3 Dow (pages 48 and 56)
December first trading day Dow up 8 of last 12*

MONDAY

1

*Women are expected to do twice as much as men in half the time
and for no credit. Fortunately, this isn't difficult.*
— Charlotte Whitton (Former Ottawa Mayor,
feminist, 1896–1975)

TUESDAY

*Don't compete. Create. Find out what everyone else
is doing and then don't do it.*
— Joel Weldon

WEDNESDAY

*Averaging down in a bear market is tantamount to
taking a seat on the down escalator at Macy's.*
— Richard Russell (*Dow Theory Letters*, 1984)

THURSDAY

The possession of gold has ruined fewer men than the lack of it.
— Thomas Bailey Aldridge (1903)

FRIDAY

A man will fight harder for his interests than his rights.
— Napoleon Bonaparte (1815)

SATURDAY

SUNDAY

WALL STREET'S ONLY "FREE LUNCH" NOW SERVED IN LATE DECEMBER

As investors normally tend to get rid of their losers near year-end for tax purposes, these stocks are often hammered down to bargain levels. Over the years the *Almanac* has shown that New York Stock Exchange stocks selling at their lows at mid-December will usually outperform the market by February 15 in the following year. Preferred stocks, closed-end funds, splits and new issues are eliminated. When there are a huge number of new lows, stocks down the most are selected, even though there are usually good reasons why some stocks have been battered.

BARGAIN STOCKS VS. THE MARKET

60-Day Period Dec 15 - Feb 15	New Lows Around Dec 15	% Change Around Feb 15	% Change NYSE Composite	Bargain Stocks Advantage
1974-75	112	48.9%	22.1%	26.8%
1975-76	21	34.9	14.9	20.0
1976-77	2	1.3	— 3.3	4.6
1977-78	15	2.8	— 4.5	7.3
1978-79	43	11.8	3.9	7.9
1979-80	5	9.3	6.1	3.2
1980-81	14	7.1	— 2.0	9.1
1981-82	21	— 2.6	— 7.4	4.8
1982-83	4	33.0	9.7	23.3
1983-84	13	— 3.2	— 3.8	0.6
1984-85	32	19.0	12.1	6.9
1985-86	4	— 22.5	3.9	— 26.4
1986-87	22	9.3	12.5	— 3.2
1987-88	23	13.2	6.8	6.4
1988-89	14	30.0	6.4	23.6
1989-90	25	— 3.1	— 4.8	1.7
1990-91	18	18.8	12.6	6.2
1991-92	23	51.1	7.7	43.4
1992-93	9	8.7	0.6	8.1
1993-94	10	— 1.4	2.0	— 3.4
1994-95	25	14.6	5.7	8.9
1995-96	5	— 11.3	4.5	—15.8
1996-97	16	13.9	11.2	2.7
1997-98	29	9.9	5.7	4.2
1998-99	40	— 2.8	4.3	— 7.1
1999-00	26[1]	8.9	— 5.4	14.3
2000-01	51[2]	44.4	0.1	44.3
2001-02	12[3]	31.4	— 2.3	33.7
28-Year Totals		**375.4%**	**119.3%**	**256.1%**
Average		**13.4%**	**4.3%**	**9.1%**

[1] Chosen 12/29/99 [2] Chosen 12/27/00 [3] Chosen 12/26/01, includes NASDAQ stocks, % Change through 1/16/02

However, as tax selling in recent years seems to be continuing down to the last few days of the year, "scavengers" have been given an even better opportunity. So, we've altered the strategy the last three years to make our selections from NYSE stocks making new lows on the fourth to last trading day of the year. We tweaked the strategy in 2002 further. Presented with only two NYSE stocks left after our screens, we turned to the NASDAQ National Market and selected 10 more using the same criteria and emailed them to our *Almanac Investor* newsletter subscribers. And, noticing the tendency over the past few years for these stocks to start giving back their gains in January, we advised subscribers to sell on January 16, 2002, giving the 12-stock basket an average 31.4% gain in just three weeks versus a 2.3% loss for the NYSE Composite index. To receive a free copy of the list of stocks selected December 26, 2002, send an email to **service@hirschorg.com**.

Examination of December trades by NYSE members through the years shows they tend to buy on balance during this month, contrary to other months.

DECEMBER

MONDAY 8

In all recorded history, there has not been one economist who has had to worry about where the next meal would come from.
— Peter Drucker

FOMC Meeting

TUESDAY 9

The less a man knows about the past and the present the more insecure must be his judgment of the future.
— Sigmund Freud

WEDNESDAY 10

Marx's great achievement was to place the system of capitalism on the defensive.
— Charles A. Madison (1977)

THURSDAY 11

The word "crisis" in Chinese is composed of two characters: the first, the symbol of danger; the second, opportunity.
— Anonymous

FRIDAY 12

In the course of evolution and a higher civilization we might be able to get along comfortably without Congress, but without Wall Street, never.
— Henry Clews (1900)

SATURDAY 13

SUNDAY 14

JANUARY EFFECT STARTS IN MID-DECEMBER

We always hear about the January Effect, but now we have a graph revealing that it does indeed exist. Ned Davis Research has taken the 24 years of daily data for the Russell 2000 index of smaller companies and divided by the Russell 1000 index of largest companies. Then they compressed the 24 years into a single year to show an idealized yearly pattern. When the graph is descending, big blue chips are outperforming smaller companies; when the graph is rising, smaller companies are moving up faster than their larger brethren.

In a typical year the smaller fry stay on the sidelines while the big boys are on the field; suddenly, in mid-December, the smaller fry take over and take off. This is known as the "January Effect." So many year-end dividends, payouts and bonuses could be a factor. Another major move is quite evident just before Labor Day. Possibly because individual investors are back from vacations. Also note the move off the low point in late November. Perhaps we should rename this small stock pattern the "December Effect"?

The data for the bottom graph were provided by Global Financial Data and show the actual ratio of the Russell 2000 divided by the Russell 1000 from 1979. We see the smaller companies having the upper hand for five years into 1983, then falling behind for about eight years, coming back after the Persian Gulf War and moving up more until 1994. For six years the picture had been bleak for small fry as the blue chips and tech stocks moved to stratospheric PE ratios. But note the small-cap spikes in late 1999, late 2000 and the continuing uptrend into mid-2002. We still seem poised for a continuation of outperformance from stocks with lower market capitalizations for more years to come.

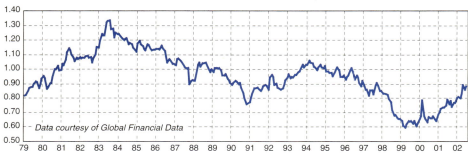

DECEMBER

Small Cap Strength Starts In Mid-December
Monday Before Triple Witching Dow Up 7 of last 12

MONDAY

15

Let us have the courage to stop borrowing to meet the continuing deficits. Stop the deficits.
— Franklin D. Roosevelt (1932)

TUESDAY
16

No nation ought to be without debt. A national debt is a national blessing.
— Thomas Paine (1776)

WEDNESDAY
17

If I had my life to live over again, I would elect to be a trader of goods rather than a student of science. I think barter is a noble thing.
— Albert Einstein (1934)

THURSDAY
18

You must automate, emigrate, or evaporate.
— James A. Baker (General Electric)

December Triple Witching Up 9 of Last 12

FRIDAY

19

If you don't know who you are, the stock market is an expensive place to find out.
— George Goodman (1959)

Chanukah

SATURDAY
20

SUNDAY
21

IF SANTA CLAUS SHOULD FAIL TO CALL BEARS MAY COME TO BROAD & WALL

Santa Claus tends to come to Wall Street nearly every year, bringing a short, sweet, respectable rally within the last five days of the year and the first two in January. This has been good for an average 1.7% gain since 1969 (1.5% since 1950). Santa's failure to show tends to precede bear markets, or times stocks could be purchased later in the year at much lower prices. Such occasions provide opportunities for long-term players to at least write options on their stocks. We discovered this phenomenon in 1972.

DAILY % CHANGE IN S&P COMPOSITE INDEX AT YEAR END

	Trading Days Before Year-End						First Days in January			Rally %
	6	5	4	3	2	1	1	2	3	Change
1969	−0.4	1.1	0.8	−0.7	0.4	0.5	1.0	0.5	−0.7	3.6
1970	0.1	0.6	0.5	1.1	0.2	−0.1	−1.1	0.7	0.6	1.9
1971	−0.4	0.2	1.0	0.3	−0.4	0.3	−0.4	0.4	1.0	1.3
1972	−0.3	−0.7	0.6	0.4	0.5	1.0	0.9	0.4	−0.1	3.1
1973	−1.1	−0.7	3.1	2.1	−0.2	0.01	0.1	2.2	−0.9	6.7
1974	−1.4	1.4	0.8	−0.4	0.03	2.1	2.4	0.7	0.5	7.2
1975	0.7	0.8	0.9	−0.1	−0.4	0.5	0.8	1.8	1.0	4.3
1976	0.1	1.2	0.7	−0.4	0.5	0.5	−0.4	−1.2	−0.9	0.8
1977	0.8	0.9	N/C	0.1	0.2	0.2	−1.3	−0.3	−0.8	−0.3
1978	0.03	1.7	1.3	−0.9	−0.4	−0.2	0.6	1.1	0.8	3.3
1979	−0.6	0.1	0.1	0.2	−0.1	0.1	−2.0	−0.5	1.2	−2.2
1980	−0.4	0.4	0.5	−1.1	0.2	0.3	0.4	1.2	0.1	2.0
1981	−0.5	0.2	−0.2	−0.5	0.5	0.2	0.2	−2.2	−0.7	−1.8
1982	0.6	1.8	−1.0	0.3	−0.7	0.2	−1.6	2.2	0.4	1.2
1983	−0.2	−0.03	0.9	0.3	−0.2	0.05	−0.5	1.7	1.2	2.1
1984	−0.5	0.8	−0.2	−0.4	0.3	0.6	−1.1	−0.5	−0.5	−0.6
1985	−1.1	−0.7	0.2	0.9	0.5	0.3	−0.8	0.6	−0.1	1.1
1986	−1.0	0.2	0.1	−0.9	−0.5	−0.5	1.8	2.3	0.2	2.4
1987	1.3	−0.5	−2.6	−0.4	1.3	−0.3	3.6	1.1	0.1	2.2
1988	−0.2	0.3	−0.4	0.1	0.8	−0.6	−0.9	1.5	0.2	0.9
1989	0.6	0.8	−0.2	0.6	0.5	0.8	1.8	−0.3	−0.9	4.1
1990	0.5	−0.6	0.3	−0.8	0.1	0.5	−1.1	−1.4	−0.3	−3.0
1991	2.5	0.6	1.4	0.4	2.1	0.5	0.04	0.5	−0.3	5.7
1992	−0.3	0.2	−0.1	−0.3	0.2	−0.7	−0.1	−0.2	0.04	−1.1
1993	0.01	0.7	0.1	−0.1	−0.4	−0.5	−0.2	0.3	0.1	−0.1
1994	0.01	0.2	0.4	−0.3	0.1	−0.4	−0.03	0.3	−0.1	0.2
1995	0.8	0.2	0.4	0.04	−0.1	0.3	0.8	0.1	−0.6	1.8
1996	−0.3	0.5	0.6	0.1	−0.4	−1.7	−0.5	1.5	−0.1	0.1
1997	−1.5	−0.7	0.4	1.8	1.8	−0.04	0.5	0.2	−1.1	4.0
1998	2.1	−0.2	−0.1	1.3	−0.8	−0.2	−0.1	1.4	2.2	1.3
1999	1.6	−0.1	0.04	0.4	0.1	0.3	−1.0	−3.8	0.2	−4.0
2000	0.8	2.4	0.7	1.0	0.4	−1.0	−2.8	5.0	−1.1	5.7
2001	0.4	0.0	0.4	0.7	0.3	−1.1	0.6	0.9	0.6	1.8
Avg	0.08	0.40	0.35	0.14	0.20	0.05	−0.02	0.55	0.02	1.7

The couplet above was certainly on the mark in 2000, as the period suffered a horrendous 4.0% loss. On January 14, 2000 the Dow started its 20-month 29.7% slide to the September 2001 lows and NASDAQ's bubble burst eight weeks later, falling 37.3% in 10 weeks, and eventually dropping 71.8% by September 2001. This is reminiscent of the Dow during the Depression, when the Dow initially fell 47.9% in just over two months from 381.17 September 3, 1929 only to end down 89.2% at the bottom of 41.22 July 8, 1932, its low of the century. (At press time, July 2002, Dow −34.3%, NASDAQ −75.7%, off their respective 2000 highs.) Saddam Hussein cancelled Christmas by invading Kuwait in 1990. Less bullishness on last day is due to last-minute portfolio restructuring. Pushing gains and losses into the next tax year affects year's first trading day.

DECEMBER

MONDAY 22

The worst trades are generally when people freeze and start to pray and hope rather than take some action.
— Robert Mnuchin (Goldman, Sachs)

TUESDAY 23

A good trader has to have three things: a chronic inability to accept things at face value, to feel continuously unsettled, and to have humility.
— Michael Steinhardt

Day before Christmas Dow up 8 of last 12
Watch for Santa Claus Rally (page 116)

WEDNESDAY 24

The pursuit of gain is the only way in which people can serve the needs of others whom they do not know.
— Friedrich von Hayek (*Counterrevolution of Science*)

Christmas Day
(Market Closed)

THURSDAY 25

Cheapening the cost of necessities and conveniences of life is the most powerful agent of civilization and progress.
— Thomas Elliott Perkins (1888)

(Shortened Trading Day)
Day after Christmas Dow up 9 of last 11
New Lows perform better when selected last settlement day of year (page 112)

FRIDAY 26

In the market, yesterday is a memory and tomorrow is a vision. And looking back is a lot easier than looking ahead.
— Frankie Joe

SATURDAY 27

January Sector Seasonalities: Bullish:
SOX; Bearish: XNG (page 118)

SUNDAY 28

SECTOR SEASONALITY: SELECTED PERCENTAGE PLAYS

Sector seasonality, a study by Merrill Lynch, was featured in the first *Stock Trader's Almanac* (1968). It showed that buying aerospace, agriculture, air conditioning, eastern railroads, fire/casualty insurance, machine tools, and meatpacking sectors around September or October and selling in the first few months of the 1954-1964 years gained more than triple the profit than holding them for the ten years. This didn't include interest or profits made the rest of the year.

From the seasonality studies on sectors by Jon D. Markman, Managing Editor at CNBC on MSN Money, in his book, *Online Investing*, and his online *SuperModels*, we have fashioned the sector index seasonality table below. It is similar in style to the "Best Six Months" on page 50 and hypothetically offers even greater possibilities. Also, see Exchange Traded Funds on page 189.

SECTOR INDEX SEASONALITY TABLE

Symbol	Sector Index		Months of Streak Start	End	Avg.% Return
XNG	Natural Gas	(Bearish)	January	January	– 5.3%
SOX	PHLX Semiconductor		January	January	10.9
MSH	Morgan Stanley High-Tech	(Bearish)	February	February	– 3.3
XTC	N. Amer Telecomm	(Bearish)	February	August	– 7.5
XNG	Natural Gas		February	May	16.7
BTK	Biotechnology	(Bearish)	March	March	– 6.8
XAL	Airline		March	April	10.2
FPP	PHLX Forest/Pap		March	April	9.2
XOI	Oil		March	May	8.4
UTY	PHLX Utility		April	December	7.3
FPP	PHLX Forest/Pap	(Bearish)	May	September	– 6.7
SOX	PHLX Semiconductor	(Bearish)	May	May	– 3.6
XNG	Natural Gas	(Bearish)	June	July	– 5.6
RUT	Russell 2000	(Bearish)	July	October	– 4.4
XAL	Airline	(Bearish)	August	September	–16.1
BTK	Biotechnology		August	February	35.4
CYC	Morgan Stanley Cyclical	(Bearish)	August	September	– 4.8
CMR	Morgan Stanley Consumer		September	January	11.7
XTC	N. Amer Telecomm		September	January	12.7
XOI	Oil	(Bearish)	September	November	– 2.0
DRG	Pharmaceutical		September	January	15.1
SOX	PHLX Semiconductor	(Bearish)	September	September	– 5.8
XAL	Airline		October	April	26.5
MSH	Morgan Stanley High-Tech		October	January	18.1
BKX	PHLX Banking		October	May	13.8
FPP	PHLX Forest/Pap		October	April	14.1
XAU	PHLX Gold/Silver	(Bearish)	October	November	– 7.0
SOX	PHLX Semiconductor		October	April	30.3
XBD	Securities Broker/Dealer		October	April	28.0
XCI	Computer Tech		November	January	10.3
CYC	Morgan Stanley Cyclical		November	April	12.1
NDX	Nasdaq 100		November	January	11.6
COMP	Nasdaq Composite		November	January	11.0
PSE	Pacfic SE High-Tech		November	February	15.7
XOI	Oil		December	May	11.2
XAU	PHLX Gold/Silver		December	May	7.1
RUT	Russell 2000		December	May	11.9
XBD	Securities Broker/Dealer		December	April	20.9

DECEMBER/JANUARY 2004

Almanac Investor FREE LUNCH Menu of New Lows served to newsletter subscribers, email service@hirschorg.com for details

MONDAY

29

If you don't profit from your investment mistakes, someone else will.
— Yale Hirsch

TUESDAY

30

Major bottoms are usually made when analysts cut their earnings estimates and companies report earnings which are below expectations.
— Edward Babbitt, Jr. (Avatar Associates)

Last Day Of Year NASDAQ Up 29 Of 31 Dow down 5 of last 6

WEDNESDAY

31

The worst bankrupt in the world is the person who has lost his enthusiasm.
— H.W. Arnold

New Year's Day
(Market Closed)

THURSDAY

1

Man's mind, once stretched by a new idea, never regains its original dimensions.
— Oliver Wendell Holmes

Average January gains last 32 years: NAS 4.1%, Dow 2.2%, S&P 2.1%

FRIDAY

2

It's no coincidence that three of the top five stock option traders in a recent trading contest were all former Marines.
— Robert Prechter, Jr. (*Elliott Wave Theorist*)

SATURDAY
3

SUNDAY

4

NASDAQ COMPOSITE MARKET PROBABILITY CALENDAR 2003
THE % CHANCE OF THE MARKET RISING ON ANY TRADING DAY OF THE YEAR
(Based on the number of times the NASDAQ rose on a particular trading day during January 1971-December 2001)

Date	Jan	Feb	Mar	Apr	May	Jun	Jul	Aug	Sep	Oct	Nov	Dec
1	H	S	S	35.5	58.1	S	54.8	54.8	H	45.2	S	61.3
2	48.4	S	S	61.3	74.2	61.3	51.6	S	54.8	64.5	S	64.5
3	74.2	67.7	67.7	64.5	S	77.4	41.9	S	64.5	54.8	67.7	67.7
4	S	74.2	61.3	54.8	S	61.3	H	41.9	61.3	S	48.4	58.1
5	S	67.7	74.2	S	67.7	61.3	S	51.6	58.1	S	74.2	45.2
6	58.1	67.7	54.8	S	54.8	61.3	S	64.5	S	64.5	51.6	S
7	67.7	54.8	58.1	54.8	58.1	S	48.4	64.5	S	64.5	45.2	S
8	51.6	S	S	64.5	58.1	S	64.5	38.7	54.8	61.3	S	51.6
9	61.3	S	S	71.0	58.1	48.4	64.5	S	41.9	45.2	S	41.9
10	51.6	48.4	61.3	54.8	S	45.2	64.5	S	45.2	48.4	54.8	41.9
11	S	48.4	64.5	58.1	S	58.1	71.0	51.6	58.1	S	71.0	45.2
12	S	67.7	51.6	S	41.9	64.5	S	51.6	51.6	S	61.3	35.5
13	64.5	54.8	74.2	S	58.1	61.3	S	64.5	S	74.2	48.4	S
14	67.7	61.3	51.6	64.5	61.3	S	77.4	61.3	S	61.3	58.1	S
15	74.2	S	S	54.8	58.1	S	67.7	54.8	38.7	48.4	S	45.2
16	74.2	S	S	58.1	45.2	48.4	48.4	S	38.7	48.4	S	58.1
17	77.4	H	54.8	51.6	S	38.7	54.8	S	38.7	41.9	51.6	54.8
18	S	58.1	64.5	H	S	45.2	29.0	38.7	58.1	S	45.2	58.1
19	S	51.6	38.7	S	51.6	64.5	S	35.5	58.1	S	51.6	54.8
20	H	51.6	35.5	S	45.2	51.6	S	67.7	S	64.5	67.7	S
21	51.6	38.7	61.3	54.8	54.8	S	51.6	54.8	S	45.2	58.1	S
22	48.4	S	S	54.8	45.2	S	41.9	54.8	58.1	64.5	S	54.8
23	51.6	S	S	54.8	58.1	54.8	45.2	S	45.2	38.7	S	64.5
24	54.8	48.4	54.8	51.6	S	51.6	54.8	S	51.6	45.2	54.8	71.0
25	S	54.8	35.5	51.6	S	45.2	58.1	51.6	48.4	S	74.2	H
26	S	61.3	54.8	S	H	54.8	S	58.1	48.4	S	64.5	74.2
27	45.2	54.8	54.8	S	48.4	71.0	S	54.8	S	29.0	H	S
28	64.5	61.3	48.4	71.0	58.1	S	45.2	58.1	S	38.7	71.0	S
29	58.1		S	61.3	48.4	S	48.4	74.2	48.4	54.8	S	54.8
30	61.3		S	77.4	74.2	77.4	48.4	S	54.8	58.1	S	74.2
31	71.0		71.0		S		58.1	S		71.0		93.5

Based on NASDAQ composite, prior to Feb. 5, 1971 based on National Quotation Bureau indices

DOW JONES INDUSTRIALS MARKET PROBABILITY CALENDAR 2003
THE % CHANCE OF THE MARKET RISING ON ANY TRADING DAY OF THE YEAR
(Based on the number of times the DJIA rose on a particular trading day during January 1953-December 2001)

Date	Jan	Feb	Mar	Apr	May	Jun	Jul	Aug	Sep	Oct	Nov	Dec
1	H	S	S	57.1	55.1	S	65.3	46.9	H	51.0	S	46.9
2	55.1	S	S	55.1	65.3	57.1	65.3	S	63.3	63.3	S	59.2
3	75.5	55.1	67.3	53.1	S	53.1	61.2	S	57.1	51.0	63.3	63.3
4	S	57.1	71.4	59.2	S	55.1	H	44.9	61.2	S	53.1	59.2
5	S	40.8	59.2	S	57.1	57.1	S	46.9	42.9	S	69.4	44.9
6	46.9	53.1	51.0	S	49.0	53.1	S	53.1	S	59.2	53.1	S
7	57.1	44.9	46.9	53.1	42.9	S	55.1	55.1	S	51.0	44.9	S
8	49.0	S	S	63.3	49.0	S	63.3	44.9	44.9	53.1	S	40.8
9	46.9	S	S	67.3	51.0	38.8	57.1	S	42.9	38.8	S	53.1
10	44.9	38.8	57.1	61.2	S	34.7	55.1	S	53.1	38.8	63.3	59.2
11	S	42.9	61.2	61.2	S	57.1	34.7	46.9	57.1	S	57.1	40.8
12	S	63.3	51.0	S	46.9	61.2	S	53.1	44.9	S	59.2	49.0
13	49.0	42.9	57.1	S	49.0	57.1	S	49.0	S	55.1	44.9	S
14	61.2	49.0	49.0	71.4	55.1	S	65.3	63.3	S	59.2	49.0	S
15	57.1	S	S	63.3	53.1	S	49.0	55.1	53.1	53.1	S	46.9
16	61.2	S	S	57.1	46.9	46.9	49.0	S	51.0	55.1	S	55.1
17	55.1	H	59.2	42.9	S	46.9	55.1	S	46.9	46.9	49.0	51.0
18	S	49.0	65.3	H	S	42.9	28.6	42.9	36.7	S	38.8	61.2
19	S	40.8	46.9	S	44.9	55.1	S	44.9	44.9	S	61.2	57.1
20	H	44.9	38.8	S	53.1	51.0	S	59.2	S	57.1	67.3	S
21	46.9	61.2	49.0	53.1	46.9	S	49.0	49.0	S	55.1	59.2	S
22	38.8	S	S	46.9	28.6	S	51.0	51.0	44.9	51.0	S	53.1
23	59.2	S	S	49.0	59.2	44.9	46.9	S	42.9	38.8	S	46.9
24	49.0	36.7	38.8	53.1	S	38.8	46.9	S	53.1	51.0	65.3	67.3
25	S	44.9	46.9	59.2	S	51.0	59.2	51.0	55.1	S	57.1	H
26	S	63.3	51.0	S	H	44.9	S	44.9	46.9	S	51.0	71.4
27	57.1	44.9	59.2	S	38.8	55.1	S	53.1	S	24.5	H	S
28	57.1	53.1	38.8	53.1	42.9	S	55.1	42.9	S	49.0	53.1	S
29	49.0		S	46.9	53.1	S	51.0	61.2	46.9	55.1	S	53.1
30	65.3		S	55.1	63.3	57.1	63.3	S	42.9	61.2	S	61.2
31	61.2		44.9		S		55.1	S		53.1		59.2

S&P 500 MARKET PROBABILITY CALENDAR 2003

THE % CHANCE OF THE MARKET RISING ON ANY TRADING DAY OF THE YEAR*

(Based on the number of times the S&P 500 rose on a particular trading day during **January 1953-December 2001**)

Date	Jan	Feb	Mar	Apr	May	Jun	Jul	Aug	Sep	Oct	Nov	Dec
1	H	S	S	61.2	55.1	S	71.4	49.0	H	46.9	S	49.0
2	44.9	S	S	55.1	73.5	57.1	63.3	S	65.3	71.4	S	55.1
3	75.5	57.1	61.2	55.1	S	61.2	53.1	S	55.1	55.1	63.3	63.3
4	S	59.2	67.3	57.1	S	55.1	H	42.9	61.2	S	55.1	61.2
5	S	53.1	63.3	S	61.2	55.1	S	49.0	42.9	S	71.4	40.8
6	49.0	49.0	46.9	S	42.9	53.1	S	55.1	S	61.2	49.0	S
7	49.0	51.0	49.0	57.1	42.9	S	59.2	57.1	S	51.0	44.9	S
8	44.9	S	S	61.2	51.0	S	67.3	40.8	49.0	55.1	S	46.9
9	51.0	S	S	65.3	49.0	38.8	57.1	S	49.0	36.7	S	53.1
10	49.0	40.8	59.2	49.0	S	40.8	53.1	S	53.1	44.9	63.3	46.9
11	S	38.8	61.2	55.1	S	59.2	42.9	51.0	61.2	S	67.3	44.9
12	S	65.3	51.0	S	51.0	63.3	S	49.0	46.9	S	57.1	40.8
13	57.1	49.0	63.3	S	49.0	57.1	S	49.0	S	53.1	44.9	S
14	63.3	42.9	46.9	63.3	55.1	S	73.5	65.3	S	51.0	53.1	S
15	65.3	S	S	61.2	55.1	S	59.2	59.2	53.1	51.0	S	49.0
16	57.1	S	S	55.1	53.1	51.0	44.9	S	51.0	55.1	S	55.1
17	59.2	H	65.3	44.9	S	42.9	59.2	S	49.0	42.9	57.1	53.1
18	S	49.0	67.3	H	S	40.8	26.5	42.9	42.9	S	40.8	51.0
19	S	38.8	46.9	S	44.9	55.1	S	44.9	51.0	S	59.2	51.0
20	H	49.0	42.9	S	49.0	57.1	S	59.2	S	63.3	65.3	S
21	53.1	53.1	42.9	53.1	55.1	S	44.9	46.9	S	55.1	61.2	S
22	49.0	S	S	49.0	38.8	S	42.9	51.0	55.1	51.0	S	49.0
23	59.2	S	S	44.9	53.1	44.9	44.9	S	40.8	34.7	S	44.9
24	61.2	44.9	53.1	49.0	S	36.7	46.9	S	51.0	44.9	67.3	65.3
25	S	38.8	40.8	61.2	S	42.9	59.2	44.9	53.1	S	59.2	H
26	S	61.2	53.1	S	H	51.0	S	42.9	55.1	S	55.1	73.5
27	51.0	49.0	57.1	S	42.9	63.3	S	53.1	S	30.6	H	S
28	55.1	61.2	32.7	53.1	44.9	S	55.1	49.0	S	59.2	53.1	S
29	46.9		S	46.9	53.1	S	53.1	65.3	51.0	61.2	S	55.1
30	67.3		S	61.2	61.2	55.1	65.3	S	46.9	59.2	S	67.3
31	67.3		42.9		S		67.3	S		53.1		69.4

See new trends developing on pages 80, 88, 92 and 136

RECENT S&P 500 MARKET PROBABILITY CALENDAR 2003

THE % CHANCE OF THE MARKET RISING ON ANY TRADING DAY OF THE YEAR*

(Based on the number of times the S&P 500 rose on a particular trading day during **January 1981-December 2001****)

Date	Jan	Feb	Mar	Apr	May	Jun	Jul	Aug	Sep	Oct	Nov	Dec
1	H	S	S	61.9	57.1	S	76.2	47.6	H	57.1	S	57.1
2	38.1	S	S	52.4	71.4	57.1	47.6	S	47.6	61.9	S	61.9
3	71.4	42.9	52.4	42.9	S	66.7	33.3	S	47.6	47.6	76.2	61.9
4	S	66.7	57.1	57.1	S	52.4	H	42.9	52.4	S	52.4	38.1
5	S	71.4	61.9	S	57.1	52.4	S	52.4	33.3	S	61.9	42.9
6	47.6	47.6	42.9	S	33.3	52.4	S	42.9	S	57.1	47.6	S
7	47.6	57.1	47.6	47.6	38.1	S	52.4	52.4	S	42.9	38.1	S
8	47.6	S	S	66.7	47.6	S	66.7	42.9	47.6	61.9	S	42.9
9	52.4	S	S	61.9	61.9	28.6	47.6	S	47.6	23.8	S	47.6
10	42.9	38.1	61.9	38.1	S	42.9	66.7	S	52.4	38.1	61.9	42.9
11	S	33.3	47.6	52.4	S	52.4	61.9	38.1	57.1	S	57.1	42.9
12	S	76.2	42.9	S	52.4	61.9	S	47.6	52.4	S	52.4	28.6
13	57.1	57.1	61.9	S	61.9	66.7	S	47.6	S	71.4	52.4	S
14	57.1	42.9	38.1	57.1	66.7	S	90.5	66.7	S	61.9	61.9	S
15	81.0	S	S	71.4	57.1	S	57.1	52.4	47.6	57.1	S	47.6
16	71.4	S	S	47.6	52.4	52.4	57.1	S	42.9	52.4	S	47.6
17	57.1	H	71.4	42.9	S	52.4	71.4	S	33.3	33.3	57.1	57.1
18	S	57.1	71.4	H	S	33.3	23.8	61.9	52.4	S	38.1	52.4
19	S	38.1	42.9	S	47.6	57.1	S	52.4	42.9	S	61.9	47.6
20	H	42.9	47.6	S	57.1	71.4	S	61.9	S	57.1	61.9	S
21	42.9	42.9	47.6	61.9	42.9	S	38.1	47.6	S	57.1	66.7	S
22	38.1	S	S	38.1	28.6	S	33.3	61.9	52.4	61.9	S	57.1
23	47.6	S	S	52.4	71.4	38.1	38.1	S	33.3	28.6	S	57.1
24	47.6	52.4	52.4	42.9	S	28.6	38.1	S	38.1	33.3	71.4	61.9
25	S	38.1	52.4	66.7	S	33.3	81.0	42.9	52.4	S	61.9	H
26	S	61.9	47.6	S	H	52.4	S	57.1	52.4	S	57.1	61.9
27	52.4	52.4	57.1	S	52.4	66.7	S	47.6	S	38.1	H	S
28	52.4	61.9	23.8	52.4	47.6	S	52.4	47.6	S	52.4	42.9	S
29	57.1		S	52.4	52.4	S	47.6	52.4	57.1	66.7	S	61.9
30	66.7		S	66.7	47.6	47.6	66.7	S	57.1	71.4	S	66.7
31	81.0		47.6		S		66.7	S		61.9		47.6

* See new trends developing on pages 80, 88, 92 and 136 *** Based on most recent 21-year period*

2004 STRATEGY CALENDAR
(Option expiration dates encircled)

	MONDAY	TUESDAY	WEDNESDAY	THURSDAY	FRIDAY	SATURDAY	SUNDAY
JANUARY	29	30	31	1 JANUARY New Year's Day	2	3	4
	5	6	7	8	9	10	11
	12	13	14	15	(16)	17	18
	19 Martin Luther King Day	20	21	22	23	24	25
	26	27	28	29	30	31	1 FEBRUARY
FEBRUARY	2	3	4	5	6	7	8
	9	10	11	12	13	14 ♥	15
	16 Presidents' Day	17	18	19	(20)	21	22
	23	24	25 Ash Wednesday	26	27	28	29
MARCH	1 MARCH	2	3	4	5	6	7
	8	9	10	11	12	13	14
	15	16	17 ♣ St. Patrick's Day	18	(19)	20	21
	22	23	24	25	26	27	28
	29	30	31	1 APRIL	2	3	4
APRIL	5	6 Passover	7	8	9 Good Friday	10	11 Easter
	12	13	14	15	(16)	17	18
	19	20	21	22	23	24	25
	26	27	28	29	30	1 MAY	2
MAY	3	4	5	6	7	8	9 Mother's Day
	10	11	12	13	14	15	16
	17	18	19	20	(21)	22	23
	24	25	26	27	28	29	30
	31 Memorial Day	1 JUNE	2	3	4	5	6
JUNE	7	8	9	10	11	12	13
	14	15	16	17	(18)	19	20 Father's Day
	21	22	23	24	25	26	27

Market closed on shaded weekdays; closes early when half-shaded.

2004 STRATEGY CALENDAR
(Option expiration dates encircled)

MONDAY	TUESDAY	WEDNESDAY	THURSDAY	FRIDAY	SATURDAY	SUNDAY	
28	29	30	1 JULY	2	3	4 Independence Day	
5	6	7	8	9	10	11	
12	13	14	15	(16)	17	18	JULY
19	20	21	22	23	24	25	
26	27	28	29	30	31	1 AUGUST	
2	3	4	5	6	7	8	
9	10	11	12	13	14	15	
16	17	18	19	(20)	21	22	AUGUST
23	24	25	26	27	28	29	
30	31	1 SEPTEMBER	2	3	4	5	
6 Labor Day	7	8	9	10	11	12	
13	14	15	16 Rosh Hashanah	(17)	18	19	SEPTEMBER
20	21	22	23	24	25 Yom Kippur	26	
27	28	29	30	1 OCTOBER	2	3	
4	5	6	7	8	9	10	
11 Columbus Day	12	13	14	(15)	16	17	OCTOBER
18	19	20	21	22	23	24	
25	26	27	28	29	30	31	
1 NOVEMBER	2 Election Day	3	4	5	6	7	
8	9	10	11 Veteran's Day	12	13	14	
15	16	17	18	(19)	20	21	NOVEMBER
22	23	24	25 Thanksgiving	26	27	28	
29	30	1 DECEMBER	2	3	4	5	
6	7	8 Chanukah	9	10	11	12	
13	14	15	16	(17)	18	19	DECEMBER
20	21	22	23	24	25 Christmas	26	
27	28	29	30	31			

DECENNIAL CYCLE: A MARKET PHENOMENON

By arranging each year's market gain or loss so the first and succeeding years of each decade fall into the same column, certain interesting patterns emerge—strong fifth and eighth years, weak seventh and zero years.

This fascinating phenomenon was first presented by Edgar Lawrence Smith in *Common Stocks and Business Cycles* (William-Frederick Press, 1959). Anthony Gaubis co-pioneered the decennial pattern with Smith.

When Smith first cut graphs of market prices into ten-year segments and placed them above one another, he observed that each decade tended to have three bull market cycles and that the longest and strongest bull markets seem to favor the middle years of a decade.

Don't place too much emphasis on the decennial cycle nowadays, other than the extraordinary fifth and zero years, as the stock market is more influenced by the quadrennial presidential election cycle, shown on page 127. Also, the last half-century, which has been the most prosperous in US history, has distributed the returns among most years of the decade. Interestingly, NASDAQ suffered its worst bear market ever in a zero year, giving us the rare experience of witnessing a bubble burst.

With the market still in the bear's clutches through 2001 and press time 2002, we look forward to 2003, as we haven't had a loss in a pre-presidential year since 1939. (See Pre-Election Year column page 127!)

THE TEN-YEAR STOCK MARKET CYCLE

Annual % Change In Dow Jones Industrial Average
Year Of Decade

DECADES	1st	2nd	3rd	4th	5th	6th	7th	8th	9th	10th
1881-1890	3.0	-2.9	-8.5	-18.8	20.1	12.4	-8.4	4.8	5.5	-14.1
1891-1900	17.6	-6.6	-24.6	-0.6	2.3	-1.7	21.3	22.5	9.2	7.0
1901-1910	-8.7	-0.4	-23.6	41.7	38.2	-1.9	-37.7	46.6	15.0	-17.9
1911-1920	0.4	7.6	-10.3	-5.4	81.7	-4.2	-21.7	10.5	30.5	-32.9
1921-1930	12.7	21.7	-3.3	26.2	30.0	0.3	28.8	48.2	-17.2	-33.8
1931-1940	-52.7	-23.1	66.7	4.1	38.5	24.8	-32.8	28.1	-2.9	-12.7
1941-1950	-15.4	7.6	13.8	12.1	26.6	-8.1	2.2	-2.1	12.9	17.6
1951-1960	14.4	8.4	-3.8	44.0	20.8	2.3	-12.8	34.0	16.4	-9.3
1961-1970	18.7	-10.8	17.0	14.6	10.9	-18.9	15.2	4.3	-15.2	4.8
1971-1980	6.1	14.6	-16.6	-27.6	38.3	17.9	-17.3	-3.1	4.2	14.9
1981-1990	-9.2	19.6	20.3	-3.7	27.7	22.6	2.3	11.8	27.0	-4.3
1991-2000	20.3	4.2	13.7	2.1	33.5	26.0	22.6	16.1	25.2	-6.2
2001-2010	-7.1									
Total % Change	0.1%	39.9%	40.8%	88.7%	368.6%	71.5%	-38.3%	221.7%	110.6%	-86.9%
Up Years	8	7	5	7	12	7	6	10	9	4
Down Years	5	5	7	5	0	5	6	2	3	8

Based on annual close *Cowles indices 1881-1885*

PRESIDENTIAL ELECTION/STOCK MARKET CYCLE THE 169-YEAR SAGA CONTINUES

It is no mere coincidence that the last two years (pre-election year and election year) of the 43 administrations since 1833 produced a total net market gain of 717.5%, dwarfing the 244.4% gain of the first two years of these administrations.

Presidential elections every four years have a profound impact on the economy and the stock market. Wars, recessions and bear markets tend to start or occur in the first half of the term; prosperous times and bull markets, in the latter half.

Looking at the track record of pre-election years gives us something to look forward to in 2003, a potential 50% move from the midterm year's (2002) bottom to the high in 2003. (See page 78.)

STOCK MARKET ACTION SINCE 1833
Annual % Change In Dow Jones Industrial Average[1]

4-Year Cycle Beginning	Elected President	Post-Election Year	Mid-Term Year	Pre-Election Year	Election Year
1833	Jackson (D)	− 0.9	13.0	3.1	−11.7
1837	Van Buren (D)	−11.5	1.6	−12.3	5.5
1841*	W.H. Harrison (W)**	−13.3	−18.1	45.0	15.5
1845*	Polk (D)	8.1	−14.5	1.2	− 3.6
1849*	Taylor (W)**	N/C	18.7	− 3.2	19.6
1853*	Pierce (D)	−12.7	−30.2	1.5	4.4
1857	Buchanan (D)	−31.0	14.3	−10.7	14.0
1861*	Lincoln (R)	− 1.8	55.4	38.0	6.4
1863	Lincoln (R)**	− 8.5	3.6	1.6	10.8
1869	Grant (R)	1.7	5.6	7.3	6.8
1873	Grant (R)	−12.7	2.8	− 4.1	−17.9
1877	Hayes (R)	− 9.4	6.1	43.0	18.7
1881	Garfield (R)**	3.0	− 2.9	− 8.5	−18.8
1885*	Cleveland (D)	20.1	12.4	− 8.4	4.8
1889*	B. Harrison (R)	5.5	−14.1	17.6	− 6.6
1893*	Cleveland (D)	−24.6	− 0.6	2.3	− 1.7
1897*	McKinley (R)	21.3	22.5	9.2	7.0
1901	McKinley (R)**	− 8.7	− 0.4	−23.6	41.7
1905	T. Roosevelt (R)	38.2	− 1.9	−37.7	46.6
1909	Taft (R)	15.0	−17.9	0.4	7.6
1913*	Wilson (D)	−10.3	− 5.4	81.7	− 4.2
1917	Wilson (D)	−21.7	10.5	30.5	−32.9
1921*	Harding (R)**	12.7	21.7	− 3.3	26.2
1925	Coolidge (R)	30.0	0.3	28.8	48.2
1929	Hoover (R)	−17.2	−33.8	−52.7	−23.1
1933*	F. Roosevelt (D)	66.7	4.1	38.5	24.8
1937	F. Roosevelt (D)	−32.8	28.1	− 2.9	−12.7
1941	F. Roosevelt (D)	−15.4	7.6	13.8	12.1
1945	F. Roosevelt (D)**	26.6	− 8.1	2.2	− 2.1
1949	Truman (D)	12.9	17.6	14.4	8.4
1953*	Eisenhower (R)	− 3.8	44.0	20.8	2.3
1957	Eisenhower (R)	−12.8	34.0	16.4	− 9.3
1961*	Kennedy (D)**	18.7	−10.8	17.0	14.6
1965	Johnson (D)	10.9	−18.9	15.2	4.3
1969*	Nixon (R)	−15.2	4.8	6.1	14.6
1973	Nixon (R)***	−16.6	−27.6	38.3	17.9
1977*	Carter (D)	−17.3	− 3.1	4.2	14.9
1981*	Reagan (R)	− 9.2	19.6	20.3	− 3.7
1985	Reagan (R)	27.7	22.6	2.3	11.8
1989	G. H. W. Bush (R)	27.0	− 4.3	20.3	4.2
1993*	Clinton (D)	13.7	2.1	33.5	26.0
1997	Clinton (D)	22.6	16.1	25.2	− 6.2
2001*	G. W. Bush (R)	− 7.1			
	Total % Gain	67.9 %	176.5%	432.3%	285.2%
	# Up	19	25	31	28
	# Down	23	17	11	14

*Party in power ousted **Death in office ***Resigned D—Democrat, W—Whig, R—Republican

[1] Based on annual close, prior to 1886 based on Cowles and other indices

BULL AND BEAR MARKETS SINCE 1900

— Beginning —		— Ending —		Bull		Bear	
Date	DJIA	Date	DJIA	% Gain	Days	% Change	Days
9/24/00	52.96	6/17/01	78.26	47.8%	266	− 46.1%	875
11/9/03	42.15	1/19/06	103.00	144.4	802	− 48.5	665
11/15/07	53.00	11/19/09	100.53	89.7	735	− 27.4	675
9/25/11	72.94	9/30/12	94.15	29.1	371	− 43.5	815
12/24/14	53.17	11/21/16	110.15	107.2	698	− 40.1	393
12/19/17	65.95	11/3/19	119.62	81.4	684	− 46.6	660
8/24/21	63.90	3/20/23	105.38	64.9	573	− 18.6	221
10/27/23	85.76	9/3/29	381.17	344.5	2138	− 47.9	71
11/13/29	198.69	4/17/30	294.07	48.0	155	− 86.0	813
7/8/32	41.22	9/7/32	79.93	93.9	61	− 37.2	173
2/27/33	50.16	2/5/34	110.74	120.8	343	− 22.8	171
7/26/34	85.51	3/10/37	194.40	127.3	958	− 49.1	386
3/31/38	98.95	11/12/38	158.41	60.1	226	− 23.3	147
4/8/39	121.44	9/12/39	155.92	28.4	157	− 40.4	959
4/28/42	92.92	5/29/46	212.50	128.7	1492	− 23.2	353
5/17/47	163.21	6/15/48	193.16	18.4	395	− 16.3	363
6/13/49	161.60	1/5/53	293.79	81.8	1302	− 13.0	252
9/14/53	255.49	4/6/56	521.05	103.9	935	− 19.4	564
10/22/57	419.79	1/5/60	685.47	63.3	805	− 17.4	294
10/25/60	566.05	12/13/61	734.91	29.8	414	− 27.1	195
6/26/62	535.76	2/9/66	995.15	85.7	1324	− 25.2	240
10/7/66	744.32	12/3/68	985.21	32.4	788	− 35.9	539
5/26/70	631.16	4/28/71	950.82	50.6	337	− 16.1	209
11/23/71	797.97	1/11/73	1051.70	31.8	415	− 45.1	694
12/6/74	577.60	9/21/76	1014.79	75.7	655	− 26.9	525
2/28/78	742.12	9/8/78	907.74	22.3	192	− 16.4	591
4/21/80	759.13	4/27/81	1024.05	34.9	371	− 24.1	472
8/12/82	776.92	11/29/83	1287.20	65.7	474	− 15.6	238
7/24/84	1086.57	8/25/87	2722.42	150.6	1127	− 36.1	55
10/19/87	1738.74	7/17/90	2999.75	72.5	1002	− 21.2	86
10/11/90	2365.10	7/17/98	9337.97	294.8	2836	− 19.3	45
8/31/98	7539.07	1/14/00	11722.98	55.5	501	− 29.7	616
9/21/01	8235.81	3/19/02	10635.25	29.1	179	− 27.6*	126*
7/23/02	7702.34	*At Press Time					

Based on Dow Jones industrial average
The NYSE was closed from 7/31/1914 to 12/11/1914 due to World War I.

1900-2000 Data: Ned Davis Research

Bear markets begin at the end of one bull market and end at the start of the next bull market (7/17/90 to 10/11/90 as an example). The high at Dow 3978.36 on January 31, 1994 was followed by a 9.7 percent correction. A 10.3 percent correction occurred between the May 22, 1996 closing high of 5778 and the intraday low on July 16, 1996. The longest bull market on record ended on July 17, 1998 and the shortest bear market on record ended on August 31, 1998 when the new bull market began. The greatest bull super cycle in history, that began 8/12/82, finally gave way in 2001, when the DJIA closed below its previous year's low for the first time since August 1982 on March 20, 2001 at 9720.76. NASDAQ suffered its worst loss ever, down 75.7% at press time.

DIRECTORY OF TRADING PATTERNS & DATABANK

CONTENTS

- 130 A Typical Day In The Market
- 131 Through the Week On A Half-Hourly Basis
- 132 Monday Reverts To Its Old Bear Market Pattern
  Worst Day Of Week Last Two Years
- 133 NASDAQ Days Of The Week
- 134 S&P Daily Performance Each Year Since 1952
- 135 NASDAQ Daily Performance Each Year Since 1971
- 136 Monthly Cash Inflows Into S&P Stocks
- 137 Monthly Cash Inflows Into NASDAQ Stocks
- 138 November, December, January-Year's Best Three Month Span
- 139 November Through June-NASDAQ's Eight-Month Run
- 140 Standard & Poor's 500 Monthly Percent Changes
- 142 Standard & Poor's 500 Monthly Closing Prices
- 144 Dow Jones Industrials Monthly Percent Changes
- 146 Dow Jones Industrials Monthly Point Changes
- 148 Dow Jones Industrials Monthly Closing Prices
- 150 NASDAQ Composite Monthly Percent Changes
- 152 NASDAQ Composite Monthly Closing Prices
- 154 Largest One-Day Dow Gains And Losses
- 155 Largest One-Day NASDAQ Gains And Losses
- 156 Largest Weekly Dow Gains And Losses
- 157 Largest Weekly NASDAQ Gains And Losses
- 158 Largest Monthly Dow Gains And Losses
- 159 Largest Monthly NASDAQ Gains And Losses
- 160 Largest Yearly Dow & NASDAQ Gains And Losses

A TYPICAL DAY IN THE MARKET

Half-hourly data became available for the Dow Jones industrial average starting in January 1987. The NYSE switched 10:00am openings to 9:30am in October 1985. Below is the comparison between half-hourly performance 1987-May 2002 and hourly November 1963-June 1985. Stronger openings and closings in a more bullish climate are evident. Morning and afternoon weakness appear an hour earlier.

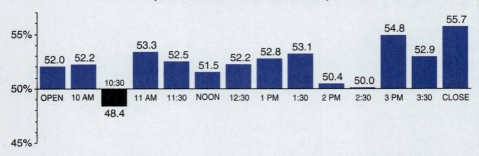

Based on the number of times the Dow Jones industrial average increased over previous half-hour

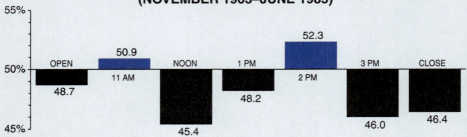

Based on the number of times the Dow Jones industrial average increased over previous hour

On the opposite page, half-hourly movements since January 1987 are separated by day of the week. From 1953 to 1989 Monday was the worst day of the week, especially during long bear markets, but times changed. Monday reversed positions and became the best day of the week, and on the plus side twelve years in a row from 1990 to 2000. But as the bear has returned Monday has been a net loser in 2001 and 2002 so far. (See page 80.) Fridays have been down the last three years and a net loser since 1990. On all days stocks do tend to firm up near the close.

THROUGH THE WEEK ON A HALF-HOURLY BASIS

From the chart showing the percentage of times the Dow Jones industrial average rose over the preceding half-hour (January 1987—May 2002*) the typical week unfolds.

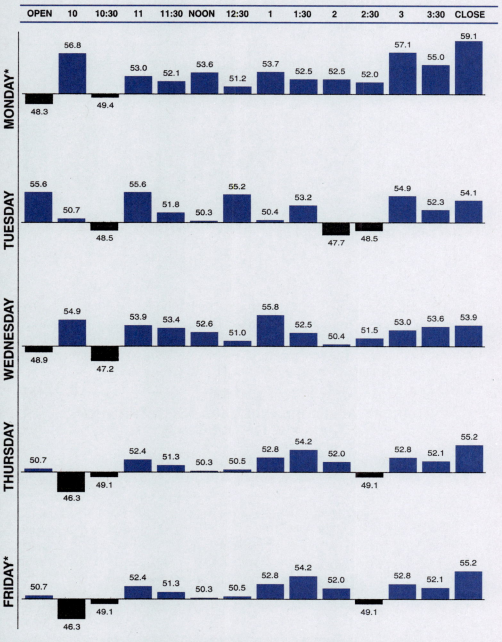

*Research indicates that where Tuesday is the first trading day of the week, it follows the Monday pattern. Therefore, all such Tuesdays were combined with the Mondays here. Thursdays that are the final trading day of a given week behave like Fridays, and were similarly grouped with Fridays.

MONDAY REVERTS TO ITS OLD BEAR PATTERN WORST DAY OF WEEK LAST TWO YEARS

Between 1952 and 1989 Monday was the worst trading day of the week. The first trading day of the week (including Tuesday, when Monday is a holiday) rose only 44.5% of the time, while the other trading days closed higher 54.7% of the time. (NYSE Saturday trading discontinued June 1952.)

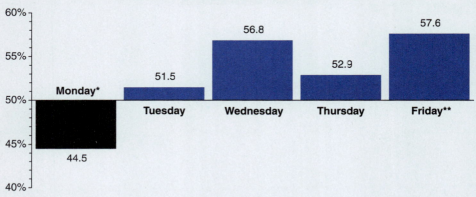

A dramatic reversal occurred during the 1990-2000 bull market—Monday became the most powerful day of the week. Throughout the recent bear market Monday has returned to its old ways and Friday has become a day to avoid, as traders are not inclined to stay long over the weekend during uncertain market times. Mid-week has been most bullish the last two years, see page 80.

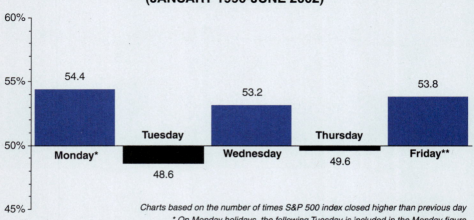

Charts based on the number of times S&P 500 index closed higher than previous day
* On Monday holidays, the following Tuesday is included in the Monday figure
** On Friday holidays, the preceding Thursday is included in the Friday figure

NASDAQ DAYS OF THE WEEK

Despite 20 years less data, daily trading patterns on NASDAQ through 1989 appear to be fairly similar to the S&P across on page 132 except for more bullishness on Thursdays. During the mostly flat markets of the 1970s and early 1980s, it would appear that apprehensive investors decided to throw in the towel over weekends and sell on Mondays and Tuesdays.

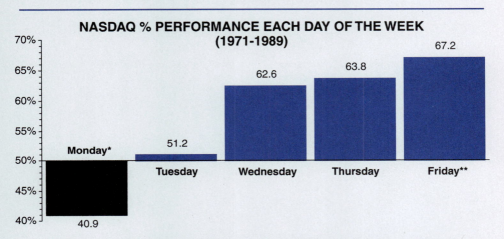

Notice the vast difference in the daily trading pattern between NASDAQ and S&P from January 1, 1990 to recent times. The reason for so much more bullishness is that NASDAQ moved up 1010%, over three times as much during the 1990-2000 period. The gain for the S&P was 332% and for the Dow Jones industrials, 326%. With the "Bubble of 2000" burst, NASDAQ's weekly patterns are beginning to move in step with the rest of the market. Notice on page 135 Monday's weakness during the 2000 to 2002 bear cycle.

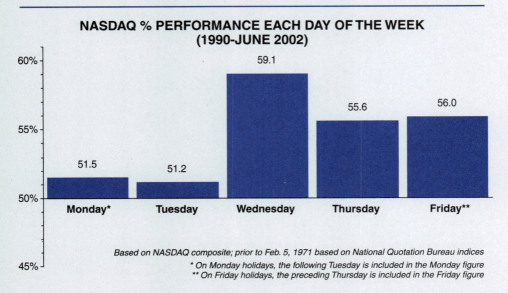

Based on NASDAQ composite; prior to Feb. 5, 1971 based on National Quotation Bureau indices
* On Monday holidays, the following Tuesday is included in the Monday figure
** On Friday holidays, the preceding Thursday is included in the Friday figure

S&P DAILY PERFORMANCE EACH YEAR SINCE 1952

To determine if market trend alters performance of different days of the week, the sixteen bear years of 1953, '57, '60, '62, '66, '69, '70, '73, '74, '77, '81, '84, '90, '94, 2000 and 2001 were separated from the 34 bull market years. While Tuesday and Thursday did not vary much on average between bull and bear years, Mondays and Fridays were sharply affected. There was a swing of 10.4 percentage points in Monday's and 11.0 in Friday's performance. Mondays were much stronger during the bullish period 1990-2000.

PERCENTAGE OF TIMES MARKET CLOSED HIGHER THAN PREVIOUS DAY (JUNE 1952–JUNE 2002)

	Monday*	Tuesday	Wednesday	Thursday	Friday**
1952	48.4%	55.6%	58.1%	51.9%	66.7%
1953	34.6	52.1	54.9	59.6	54.7
1954	50.0	57.4	63.5	59.2	73.1
1955	50.0	45.7	63.5	60.0	78.8
1956	37.7	39.6	45.8	50.0	59.6
1957	26.9	54.0	66.7	48.9	44.2
1958	59.6	52.0	58.8	68.1	73.1
1959	40.4	53.1	55.8	48.9	69.8
1960	34.6	50.0	44.2	54.0	59.6
1961	53.8	52.2	64.0	56.0	63.5
1962	28.3	52.1	54.0	53.1	48.1
1963	46.2	63.3	51.0	57.4	69.2
1964	40.4	48.0	61.5	58.7	77.4
1965	46.2	57.4	55.8	51.0	71.2
1966	36.5	47.8	53.8	42.0	57.7
1967	38.5	50.0	60.8	64.0	69.2
1968[1]	49.1	55.3	63.0	40.4	55.8
1969	32.7	45.8	50.0	67.4	50.0
1970	40.4	44.0	65.4	46.8	52.8
1971	44.2	62.5	55.8	57.1	50.0
1972	38.5	60.9	57.7	51.0	67.3
1973	32.1	51.1	52.9	44.9	44.2
1974	32.7	57.1	51.0	36.7	30.8
1975	53.8	38.8	61.5	56.3	55.8
1976	55.8	55.3	55.8	40.8	58.5
1977	40.4	40.4	46.2	53.1	53.8
1978	51.9	43.5	59.6	54.0	48.1
1979	54.7	53.2	58.8	66.0	44.2
1980	55.8	56.3	69.8	35.4	55.8
1981	44.2	38.8	55.8	53.2	47.2
1982	46.2	39.6	44.2	44.9	50.0
1983	55.8	46.8	61.5	50.0	55.8
1984	39.6	63.8	31.4	46.0	44.2
1985	44.2	61.2	54.9	56.3	53.8
1986	51.9	44.9	67.3	58.3	55.8
1987	51.9	57.1	63.5	61.7	49.1
1988	51.9	61.7	51.9	48.0	59.6
1989	51.9	47.8	69.2	58.0	69.2
1990	67.9	53.2	52.9	40.0	51.9
1991	44.2	46.9	52.9	49.0	51.9
1992	51.9	49.0	53.8	56.3	45.3
1993	65.4	41.7	55.8	44.9	48.1
1994	55.8	46.8	52.9	48.0	59.6
1995	63.5	56.5	63.5	62.0	63.5
1996	54.7	44.9	51.0	57.1	63.5
1997	67.3	69.4	42.3	41.7	57.7
1998	57.7	62.5	57.7	37.5	61.5
1999	46.2	29.8	66.7	53.1	59.6
2000	51.9	43.5	40.4	56.0	46.2
2001	45.3	51.1	44.0	59.2	43.1
2002[2]	36.0	36.4	57.7	40.0	48.0
Average	**47.1**	**50.7**	**55.9**	**52.0**	**56.6**
34 Bull Years	**50.6**	**51.8**	**58.1**	**53.1**	**60.3**
16 Bear Years	**40.2**	**49.5**	**51.0**	**50.6**	**49.3**

Based on S&P 500

[1] Excludes last six months of four-day market weeks. [2] Six months only. Not included in averages.
* On Monday holidays, the following Tuesday is included in the Monday figure
** On Friday holidays, the preceding Thursday is included in the Friday figure

NASDAQ DAILY PERFORMANCE EACH YEAR SINCE 1971

Bear in mind again, as on page 133, that during the tech stock explosion of the late 1990s NASDAQ soared in comparison to the Dow and S&P. Even after tumbling back to earth with a post-millennial hangover, NASDAQ tech stocks still outpace the blue chips and big caps—but not by nearly as much as they did. From January 1, 1971 through July 23, 2002, NASDAQ moved up an impressive 1272%. The S&P (up 766%) and the Dow (up 818%) gained almost two thirds as much.

Monday's performance on NASDAQ has also returned to its bearish ways of the past in the last three years. Another pattern, that cannot be seen here, is that when major stocks become overextended for some period of time, nervous traders will sell off positions on Friday. And when the world doesn't collapse over the weekend, come back in and push up Mondays. Conversely, when Fridays close down and those traders that sold don't come back in on Monday, watch out. This can lead to further declines, especially when a cluster of "Down Fridays, Down Mondays" develops. See page 68.

PERCENTAGE OF TIMES NASDAQ CLOSED HIGHER THAN PREVIOUS DAY
(1971-JUNE 2002)

	Monday*	Tuesday	Wednesday	Thursday	Friday**
1971	51.9%	52.1%	59.6%	65.3%	71.2%
1972	30.8	60.9	63.5	57.1	78.8
1973	34.0	48.9	52.9	53.1	48.1
1974	30.8	46.9	51.0	49.0	42.3
1975	42.3	42.9	63.5	64.6	63.5
1976	50.0	63.8	67.3	59.2	58.5
1977	50.0	42.6	53.8	61.2	73.1
1978	48.1	47.8	71.2	72.0	84.6
1979	45.3	53.2	64.7	86.0	82.7
1980	44.2	64.6	84.9	52.1	73.1
1981	42.3	32.7	67.3	76.6	69.8
1982	36.5	47.9	61.5	51.0	61.5
1983	42.3	42.6	67.3	68.0	73.1
1984	22.6	53.2	35.3	52.0	51.9
1985	36.5	59.2	62.7	68.8	67.3
1986	38.5	55.1	65.4	72.9	75.0
1987	42.3	49.0	65.4	68.1	66.0
1988	50.0	55.3	61.5	66.0	63.5
1989	38.5	54.3	71.2	70.0	73.1
1990	54.7	42.6	60.8	46.0	55.8
1991	51.9	59.2	66.7	65.3	51.9
1992	46.2	53.1	59.6	60.4	45.3
1993	55.8	56.3	69.2	57.1	67.3
1994	51.9	46.8	54.9	52.0	55.8
1995	50.0	52.2	63.5	62.0	63.5
1996	50.9	57.1	64.7	61.2	63.5
1997	65.4	59.2	53.8	52.1	55.8
1998	59.6	58.3	63.5	46.8	58.5
1999	61.5	40.4	63.5	57.1	65.4
2000	40.4	41.3	42.3	60.0	57.7
2001	41.5	57.8	52.0	55.1	47.1
2002[1]	40.0	40.9	53.8	48.0	40.0
Average	**45.4%**	**51.5%**	**61.4%**	**60.9%**	**63.4%**
22 Bull Years	**47.6%**	**53.5%**	**64.7%**	**62.6%**	**66.8%**
9 Bear Years	**40.1%**	**46.6%**	**53.5%**	**56.9%**	**54.9%**

Based on NASDAQ composite; prior to Feb. 5, 1971 based on National Quotation Bureau indices
[1] *Six months only. Not included in averages.*
* On Monday holidays, the following Tuesday is included in the Monday figure
** On Friday holidays, the preceding Thursday is included in the Friday figure

MONTHLY CASH INFLOWS INTO S&P STOCKS

For many years, the last trading day of the month plus the first four of the following month were the best market days of the month. This pattern is quite clear in the first chart showing these five consecutive trading days towering above the other 16 trading days of the average month in the 1953-1981 period. The rationale was that individuals and institutions tended to operate similarly, causing a massive flow of cash into stocks near beginnings of months.

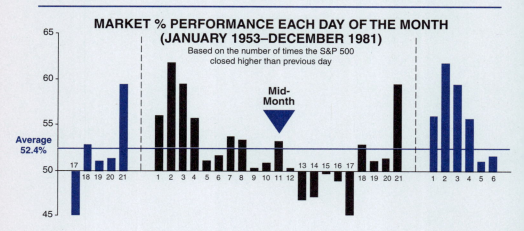

Clearly, "front-running" traders took advantage of this phenomenon, drastically altering the previous pattern. The second chart from 1982 onward shows the trading shift caused by these "anticipators" to the last three trading days of the month plus the first two. Another astonishing development shows the ninth, tenth, and eleventh trading days rising strongly as well. Perhaps the enormous growth of 401(k) retirement plans (participants' salaries are usually paid twice monthly) is responsible for this new mid-month bulge. First trading days of the month have produced the greatest gains in recent years (see pages 62, 88 and 92).

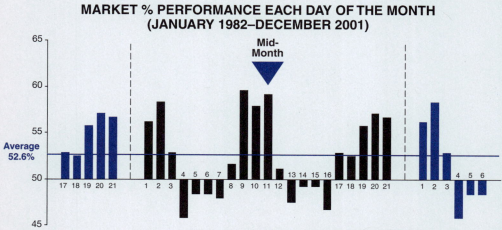

TRADING DAYS (excluding Saturdays, Sundays, and holidays)

MONTHLY CASH INFLOWS INTO NASDAQ STOCKS

NASDAQ stocks moved up 57.9% of the time through 1981 compared to 52.4% for the S&P across the page. Ends and beginnings of the month are fairly similar, specifically the last plus the first four trading days. But notice how investors kept piling into NASDAQ stocks for six additional days. NASDAQ rose 118.5% from January 1, 1971 to December 31, 1981 compared to 33.0% for the S&P.

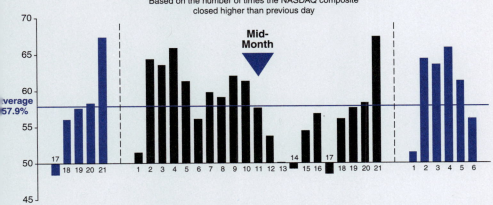

With markets back to earth, the S&P and NASDAQ are on par now, climbing 836.8% and 895.9% respectively over the next 20 years. Last three, first three and middle three days rose the most. Where the S&P has eight days of the month that go down more often than up, NASDAQ only has one. NASDAQ still exhibits the most strength on the last trading day of the month, and the last trading day of December has only been down twice in 31 years.

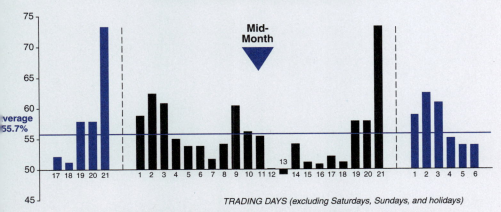

Based on NASDAQ composite, prior to Feb. 5, 1971 based on National Quotation Bureau indices

NOVEMBER, DECEMBER, AND JANUARY YEAR'S BEST THREE-MONTH SPAN

The most important observation to be made from a chart showing the average monthly percent change in market prices since 1950 is that institutions (mutual funds, pension funds, banks, etc.) determine the trading patterns in today's market.

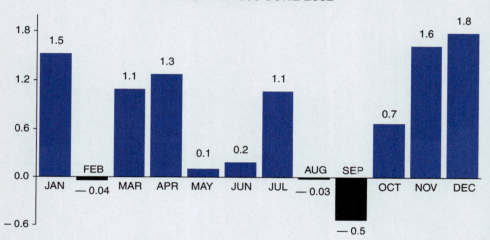

Average month-to-month % change in S&P 500
(Based on monthly closing prices)

The "investment calendar" reflects the annual, semi-annual and quarterly operations of institutions during January, April and July. October, besides being a "tight money" month, and the last campaign month before elections, is also the time when most bear markets seem to end, as in 1946, 1957, 1960, 1962, 1966, 1974, 1987, 1990 and 1998. (August and September tend to combine to make the worst consecutive two-month period.)

Unusual year-end strength comes from corporate and private pension funds, producing a 4.9% gain on average between November 1 and January 31. September's dismal performance makes it the worst month of the year. In the last eighteen years it has only been up six times.

Best months in pre-election years since 1950: January (13-0), April (12-1), March (11-2) and December (10-3).

See page 48 for monthly performance tables for the S&P 500 and the Dow Jones industrials. See pages 50 and 52 for unique six-month switching strategies.

On page 74 you can see how the first month of the first three quarters far outperforms the second and the third months since 1950. Individual monthly performance is also shown for each year starting with 1991.

NOVEMBER THROUGH JUNE
NASDAQ'S EIGHT-MONTH RUN

The two-year and four-month rout of 75.7% in NASDAQ stocks between March 10, 2000 and July 23, 2002 (at press time) brought several horrendous monthly losses. The two greatest were in November 2000 (-22.9%) and February 2001 (-22.4%), which severely affected those months' average performance over the 31-year period. January's 4.1% average gain is still awesome, and 2.7 times better than what the S&P did in January.

Bear in mind when comparing NASDAQ to the S&P across the page that there are 21 fewer years of data here. During this 31½-year (1971-June 2002) period NASDAQ, at its June 28, 2002 1463.21 close, grew 1532.9%, while the S&P and the Dow rose only 974.1% and 1001.8%, respectively. On page 56 you can see a statistical monthly comparison between NASDAQ, which grew at 9.05% a year, and the Dow, 7.59% (S&P 7.49%).

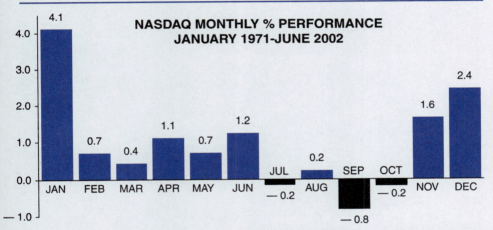

Average month-to-month % change in NASDAQ composite, prior to Feb. 5, 1971 based on National Quotation Bureau indices
(Based on monthly closing prices)

An enormous bear market has made a whale of a difference to compounded rates of return. Calculating from January 1, 1971 to their respective 2000 tops had inflated NASDAQ to a 14.4% annual rate of return, compared to 9.2% for the Dow and 9.8% for the S&P.

What a difference a year can make. During 2000 and 2001 we experienced an unusual divergence. When you were asked, "How'd the market do today?" You often responded, "Which market?" This resulted from the Dow and the Nasdaq going in opposite directions on the same day. We also heard of the "New Economy" stocks versus the "Old Economy" stocks. With so many casualties and dot bombs it seems that the "Old Economy" has engulfed the "New Economy" and we now have one economy—Internet and all.

Just before the runaway technology-dominated NASDAQ took center stage, technology comprised just 8.8% of the S&P 500 in 1990. By 1995 the sector grew to be 12.2% of the S&P. However, at the NASDAQ peak in March 2000, the group represented 35% of the S&P 500. Twenty-eight months later in July 2002, after a thorough shellacking, the percentage dropped sharply to 15.5%.

STANDARD & POOR'S 500
MONTHLY PERCENT CHANGES

	JAN	FEB	MAR	APR	MAY	JUN
1950	1.7%	1.0%	0.4%	4.5%	3.9%	— 5.8%
1951	6.1	0.6	— 1.8	4.8	— 4.1	— 2.6
1952	1.6	— 3.6	4.8	— 4.3	2.3	4.6
1953	— 0.7	— 1.8	— 2.4	— 2.6	— 0.3	— 1.6
1954	5.1	0.3	3.0	4.9	3.3	0.1
1955	1.8	0.4	— 0.5	3.8	— 0.1	8.2
1956	— 3.6	3.5	6.9	— 0.2	— 6.6	3.9
1957	— 4.2	— 3.3	2.0	3.7	3.7	— 0.1
1958	4.3	— 2.1	3.1	3.2	1.5	2.6
1959	0.4	— 0.02	0.1	3.9	1.9	— 0.4
1960	— 7.1	0.9	— 1.4	— 1.8	2.7	2.0
1961	6.3	2.7	2.6	0.4	1.9	— 2.9
1962	— 3.8	1.6	— 0.6	— 6.2	— 8.6	— 8.2
1963	4.9	— 2.9	3.5	4.9	1.4	— 2.0
1964	2.7	1.0	1.5	0.6	1.1	1.6
1965	3.3	— 0.1	— 1.5	3.4	— 0.8	— 4.9
1966	0.5	— 1.8	— 2.2	2.1	— 5.4	— 1.6
1967	7.8	0.2	3.9	4.2	— 5.2	1.8
1968	— 4.4	— 3.1	0.9	8.2	1.1	0.9
1969	— 0.8	— 4.7	3.4	2.1	— 0.2	— 5.6
1970	— 7.6	5.3	0.1	— 9.0	— 6.1	— 5.0
1971	4.0	0.9	3.7	3.6	— 4.2	0.1
1972	1.8	2.5	0.6	0.4	1.7	— 2.2
1973	— 1.7	— 3.7	— 0.1	— 4.1	— 1.9	— 0.7
1974	— 1.0	— 0.4	— 2.3	— 3.9	— 3.4	— 1.5
1975	12.3	6.0	2.2	4.7	4.4	4.4
1976	11.8	— 1.1	3.1	— 1.1	— 1.4	4.1
1977	— 5.1	— 2.2	— 1.4	0.02	— 2.4	4.5
1978	— 6.2	— 2.5	2.5	8.5	0.4	— 1.8
1979	4.0	— 3.7	5.5	0.2	— 2.6	3.9
1980	5.8	— 0.4	—10.2	4.1	4.7	2.7
1981	— 4.6	1.3	3.6	— 2.3	— 0.2	— 1.0
1982	— 1.8	— 6.1	— 1.0	4.0	— 3.9	— 2.0
1983	3.3	1.9	3.3	7.5	— 1.2	3.5
1984	— 0.9	— 3.9	1.3	0.5	— 5.9	1.7
1985	7.4	0.9	— 0.3	— 0.5	5.4	1.2
1986	0.2	7.1	5.3	— 1.4	5.0	1.4
1987	13.2	3.7	2.6	— 1.1	0.6	4.8
1988	4.0	4.2	— 3.3	0.9	0.3	4.3
1989	7.1	— 2.9	2.1	5.0	3.5	— 0.8
1990	— 6.9	0.9	2.4	— 2.7	9.2	— 0.9
1991	4.2	6.7	2.2	0.03	3.9	— 4.8
1992	— 2.0	1.0	— 2.2	2.8	0.1	— 1.7
1993	0.7	1.0	1.9	— 2.5	2.3	0.1
1994	3.3	— 3.0	— 4.6	1.2	1.2	— 2.7
1995	2.4	3.6	2.7	2.8	3.6	2.1
1996	3.3	0.7	0.8	1.3	2.3	0.2
1997	6.1	0.6	— 4.3	5.8	5.9	4.3
1998	1.0	7.0	5.0	0.9	— 1.9	3.9
1999	4.1	— 3.2	3.9	3.8	— 2.5	5.4
2000	— 5.1	— 2.0	9.7	— 3.1	— 2.2	2.4
2001	3.5	— 9.2	— 6.4	7.7	0.5	— 2.5
2002	— 1.6	— 2.1	3.7	— 6.1	— 0.9	— 7.2

STANDARD & POOR'S 500 MONTHLY PERCENT CHANGES

JUL	AUG	SEP	OCT	NOV	DEC		Year's Change
0.8%	3.3%	5.6%	0.4%	— 0.1%	4.6%	**1950**	21.8%
6.9	3.9	— 0.1	— 1.4	— 0.3	3.9	**1951**	16.5
1.8	— 1.5	— 2.0	— 0.1	4.6	3.5	**1952**	11.8
2.5	— 5.8	0.1	5.1	0.9	0.2	**1953**	— 6.6
5.7	— 3.4	8.3	— 1.9	8.1	5.1	**1954**	45.0
6.1	— 0.8	1.1	— 3.0	7.5	— 0.1	**1955**	26.4
5.2	— 3.8	— 4.5	0.5	— 1.1	3.5	**1956**	2.6
1.1	— 5.6	— 6.2	— 3.2	1.6	— 4.1	**1957**	— 14.3
4.3	1.2	4.8	2.5	2.2	5.2	**1958**	38.1
3.5	— 1.5	— 4.6	1.1	1.3	2.8	**1959**	8.5
— 2.5	2.6	— 6.0	— 0.2	4.0	4.6	**1960**	— 3.0
3.3	2.0	— 2.0	2.8	3.9	0.3	**1961**	23.1
6.4	1.5	— 4.8	0.4	10.2	1.3	**1962**	— 11.8
— 0.3	4.9	— 1.1	3.2	— 1.1	2.4	**1963**	18.9
1.8	— 1.6	2.9	0.8	— 0.5	0.4	**1964**	13.0
1.3	2.3	3.2	2.7	— 0.9	0.9	**1965**	9.1
— 1.3	— 7.8	— 0.7	4.8	0.3	— 0.1	**1966**	— 13.1
4.5	— 1.2	3.3	— 2.9	0.1	2.6	**1967**	20.1
— 1.8	1.1	3.9	0.7	4.8	— 4.2	**1968**	7.7
— 6.0	4.0	— 2.5	4.4	— 3.5	— 1.9	**1969**	— 11.4
7.3	4.4	3.3	— 1.1	4.7	5.7	**1970**	0.1
— 4.1	3.6	— 0.7	— 4.2	— 0.3	8.6	**1971**	10.8
0.2	3.4	— 0.5	0.9	4.6	1.2	**1972**	15.6
3.8	— 3.7	4.0	— 0.1	—11.4	1.7	**1973**	— 17.4
— 7.8	— 9.0	—11.9	16.3	— 5.3	— 2.0	**1974**	— 29.7
— 6.8	— 2.1	— 3.5	6.2	2.5	— 1.2	**1975**	31.5
— 0.8	— 0.5	2.3	— 2.2	— 0.8	5.2	**1976**	19.1
— 1.6	— 2.1	— 0.2	— 4.3	2.7	0.3	**1977**	— 11.5
5.4	2.6	— 0.7	— 9.2	1.7	1.5	**1978**	1.1
0.9	5.3	NC	— 6.9	4.3	1.7	**1979**	12.3
6.5	0.6	2.5	1.6	10.2	— 3.4	**1980**	25.8
— 0.2	— 6.2	— 5.4	4.9	3.7	— 3.0	**1981**	— 9.7
— 2.3	11.6	0.8	11.0	3.6	1.5	**1982**	14.8
— 3.3	1.1	1.0	— 1.5	1.7	— 0.9	**1983**	17.3
— 1.6	10.6	— 0.3	— 0.01	— 1.5	2.2	**1984**	1.4
— 0.5	— 1.2	— 3.5	4.3	6.5	4.5	**1985**	26.3
— 5.9	7.1	— 8.5	5.5	2.1	— 2.8	**1986**	14.6
4.8	3.5	— 2.4	—21.8	— 8.5	7.3	**1987**	2.0
— 0.5	— 3.9	4.0	2.6	— 1.9	1.5	**1988**	12.4
8.8	1.6	— 0.7	— 2.5	1.7	2.1	**1989**	27.3
— 0.5	— 9.4	— 5.1	— 0.7	6.0	2.5	**1990**	— 6.6
4.5	2.0	— 1.9	1.2	— 4.4	11.2	**1991**	26.3
3.9	— 2.4	0.9	0.2	3.0	1.0	**1992**	4.5
— 0.5	3.4	— 1.0	1.9	— 1.3	1.0	**1993**	7.1
3.1	3.8	— 2.7	2.1	— 4.0	1.2	**1994**	— 1.5
3.2	— 0.03	4.0	— 0.5	4.1	1.7	**1995**	34.1
— 4.6	1.9	5.4	2.6	7.3	— 2.2	**1996**	20.3
7.8	— 5.7	5.3	— 3.4	4.5	1.6	**1997**	31.0
— 1.2	—14.6	6.2	8.0	5.9	5.6	**1998**	26.7
— 3.2	— 0.6	— 2.9	6.3	1.9	5.8	**1999**	19.5
— 1.6	6.1	— 5.3	— 0.5	— 8.0	0.4	**2000**	— 10.1
— 1.1	— 6.4	— 8.2	1.8	7.5	0.8	**2001**	— 13.0
— 7.9						**2002**	

141

STANDARD & POOR'S 500
MONTHLY CLOSING PRICES

	JAN	FEB	MAR	APR	MAY	JUN
1950	17.05	17.22	17.29	18.07	18.78	17.69
1951	21.66	21.80	21.40	22.43	21.52	20.96
1952	24.14	23.26	24.37	23.32	23.86	24.96
1953	26.38	25.90	25.29	24.62	24.54	24.14
1954	26.08	26.15	26.94	28.26	29.19	29.21
1955	36.63	36.76	36.58	37.96	37.91	41.03
1956	43.82	45.34	48.48	48.38	45.20	46.97
1957	44.72	43.26	44.11	45.74	47.43	47.37
1958	41.70	40.84	42.10	43.44	44.09	45.24
1959	55.42	55.41	55.44	57.59	58.68	58.47
1960	55.61	56.12	55.34	54.37	55.83	56.92
1961	61.78	63.44	65.06	65.31	66.56	64.64
1962	68.84	69.96	69.55	65.24	59.63	54.75
1963	66.20	64.29	66.57	69.80	70.80	69.37
1964	77.04	77.80	78.98	79.46	80.37	81.69
1965	87.56	87.43	86.16	89.11	88.42	84.12
1966	92.88	91.22	89.23	91.06	86.13	84.74
1967	86.61	86.78	90.20	94.01	89.08	90.64
1968	92.24	89.36	90.20	97.59	98.68	99.58
1969	103.01	98.13	101.51	103.69	103.46	97.71
1970	85.02	89.50	89.63	81.52	76.55	72.72
1971	95.88	96.75	100.31	103.95	99.63	99.70
1972	103.94	106.57	107.20	107.67	109.53	107.14
1973	116.03	111.68	111.52	106.97	104.95	104.26
1974	96.57	96.22	93.98	90.31	87.28	86.00
1975	76.98	81.59	83.36	87.30	91.15	95.19
1976	100.86	99.71	102.77	101.64	100.18	104.28
1977	102.03	99.82	98.42	98.44	96.12	100.48
1978	89.25	87.04	89.21	96.83	97.24	95.53
1979	99.93	96.28	101.59	101.76	99.08	102.91
1980	114.16	113.66	102.09	106.29	111.24	114.24
1981	129.55	131.27	136.00	132.81	132.59	131.21
1982	120.40	113.11	111.96	116.44	111.88	109.61
1983	145.30	148.06	152.96	164.42	162.39	168.11
1984	163.41	157.06	159.18	160.05	150.55	153.18
1985	179.63	181.18	180.66	179.83	189.55	191.85
1986	211.78	226.92	238.90	235.52	247.35	250.84
1987	274.08	284.20	291.70	288.36	290.10	304.00
1988	257.07	267.82	258.89	261.33	262.16	273.50
1989	297.47	288.86	294.87	309.64	320.52	317.98
1990	329.08	331.89	339.94	330.80	361.23	358.02
1991	343.93	367.07	375.22	375.35	389.83	371.16
1992	408.79	412.70	403.69	414.95	415.35	408.14
1993	438.78	443.38	451.67	440.19	450.19	450.53
1994	481.61	467.14	445.77	450.91	456.50	444.27
1995	470.42	487.39	500.71	514.71	533.40	544.75
1996	636.02	640.43	645.50	654.17	669.12	670.63
1997	786.16	790.82	757.12	801.34	848.28	885.14
1998	980.28	1049.34	1101.75	1111.75	1090.82	1133.84
1999	1279.64	1238.33	1286.37	1335.18	1301.84	1372.71
2000	1394.46	1366.42	1498.58	1452.43	1420.60	1454.60
2001	1366.01	1239.94	1160.33	1249.46	1255.82	1224.42
2002	1130.20	1106.73	1147.39	1076.92	1067.14	989.82

STANDARD & POOR'S 500 MONTHLY CLOSING PRICES

JUL	AUG	SEP	OCT	NOV	DEC	
17.84	18.42	19.45	19.53	19.51	20.41	**1950**
22.40	23.28	23.26	22.94	22.88	23.77	**1951**
25.40	25.03	24.54	24.52	25.66	26.57	**1952**
24.75	23.32	23.35	24.54	24.76	24.81	**1953**
30.88	29.83	32.31	31.68	34.24	35.98	**1954**
43.52	43.18	43.67	42.34	45.51	45.48	**1955**
49.39	47.51	45.35	45.58	45.08	46.67	**1956**
47.91	45.22	42.42	41.06	41.72	39.99	**1957**
47.19	47.75	50.06	51.33	52.48	55.21	**1958**
60.51	59.60	56.88	57.52	58.28	59.89	**1959**
55.51	56.96	53.52	53.39	55.54	58.11	**1960**
66.76	68.07	66.73	68.62	71.32	71.55	**1961**
58.23	59.12	56.27	56.52	62.26	63.10	**1962**
69.13	72.50	71.70	74.01	73.23	75.02	**1963**
83.18	81.83	84.18	84.86	84.42	84.75	**1964**
85.25	87.17	89.96	92.42	91.61	92.43	**1965**
83.60	77.10	76.56	80.20	80.45	80.33	**1966**
94.75	93.64	96.71	93.90	94.00	96.47	**1967**
97.74	98.86	102.67	103.41	108.37	103.86	**1968**
91.83	95.51	93.12	97.24	93.81	92.06	**1969**
78.05	81.52	84.21	83.25	87.20	92.15	**1970**
95.58	99.03	98.34	94.23	93.99	102.09	**1971**
107.39	111.09	110.55	111.58	116.67	118.05	**1972**
108.22	104.25	108.43	108.29	95.96	97.55	**1973**
79.31	72.15	63.54	73.90	69.97	68.56	**1974**
88.75	86.88	83.87	89.04	91.24	90.19	**1975**
103.44	102.91	105.24	102.90	102.10	107.46	**1976**
98.85	96.77	96.53	92.34	94.83	95.10	**1977**
100.68	103.29	102.54	93.15	94.70	96.11	**1978**
103.81	109.32	109.32	101.82	106.16	107.94	**1979**
121.67	122.38	125.46	127.47	140.52	135.76	**1980**
130.92	122.79	116.18	121.89	126.35	122.55	**1981**
107.09	119.51	120.42	133.71	138.54	140.64	**1982**
162.56	164.40	166.07	163.55	166.40	164.93	**1983**
150.66	166.68	166.10	166.09	163.58	167.24	**1984**
190.92	188.63	182.08	189.82	202.17	211.28	**1985**
236.12	252.93	231.32	243.98	249.22	242.17	**1986**
318.66	329.80	321.83	251.79	230.30	247.08	**1987**
272.02	261.52	271.91	278.97	273.70	277.72	**1988**
346.08	351.45	349.15	340.36	345.99	353.40	**1989**
356.15	322.56	306.05	304.00	322.22	330.22	**1990**
387.81	395.43	387.86	392.46	375.22	417.09	**1991**
424.21	414.03	417.80	418.68	431.35	435.71	**1992**
448.13	463.56	458.93	467.83	461.79	466.45	**1993**
458.26	475.49	462.69	472.35	453.69	459.27	**1994**
562.06	561.88	584.41	581.50	605.37	615.93	**1995**
639.95	651.99	687.31	705.27	757.02	740.74	**1996**
954.29	899.47	947.28	914.62	955.40	970.43	**1997**
1120.67	957.28	1017.01	1098.67	1163.63	1229.23	**1998**
1328.72	1320.41	1282.71	1362.93	1388.91	1469.25	**1999**
1430.83	1517.68	1436.51	1429.40	1314.95	1320.28	**2000**
1211.23	1133.58	1040.94	1059.78	1139.45	1148.08	**2001**
911.62						**2002**

DOW JONES INDUSTRIALS
MONTHLY PERCENT CHANGES

	JAN	FEB	MAR	APR	MAY	JUN
1950	0.8%	0.8%	1.3%	4.0%	4.2%	— 6.4%
1951	5.7	1.3	— 1.6	4.5	— 3.7	— 2.8
1952	0.5	— 3.9	3.6	— 4.4	2.1	4.3
1953	— 0.7	— 1.9	— 1.5	— 1.8	— 0.9	— 1.5
1954	4.1	0.7	3.0	5.2	2.6	1.8
1955	1.1	0.7	— 0.5	3.9	— 0.2	6.2
1956	— 3.6	2.7	5.8	0.8	— 7.4	3.1
1957	— 4.1	— 3.0	2.2	4.1	2.1	— 0.3
1958	3.3	— 2.2	1.6	2.0	1.5	3.3
1959	1.8	1.6	— 0.3	3.7	3.2	0.03
1960	— 8.4	1.2	— 2.1	— 2.4	4.0	2.4
1961	5.2	2.1	2.2	0.3	2.7	— 1.8
1962	— 4.3	1.1	— 0.2	— 5.9	— 7.8	— 8.5
1963	4.7	— 2.9	3.0	5.2	1.3	— 2.8
1964	2.9	1.9	1.6	— 0.3	1.2	1.3
1965	3.3	0.1	— 1.6	3.7	— 0.5	— 5.4
1966	1.5	— 3.2	— 2.8	1.0	— 5.3	— 1.6
1967	8.2	— 1.2	3.2	3.6	— 5.0	0.9
1968	— 5.5	— 1.7	0.02	8.5	— 1.4	— 0.1
1969	0.2	— 4.3	3.3	1.6	— 1.3	— 6.9
1970	— 7.0	4.5	1.0	— 6.3	— 4.8	— 2.4
1971	3.5	1.2	2.9	4.1	— 3.6	— 1.8
1972	1.3	2.9	1.4	1.4	0.7	— 3.3
1973	— 2.1	— 4.4	— 0.4	— 3.1	— 2.2	— 1.1
1974	0.6	0.6	— 1.6	— 1.2	— 4.1	0.03
1975	14.2	5.0	3.9	6.9	1.3	5.6
1976	14.4	— 0.3	2.8	— 0.3	— 2.2	2.8
1977	— 5.0	— 1.9	— 1.8	0.8	— 3.0	2.0
1978	— 7.4	— 3.6	2.1	10.6	0.4	— 2.6
1979	4.2	— 3.6	6.6	— 0.8	— 3.8	2.4
1980	4.4	— 1.5	— 9.0	4.0	4.1	2.0
1981	— 1.7	2.9	3.0	— 0.6	— 0.6	— 1.5
1982	— 0.4	— 5.4	— 0.2	3.1	— 3.4	— 0.9
1983	2.8	3.4	1.6	8.5	— 2.1	1.8
1984	— 3.0	— 5.4	0.9	0.5	— 5.6	2.5
1985	6.2	— 0.2	— 1.3	— 0.7	4.6	1.5
1986	1.6	8.8	6.4	— 1.9	5.2	0.9
1987	13.8	3.1	3.6	— 0.8	0.2	5.5
1988	1.0	5.8	— 4.0	2.2	— 0.1	5.4
1989	8.0	— 3.6	1.6	5.5	2.5	— 1.6
1990	— 5.9	1.4	3.0	— 1.9	8.3	0.1
1991	3.9	5.3	1.1	— 0.9	4.8	— 4.0
1992	1.7	1.4	— 1.0	3.8	1.1	— 2.3
1993	0.3	1.8	1.9	— 0.2	2.9	— 0.3
1994	6.0	— 3.7	— 5.1	1.3	2.1	— 3.5
1995	0.2	4.3	3.7	3.9	3.3	2.0
1996	5.4	1.7	1.9	— 0.3	1.3	0.2
1997	5.7	0.9	— 4.3	6.5	4.6	4.7
1998	— 0.02	8.1	3.0	3.0	— 1.8	0.6
1999	1.9	— 0.6	5.2	10.2	— 2.1	3.9
2000	— 4.8	— 7.4	7.8	— 1.7	— 2.0	— 0.7
2001	0.9	— 3.6	— 5.9	8.7	1.6	— 3.8
2002	— 1.0	1.9	2.9	— 4.4	— 0.2	— 6.9

DOW JONES INDUSTRIALS
MONTHLY PERCENT CHANGES

JUL	AUG	SEP	OCT	NOV	DEC		Year's Change
0.1%	3.6%	4.4%	— 0.6%	1.2%	3.4%	1950	17.6%
6.3	4.8	0.3	— 3.2	— 0.4	3.0	1951	14.4
1.9	— 1.6	— 1.6	— 0.5	5.4	2.9	1952	8.4
2.7	— 5.1	1.1	4.5	2.0	— 0.2	1953	— 3.8
4.3	— 3.5	7.3	— 2.3	9.8	4.6	1954	44.0
3.2	0.5	— 0.3	— 2.5	6.2	1.1	1955	20.8
5.1	— 3.0	— 5.3	1.0	— 1.5	5.6	1956	2.3
1.0	— 4.8	— 5.8	— 3.3	2.0	— 3.2	1957	—12.8
5.2	1.1	4.6	2.1	2.6	4.7	1958	34.0
4.9	— 1.6	— 4.9	2.4	1.9	3.1	1959	16.4
— 3.7	1.5	— 7.3	0.04	2.9	3.1	1960	— 9.3
3.1	2.1	— 2.6	0.4	2.5	1.3	1961	18.7
6.5	1.9	— 5.0	1.9	10.1	0.4	1962	—10.8
— 1.6	4.9	0.5	3.1	— 0.6	1.7	1963	17.0
1.2	— 0.3	4.4	— 0.3	0.3	— 0.1	1964	14.6
1.6	1.3	4.2	3.2	— 1.5	2.4	1965	10.9
— 2.6	— 7.0	— 1.8	4.2	— 1.9	— 0.7	1966	—18.9
5.1	— 0.3	2.8	— 5.1	— 0.4	3.3	1967	15.2
— 1.6	1.5	4.4	1.8	3.4	— 4.2	1968	4.3
— 6.6	2.6	— 2.8	5.3	— 5.1	— 1.5	1969	—15.2
7.4	4.1	— 0.5	— 0.7	5.1	5.6	1970	4.8
— 3.7	4.6	— 1.2	— 5.4	— 0.9	7.1	1971	6.1
— 0.5	4.2	— 1.1	0.2	6.6	0.2	1972	14.6
3.9	— 4.2	6.7	1.0	—14.0	3.5	1973	—16.6
— 5.6	—10.4	—10.4	9.5	— 7.0	— 0.4	1974	—27.6
— 5.4	0.5	— 5.0	5.3	2.9	— 1.0	1975	38.3
— 1.8	— 1.1	1.7	— 2.6	— 1.8	6.1	1976	17.9
— 2.9	— 3.2	— 1.7	— 3.4	1.4	0.2	1977	—17.3
5.3	1.7	— 1.3	— 8.5	0.8	0.7	1978	— 3.1
0.5	4.9	— 1.0	— 7.2	0.8	2.0	1979	4.2
7.8	— 0.3	0.02	— 0.9	7.4	— 3.0	1980	14.9
— 2.5	— 7.4	— 3.6	0.3	4.3	— 1.6	1981	— 9.2
— 0.4	11.5	— 0.6	10.7	4.8	0.7	1982	19.6
— 1.9	1.4	1.4	— 0.6	4.1	— 1.4	1983	20.3
— 1.5	9.8	— 1.4	0.1	— 1.5	1.9	1984	— 3.7
0.9	— 1.0	— 0.4	3.4	7.1	5.1	1985	27.7
— 6.2	6.9	— 6.9	6.2	1.9	— 1.0	1986	22.6
6.3	3.5	— 2.5	—23.2	— 8.0	5.7	1987	2.3
— 0.6	— 4.6	4.0	1.7	— 1.6	2.6	1988	11.8
9.0	2.9	— 1.6	— 1.8	2.3	1.7	1989	27.0
0.9	—10.0	— 6.2	— 0.4	4.8	2.9	1990	— 4.3
4.1	0.6	— 0.9	1.7	— 5.7	9.5	1991	20.3
2.3	— 4.0	0.4	— 1.4	2.4	— 0.1	1992	4.2
0.7	3.2	— 2.6	3.5	0.1	1.9	1993	13.7
3.8	4.0	— 1.8	1.7	— 4.3	2.5	1994	2.1
3.3	— 2.1	3.9	— 0.7	6.7	0.8	1995	33.5
— 2.2	1.6	4.7	2.5	8.2	— 1.1	1996	26.0
7.2	— 7.3	4.2	— 6.3	5.1	1.1	1997	22.6
— 0.8	—15.1	4.0	9.6	6.1	0.7	1998	16.1
— 2.9	1.6	— 4.5	3.8	1.4	5.7	1999	25.2
0.7	6.6	— 5.0	3.0	— 5.1	3.6	2000	— 6.2
0.2	— 5.4	—11.1	2.6	8.6	1.7	2001	— 7.1
— 5.5						2002	

145

DOW JONES INDUSTRIALS MONTHLY POINT CHANGES

	JAN	FEB	MAR	APR	MAY	JUN
1950	1.66	1.65	2.61	8.28	9.09	— 14.31
1951	13.42	3.22	— 4.11	11.19	— 9.48	— 7.01
1952	1.46	— 10.61	9.38	— 11.83	5.31	11.32
1953	— 2.13	— 5.50	— 4.40	— 5.12	— 2.47	— 4.02
1954	11.49	2.15	8.97	15.82	8.16	6.04
1955	4.44	3.04	— 2.17	15.95	— 0.79	26.52
1956	— 17.66	12.91	28.14	4.33	— 38.07	14.73
1957	— 20.31	— 14.54	10.19	19.55	10.57	— 1.64
1958	14.33	— 10.10	6.84	9.10	6.84	15.48
1959	10.31	9.54	— 1.79	22.04	20.04	— 0.19
1960	— 56.74	7.50	— 13.53	— 14.89	23.80	15.12
1961	32.31	13.88	14.55	2.08	18.01	— 12.76
1962	— 31.14	8.05	— 1.10	— 41.62	— 51.97	— 52.08
1963	30.75	— 19.91	19.58	35.18	9.26	— 20.08
1964	22.39	14.80	13.15	— 2.52	9.79	10.94
1965	28.73	0.62	— 14.43	33.26	— 4.27	— 50.01
1966	14.25	— 31.62	— 27.12	8.91	— 49.61	— 13.97
1967	64.20	— 10.52	26.61	31.07	— 44.49	7.70
1968	— 49.64	— 14.97	0.17	71.55	— 13.22	— 1.20
1969	2.30	— 40.84	30.27	14.70	— 12.62	— 64.37
1970	— 56.30	33.53	7.98	— 49.50	— 35.63	— 16.91
1971	29.58	10.33	25.54	37.38	— 33.94	— 16.67
1972	11.97	25.96	12.57	13.47	6.55	— 31.69
1973	— 21.00	— 43.95	— 4.06	— 29.58	— 20.02	9.70
1974	4.69	4.98	— 13.85	— 9.93	— 34.58	0.24
1975	87.45	35.36	29.10	53.19	10.95	46.70
1976	122.87	— 2.67	26.84	— 2.60	— 21.62	27.55
1977	— 50.28	— 17.95	— 17.29	7.77	— 28.24	17.64
1978	— 61.25	— 27.80	15.24	79.96	3.29	— 21.66
1979	34.21	— 30.40	53.36	— 7.28	— 32.57	19.65
1980	37.11	— 12.71	— 77.39	31.31	33.79	17.07
1981	— 16.72	27.31	29.29	— 6.12	— 6.00	— 14.87
1982	— 3.90	— 46.71	— 1.62	25.59	— 28.82	— 7.61
1983	29.16	36.92	17.41	96.17	— 26.22	21.98
1984	— 38.06	— 65.95	10.26	5.86	— 65.90	27.55
1985	75.20	— 2.76	— 17.23	— 8.72	57.35	20.05
1986	24.32	138.07	109.55	— 34.63	92.73	16.01
1987	262.09	65.95	80.70	— 18.33	5.21	126.96
1988	19.39	113.40	— 83.56	44.27	— 1.21	110.59
1989	173.75	— 83.93	35.23	125.18	61.35	— 40.09
1990	—162.66	36.71	79.96	— 50.45	219.90	4.03
1991	102.73	145.79	31.68	— 25.99	139.63	—120.75
1992	54.56	44.28	— 32.20	123.65	37.76	— 78.36
1993	8.92	60.78	64.30	— 7.56	99.88	— 11.35
1994	224.27	—146.34	—196.06	45.73	76.68	—133.41
1995	9.42	167.19	146.64	163.58	143.87	90.96
1996	278.18	90.32	101.52	— 18.06	74.10	11.45
1997	364.82	64.65	—294.26	425.51	322.05	341.75
1998	— 1.75	639.22	254.09	263.56	—163.42	52.07
1999	177.40	— 52.25	479.58	1002.88	—229.30	411.06
2000	—556.59	—812.22	793.61	—188.01	—211.58	— 74.44
2001	100.51	—392.08	—616.50	856.19	176.97	—409.54
2002	—101.50	186.13	297.81	—457.72	— 20.97	—681.99
TOTALS	1237.01	107.91	1450.05	2713.80	495.92	–439.52
# Up	36	30	34	33	27	26
# Down	17	23	19	20	26	27

DOW JONES INDUSTRIALS MONTHLY POINT CHANGES

JUL	AUG	SEP	OCT	NOV	DEC	Year's Close	
0.29	7.47	9.49	— 1.35	2.59	7.81	235.41	1950
15.22	12.39	0.91	— 8.81	— 1.08	7.96	269.23	1951
5.30	— 4.52	— 4.43	— 1.38	14.43	8.24	291.90	1952
7.12	— 14.16	2.82	11.77	5.56	— 0.47	280.90	1953
14.39	— 12.12	24.66	— 8.32	34.63	17.62	404.39	1954
14.47	2.33	— 1.56	— 11.75	28.39	5.14	488.40	1955
25.03	— 15.77	— 26.79	4.60	— 7.07	26.69	499.47	1956
5.23	— 24.17	— 28.05	— 15.26	8.83	— 14.18	435.69	1957
24.81	5.64	23.46	11.13	14.24	26.19	583.65	1958
31.28	— 10.47	— 32.73	14.92	12.58	20.18	679.36	1959
— 23.89	9.26	— 45.85	0.22	16.86	18.67	615.89	1960
21.41	14.57	— 18.73	2.71	17.68	9.54	731.14	1961
36.65	11.25	— 30.20	10.79	59.53	2.80	652.10	1962
— 11.45	33.89	3.47	22.44	— 4.71	12.43	762.95	1963
9.60	— 2.62	36.89	— 2.29	2.35	— 1.30	874.13	1964
13.71	11.36	37.48	30.24	— 14.11	22.55	969.26	1965
— 22.72	— 58.97	— 14.19	32.85	— 15.48	— 5.90	785.69	1966
43.98	— 2.95	25.37	— 46.92	— 3.93	29.30	905.11	1967
— 14.80	13.01	39.78	16.60	32.69	— 41.33	943.75	1968
— 57.72	21.25	— 23.63	42.90	— 43.69	— 11.94	800.36	1969
50.59	30.46	— 3.90	— 5.07	38.48	44.83	838.92	1970
— 32.71	39.64	— 10.88	— 48.19	— 7.66	58.86	890.20	1971
— 4.29	38.99	— 10.46	2.25	62.69	1.81	1020.02	1972
34.69	— 38.83	59.53	9.48	—134.33	28.61	850.86	1973
— 44.98	— 78.85	— 70.71	57.65	— 46.86	— 2.42	616.24	1974
— 47.48	3.83	— 41.46	42.16	24.63	— 8.26	852.41	1975
— 18.14	— 10.90	16.45	— 25.26	— 17.71	57.43	1004.65	1976
— 26.23	— 28.58	— 14.38	— 28.76	11.35	1.47	831.17	1977
43.32	14.55	— 11.00	— 73.37	6.58	5.98	805.01	1978
4.44	41.21	— 9.05	— 62.88	6.65	16.39	838.74	1979
67.40	— 2.73	— 0.17	— 7.93	68.85	— 29.35	963.99	1980
— 24.54	— 70.87	— 31.49	2.57	36.43	— 13.98	875.00	1981
— 3.33	92.71	— 5.06	95.47	47.56	7.26	1046.54	1982
— 22.74	16.94	16.97	— 7.93	50.82	— 17.38	1258.64	1983
— 17.12	109.10	— 17.67	0.67	— 18.44	22.63	1211.57	1984
11.99	— 13.44	— 5.38	45.68	97.82	74.54	1546.67	1985
—117.41	123.03	—130.76	110.23	36.42	— 18.28	1895.95	1986
153.54	90.88	— 66.67	—602.75	—159.98	105.28	1938.83	1987
— 12.98	— 97.08	81.26	35.74	— 34.14	54.06	2168.57	1988
220.60	76.61	— 44.45	— 47.74	61.19	46.93	2753.20	1989
24.51	— 290.84	—161.88	— 10.15	117.32	74.01	2633.66	1990
118.07	18.78	— 26.83	52.33	—174.42	274.15	3168.83	1991
75.26	— 136.43	14.31	— 45.38	78.88	— 4.05	3301.11	1992
23.39	111.78	— 96.13	125.47	3.36	70.14	3754.09	1993
139.54	148.92	— 70.23	64.93	—168.89	95.21	3834.44	1994
152.37	— 97.91	178.52	— 33.60	319.01	42.63	5117.12	1995
—125.72	87.30	265.96	147.21	492.32	— 73.43	6448.27	1996
549.82	— 600.19	322.84	—503.18	381.05	85.12	7908.25	1997
— 68.73	—1344.22	303.55	749.48	524.45	64.88	9181.43	1998
—315.65	174.13	—492.33	392.91	147.95	619.31	11497.12	1999
74.09	693.12	—564.18	320.22	—556.65	372.36	10786.85	2000
20.41	— 573.06	—1102.19	227.58	776.42	169.94	10021.50	2001
—506.67							2002
513.22	—1475.28	—1749.70	1084.93	2231.44	2366.68		
32	29	19	30	35	38		
21	23	33	22	17	14		

DOW JONES INDUSTRIALS MONTHLY CLOSING PRICES

	JAN	FEB	MAR	APR	MAY	JUN
1950	201.79	203.44	206.05	214.33	223.42	209.11
1951	248.83	252.05	247.94	259.13	249.65	242.64
1952	270.69	260.08	269.46	257.63	262.94	274.26
1953	289.77	284.27	279.87	274.75	272.28	268.26
1954	292.39	294.54	303.51	319.33	327.49	333.53
1955	408.83	411.87	409.70	425.65	424.86	451.38
1956	470.74	483.65	511.79	516.12	478.05	492.78
1957	479.16	464.62	474.81	494.36	504.93	503.29
1958	450.02	439.92	446.76	455.86	462.70	478.18
1959	593.96	603.50	601.71	623.75	643.79	643.60
1960	622.62	630.12	616.59	601.70	625.50	640.62
1961	648.20	662.08	676.63	678.71	696.72	683.96
1962	700.00	708.05	706.95	665.33	613.36	561.28
1963	682.85	662.94	682.52	717.70	726.96	706.88
1964	785.34	800.14	813.29	810.77	820.56	831.50
1965	902.86	903.48	889.05	922.31	918.04	868.03
1966	983.51	951.89	924.77	933.68	884.07	870.10
1967	849.89	839.37	865.98	897.05	852.56	860.26
1968	855.47	840.50	840.67	912.22	899.00	897.80
1969	946.05	905.21	935.48	950.18	937.56	873.19
1970	744.06	777.59	785.57	736.07	700.44	683.53
1971	868.50	878.83	904.37	941.75	907.81	891.14
1972	902.17	928.13	940.70	954.17	960.72	929.03
1973	999.02	955.07	951.01	921.43	901.41	891.71
1974	855.55	860.53	846.68	836.75	802.17	802.41
1975	703.69	739.05	768.15	821.34	832.29	878.99
1976	975.28	972.61	999.45	996.85	975.23	1002.78
1977	954.37	936.42	919.13	926.90	898.66	916.30
1978	769.92	742.12	757.36	837.32	840.61	818.95
1979	839.22	808.82	862.18	854.90	822.33	841.98
1980	875.85	863.14	785.75	817.06	850.85	867.92
1981	947.27	974.58	1003.87	997.75	991.75	976.88
1982	871.10	824.39	822.77	848.36	819.54	811.93
1983	1075.70	1112.62	1130.03	1226.20	1199.98	1221.96
1984	1220.58	1154.63	1164.89	1170.75	1104.85	1132.40
1985	1286.77	1284.01	1266.78	1258.06	1315.41	1335.46
1986	1570.99	1709.06	1818.61	1783.98	1876.71	1892.72
1987	2158.04	2223.99	2304.69	2286.36	2291.57	2418.53
1988	1958.22	2071.62	1988.06	2032.33	2031.12	2141.71
1989	2342.32	2258.39	2293.62	2418.80	2480.15	2440.06
1990	2590.54	2627.25	2707.21	2656.76	2876.66	2880.69
1991	2736.39	2882.18	2913.86	2887.87	3027.50	2906.75
1992	3223.39	3267.67	3235.47	3359.12	3396.88	3318.52
1993	3310.03	3370.81	3435.11	3427.55	3527.43	3516.08
1994	3978.36	3832.02	3635.96	3681.69	3758.37	3624.96
1995	3843.86	4011.05	4157.69	4321.27	4465.14	4556.10
1996	5395.30	5485.62	5587.14	5569.08	5643.18	5654.63
1997	6813.09	6877.74	6583.48	7008.99	7331.04	7672.79
1998	7906.50	8545.72	8799.81	9063.37	8899.95	8952.02
1999	9358.83	9306.58	9786.16	10789.04	10559.74	10970.80
2000	10940.53	10128.31	10921.92	10733.91	10522.33	10447.89
2001	10887.36	10495.28	9878.78	10734.97	10911.94	10502.40
2002	9920.00	10106.13	10403.94	9946.22	9925.25	9243.26

DOW JONES INDUSTRIALS MONTHLY CLOSING PRICES

JUL	AUG	SEP	OCT	NOV	DEC	
209.40	216.87	226.36	225.01	227.60	235.41	**1950**
257.86	270.25	271.16	262.35	261.27	269.23	**1951**
279.56	275.04	270.61	269.23	283.66	291.90	**1952**
275.38	261.22	264.04	275.81	281.37	280.90	**1953**
347.92	335.80	360.46	352.14	386.77	404.39	**1954**
465.85	468.18	466.62	454.87	483.26	488.40	**1955**
517.81	502.04	475.25	479.85	472.78	499.47	**1956**
508.52	484.35	456.30	441.04	449.87	435.69	**1957**
502.99	508.63	532.09	543.22	557.46	583.65	**1958**
674.88	664.41	631.68	646.60	659.18	679.36	**1959**
616.73	625.99	580.14	580.36	597.22	615.89	**1960**
705.37	719.94	701.21	703.92	721.60	731.14	**1961**
597.93	609.18	578.98	589.77	649.30	652.10	**1962**
695.43	729.32	732.79	755.23	750.52	762.95	**1963**
841.10	838.48	875.37	873.08	875.43	874.13	**1964**
881.74	893.10	930.58	960.82	946.71	969.26	**1965**
847.38	788.41	774.22	807.07	791.59	785.69	**1966**
904.24	901.29	926.66	879.74	875.81	905.11	**1967**
883.00	896.01	935.79	952.39	985.08	943.75	**1968**
815.47	836.72	813.09	855.99	812.30	800.36	**1969**
734.12	764.58	760.68	755.61	794.09	838.92	**1970**
858.43	898.07	887.19	839.00	831.34	890.20	**1971**
924.74	963.73	953.27	955.52	1018.21	1020.02	**1972**
926.40	887.57	947.10	956.58	822.25	850.86	**1973**
757.43	678.58	607.87	665.52	618.66	616.24	**1974**
831.51	835.34	793.88	836.04	860.67	852.41	**1975**
984.64	973.74	990.19	964.93	947.22	1004.65	**1976**
890.07	861.49	847.11	818.35	829.70	831.17	**1977**
862.27	876.82	865.82	792.45	799.03	805.01	**1978**
846.42	887.63	878.58	815.70	822.35	838.74	**1979**
935.32	932.59	932.42	924.49	993.34	963.99	**1980**
952.34	881.47	849.98	852.55	888.98	875.00	**1981**
808.60	901.31	896.25	991.72	1039.28	1046.54	**1982**
1199.22	1216.16	1233.13	1225.20	1276.02	1258.64	**1983**
1115.28	1224.38	1206.71	1207.38	1188.94	1211.57	**1984**
1347.45	1334.01	1328.63	1374.31	1472.13	1546.67	**1985**
1775.31	1898.34	1767.58	1877.81	1914.23	1895.95	**1986**
2572.07	2662.95	2596.28	1993.53	1833.55	1938.83	**1987**
2128.73	2031.65	2112.91	2148.65	2114.51	2168.57	**1988**
2660.66	2737.27	2692.82	2645.08	2706.27	2753.20	**1989**
2905.20	2614.36	2452.48	2442.33	2559.65	2633.66	**1990**
3024.82	3043.60	3016.77	3069.10	2894.68	3168.83	**1991**
3393.78	3257.35	3271.66	3226.28	3305.16	3301.11	**1992**
3539.47	3651.25	3555.12	3680.59	3683.95	3754.09	**1993**
3764.50	3913.42	3843.19	3908.12	3739.23	3834.44	**1994**
4708.47	4610.56	4789.08	4755.48	5074.49	5117.12	**1995**
5528.91	5616.21	5882.17	6029.38	6521.70	6448.27	**1996**
8222.61	7622.42	7945.26	7442.08	7823.13	7908.25	**1997**
8883.29	7539.07	7842.62	8592.62	9116.55	9181.43	**1998**
10655.15	10829.28	10336.95	10729.86	10877.81	11497.12	**1999**
10521.98	11215.10	10650.92	10971.14	10414.49	10786.85	**2000**
10522.81	9949.75	8847.56	9075.14	9851.56	10021.50	**2001**
8736.59						**2002**

149

NASDAQ COMPOSITE
MONTHLY PERCENT CHANGES

	JAN	FEB	MAR	APR	MAY	JUN
1971	10.2%	2.6%	4.6%	6.0%	— 3.6%	— 0.4%
1972	4.2	5.5	2.2	2.5	0.9	— 1.8
1973	— 4.0	— 6.2	— 2.4	— 8.2	— 4.8	— 1.6
1974	3.0	— 0.6	— 2.2	— 5.9	— 7.7	— 5.3
1975	16.6	4.6	3.6	3.8	5.8	4.7
1976	12.1	3.7	0.4	— 0.6	— 2.3	2.6
1977	— 2.4	— 1.0	— 0.5	1.4	0.1	4.3
1978	— 4.0	0.6	4.7	8.5	4.4	0.05
1979	6.6	— 2.6	7.5	1.6	— 1.8	5.1
1980	7.0	— 2.3	— 17.1	6.9	7.5	4.9
1981	— 2.2	0.1	6.1	3.1	3.1	— 3.5
1982	— 3.8	— 4.8	— 2.1	5.2	— 3.3	— 4.1
1983	6.9	5.0	3.9	8.2	5.3	3.2
1984	— 3.7	— 5.9	— 0.7	— 1.3	— 5.9	2.9
1985	12.7	2.0	— 1.7	0.5	3.6	1.9
1986	3.3	7.1	4.2	2.3	4.4	1.3
1987	12.2	8.4	1.2	— 2.8	— 0.3	2.0
1988	4.3	6.5	2.1	1.2	— 2.3	6.6
1989	5.2	— 0.4	1.8	5.1	4.4	— 2.4
1990	— 8.6	2.4	2.3	— 3.6	9.3	0.7
1991	10.8	9.4	6.5	0.5	4.4	— 6.0
1992	5.8	2.1	— 4.7	— 4.2	1.1	— 3.7
1993	2.9	— 3.7	2.9	— 4.2	5.9	0.5
1994	3.0	— 1.0	— 6.2	— 1.3	0.2	— 4.0
1995	0.4	5.1	3.0	3.3	2.4	8.0
1996	0.7	3.8	0.1	8.1	4.4	— 4.7
1997	6.9	— 5.1	— 6.7	3.2	11.1	3.0
1998	3.1	9.3	3.7	1.8	— 4.8	6.5
1999	14.3	— 8.7	7.6	3.3	— 2.8	8.7
2000	— 3.2	19.2	— 2.6	— 15.6	— 11.9	16.6
2001	12.2	—22.4	— 14.5	15.0	— 0.3	2.4
2002	— 0.8	—10.5	6.6	— 8.5	— 4.3	— 9.4

Based on NASDAQ composite, prior to Feb. 5, 1971 based on National Quotation Bureau indices

NASDAQ COMPOSITE MONTHLY PERCENT CHANGES

JUL	AUG	SEP	OCT	NOV	DEC		Year's Change
— 2.3%	3.0%	0.6%	— 3.6%	— 1.1%	9.8%	**1971**	27.4%
— 1.8	1.7	— 0.3	0.5	2.1	0.6	**1972**	17.2
7.6	— 3.5	6.0	— 0.9	— 15.1	— 1.4	**1973**	— 31.1
— 7.9	— 10.9	— 10.7	17.2	— 3.5	— 5.0	**1974**	— 35.1
— 4.4	— 5.0	— 5.9	3.6	2.4	— 1.5	**1975**	29.8
1.1	— 1.7	1.7	— 1.0	0.9	7.4	**1976**	26.1
0.9	— 0.5	0.7	— 3.3	5.8	1.8	**1977**	7.3
5.0	6.9	— 1.6	— 16.4	3.2	2.9	**1978**	12.3
2.3	6.4	— 0.3	— 9.6	6.4	4.8	**1979**	28.1
8.9	5.7	3.4	2.7	8.0	— 2.8	**1980**	33.9
— 1.9	— 7.5	— 8.0	8.4	3.1	— 2.7	**1981**	— 3.2
— 2.3	6.2	5.6	13.3	9.3	0.04	**1982**	18.7
— 4.6	— 3.8	1.4	— 7.4	4.1	— 2.5	**1983**	19.9
— 4.2	10.9	— 1.8	— 1.2	— 1.8	2.0	**1984**	— 11.2
1.7	— 1.2	— 5.8	4.4	7.3	3.5	**1985**	31.4
— 8.4	3.1	— 8.4	2.9	— 0.3	— 2.8	**1986**	7.5
2.4	4.6	— 2.3	— 27.2	— 5.6	8.3	**1987**	— 5.4
— 1.9	— 2.8	3.0	— 1.4	— 2.9	2.7	**1988**	15.4
4.3	3.4	0.8	— 3.7	0.1	— 0.3	**1989**	19.3
— 5.2	— 13.0	— 9.6	— 4.3	8.9	4.1	**1990**	— 17.8
5.5	4.7	0.2	3.1	— 3.5	11.9	**1991**	56.8
3.1	— 3.0	3.6	3.8	7.9	3.7	**1992**	15.5
0.1	5.4	2.7	2.2	— 3.2	3.0	**1993**	14.7
2.3	6.0	— 0.2	1.7	— 3.5	0.2	**1994**	— 3.2
7.3	1.9	2.3	— 0.7	2.2	— 0.7	**1995**	39.9
— 8.8	5.6	7.5	— 0.4	5.8	— 0.1	**1996**	22.7
10.5	— 0.4	6.2	— 5.5	0.4	— 1.9	**1997**	21.6
— 1.2	— 19.9	13.0	4.6	10.1	12.5	**1998**	39.6
— 1.8	3.8	0.2	8.0	12.5	22.0	**1999**	85.6
— 5.0	11.7	— 12.7	— 8.3	— 22.9	— 4.9	**2000**	— 39.3
— 6.2	— 10.9	— 17.0	12.8	14.2	1.0	**2001**	— 21.1
— 9.2						**2002**	

NASDAQ COMPOSITE
MONTHLY CLOSING PRICES

	JAN	FEB	MAR	APR	MAY	JUN
1971	98.77	101.34	105.97	112.30	108.25	107.80
1972	118.87	125.38	128.14	131.33	132.53	130.08
1973	128.40	120.41	117.46	107.85	102.64	100.98
1974	94.93	94.35	92.27	86.86	80.20	75.96
1975	69.78	73.00	75.66	78.54	83.10	87.02
1976	87.05	90.26	90.62	90.08	88.04	90.32
1977	95.54	94.57	94.13	95.48	95.59	99.73
1978	100.84	101.47	106.20	115.18	120.24	120.30
1979	125.82	122.56	131.76	133.82	131.42	138.13
1980	161.75	158.03	131.00	139.99	150.45	157.78
1981	197.81	198.01	210.18	216.74	223.47	215.75
1982	188.39	179.43	175.65	184.70	178.54	171.30
1983	248.35	260.67	270.80	293.06	308.73	318.70
1984	268.43	252.57	250.78	247.44	232.82	239.65
1985	278.70	284.17	279.20	280.56	290.80	296.20
1986	335.77	359.53	374.72	383.24	400.16	405.51
1987	392.06	424.97	430.05	417.81	416.54	424.67
1988	344.66	366.95	374.64	379.23	370.34	394.66
1989	401.30	399.71	406.73	427.55	446.17	435.29
1990	415.81	425.83	435.54	420.07	458.97	462.29
1991	414.20	453.05	482.30	484.72	506.11	475.92
1992	620.21	633.47	603.77	578.68	585.31	563.60
1993	696.34	670.77	690.13	661.42	700.53	703.95
1994	800.47	792.50	743.46	733.84	735.19	705.96
1995	755.20	793.73	817.21	843.98	864.58	933.45
1996	1059.79	1100.05	1101.40	1190.52	1243.43	1185.02
1997	1379.85	1309.00	1221.70	1260.76	1400.32	1442.07
1998	1619.36	1770.51	1835.68	1868.41	1778.87	1894.74
1999	2505.88	2288.03	2461.40	2542.85	2470.52	2686.12
2000	3940.35	4696.69	4572.83	3860.66	3400.91	3966.11
2001	2772.73	2151.83	1840.26	2116.24	2110.49	2160.54
2002	1934.03	1731.49	1845.35	1688.23	1615.73	1463.21

Based on NASDAQ composite, prior to Feb. 5, 1971 based on National Quotation Bureau indices

NASDAQ COMPOSITE MONTHLY CLOSING PRICES

JUL	AUG	SEP	OCT	NOV	DEC	
105.27	108.42	109.03	105.10	103.97	114.12	**1971**
127.75	129.95	129.61	130.24	132.96	133.73	**1972**
108.64	104.87	111.20	110.17	93.51	92.19	**1973**
69.99	62.37	55.67	65.23	62.95	59.82	**1974**
83.19	79.01	74.33	76.99	78.80	77.62	**1975**
91.29	89.70	91.26	90.35	91.12	97.88	**1976**
100.65	100.10	100.85	97.52	103.15	105.05	**1977**
126.32	135.01	132.89	111.12	114.69	117.98	**1978**
141.33	150.44	149.98	135.53	144.26	151.14	**1979**
171.81	181.52	187.76	192.78	208.15	202.34	**1980**
211.63	195.75	180.03	195.24	201.37	195.84	**1981**
167.35	177.71	187.65	212.63	232.31	232.41	**1982**
303.96	292.42	296.65	274.55	285.67	278.60	**1983**
229.70	254.64	249.94	247.03	242.53	247.35	**1984**
301.29	297.71	280.33	292.54	313.95	324.93	**1985**
371.37	382.86	350.67	360.77	359.57	349.33	**1986**
434.93	454.97	444.29	323.30	305.16	330.47	**1987**
387.33	376.55	387.71	382.46	371.45	381.38	**1988**
453.84	469.33	472.92	455.63	456.09	454.82	**1989**
438.24	381.21	344.51	329.84	359.06	373.84	**1990**
502.04	525.68	526.88	542.98	523.90	586.34	**1991**
580.83	563.12	583.27	605.17	652.73	676.95	**1992**
704.70	742.84	762.78	779.26	754.39	776.80	**1993**
722.16	765.62	764.29	777.49	750.32	751.96	**1994**
1001.21	1020.11	1043.54	1036.06	1059.20	1052.13	**1995**
1080.59	1141.50	1226.92	1221.51	1292.61	1291.03	**1996**
1593.81	1587.32	1685.69	1593.61	1600.55	1570.35	**1997**
1872.39	1499.25	1693.84	1771.39	1949.54	2192.69	**1998**
2638.49	2739.35	2746.16	2966.43	3336.16	4069.31	**1999**
3766.99	4206.35	3672.82	3369.63	2597.93	2470.52	**2000**
2027.13	1805.43	1498.80	1690.20	1930.58	1950.40	**2001**
1328.26						**2002**

LARGEST ONE-DAY DOW GAINS AND LOSSES SINCE OCTOBER 1928 BY POINTS AND PERCENT

TOP TWENTY GAINS SINCE 1928 BY POINTS

Day	DJIA Close	Points Change	% Change
3/16/00	10630.60	499.19	4.9
7/24/02	8191.29	488.95	6.3
4/5/01	9918.05	402.63	4.2
4/18/01	10615.83	399.10	3.9
9/8/98	8020.78	380.53	5.0
9/24/01	8603.86	368.05	4.5
5/16/01	11215.92	342.95	3.2
12/5/00	10898.72	338.62	3.2
10/28/97	7498.32	337.17	4.7
10/15/98	8299.36	330.58	4.1
7/5/02	9379.50	324.53	3.6
3/15/00	10131.41	320.17	3.3
5/8/02	10141.83	305.28	3.1
4/3/00	11221.93	300.01	2.7
1/3/01	10945.75	299.60	2.8
9/1/98	7827.43	288.36	3.8
4/17/00	10582.51	276.74	2.7
1/7/00	11522.56	269.30	2.4
3/5/99	9736.08	268.68	2.8
3/1/02	10368.86	262.73	2.6

TOP TWENTY LOSSES SINCE 1928 BY POINTS

Day	DJIA Close	Points Change	% Change
9/17/01	8920.70	− 684.81	− 7.1
4/14/00	10305.77	− 617.78	− 5.7
10/27/97	7161.15	− 554.26	− 7.2
8/31/98	7539.07	− 512.61	− 6.4
10/19/87	1738.74	− 508.00	− 22.6
3/12/01	10208.25	− 436.37	− 4.1
7/19/02	8019.26	− 390.23	− 4.6
9/20/01	8376.21	− 382.92	− 4.4
10/12/00	10034.58	− 379.21	− 3.6
3/7/00	9796.03	− 374.47	− 3.7
1/4/00	10997.93	− 359.58	− 3.2
8/27/98	8165.99	− 357.36	− 4.2
3/14/01	9973.46	− 317.34	− 3.1
8/4/98	8487.31	− 299.43	− 3.4
2/18/00	10219.52	− 295.05	− 2.8
4/3/01	9485.71	− 292.22	− 3.0
1/28/00	10738.87	− 289.15	− 2.6
7/10/02	8813.50	− 282.59	− 3.1
10/29/01	9269.50	− 275.67	− 2.9
10/15/99	10019.71	− 266.90	− 2.6

TOP TWENTY GAINS SINCE 1950 BY %

Day	DJIA Close	Points Change	% Change
10/21/87	2027.85	186.84	10.1
7/24/02	8191.29	488.95	6.3
10/20/87	1841.01	102.27	5.9
5/27/70	663.20	32.04	5.1
9/8/98	8020.78	380.53	5.0
10/29/87	1938.33	91.51	5.0
3/16/00	10630.60	499.19	4.9
8/17/82	831.24	38.81	4.9
10/9/74	631.02	28.39	4.7
10/28/97	7498.32	337.17	4.7
5/29/62	603.96	27.03	4.7
1/17/91	2623.51	114.60	4.6
11/26/63	743.52	32.03	4.5
9/24/01	8603.86	368.05	4.5
11/1/78	827.79	35.34	4.5
11/3/82	1065.49	43.41	4.2
4/5/01	9918.05	402.63	4.2
10/15/98	8299.36	330.58	4.1
10/23/57	437.13	17.34	4.1
10/6/82	944.26	37.07	4.1

TOP TWENTY LOSSES SINCE 1950 BY %

Day	DJIA Close	Points Change	% Change
10/19/87	1738.74	− 508.00	− 22.6
10/26/87	1793.93	− 156.83	− 8.0
10/27/97	7161.15	− 554.26	− 7.2
9/17/01	8920.70	− 684.81	− 7.1
10/13/89	2569.26	− 190.58	− 6.9
1/8/88	1911.31	− 140.58	− 6.9
9/26/55	455.56	− 31.89	− 6.5
8/31/98	7539.07	− 512.61	− 6.4
5/28/62	576.93	− 34.95	− 5.7
4/14/00	10305.77	− 617.78	− 5.7
4/14/88	2005.64	− 101.46	− 4.8
6/26/50	213.91	− 10.44	− 4.7
7/19/02	8019.26	− 390.23	− 4.6
9/11/86	1792.89	− 86.61	− 4.6
10/16/87	2246.74	− 108.35	− 4.6
9/20/01	8376.21	− 382.92	− 4.4
8/27/98	8165.99	− 357.36	− 4.2
3/12/01	10208.25	− 436.37	− 4.1
11/30/87	1833.55	− 76.93	− 4.0
11/15/91	2943.20	− 120.31	− 3.9

TOP TEN GAINS 1928-1950 BY %

Day	DJIA Close	Points Change	% Change
3/15/33	62.10	8.26	15.3
10/6/31	99.34	12.86	14.9
10/30/29	258.47	28.40	12.3
9/21/32	75.16	7.67	11.4
8/3/32	58.22	5.06	9.5
2/11/32	78.60	6.80	9.5
11/14/29	217.28	18.59	9.4
12/18/31	80.69	6.90	9.4
2/13/32	85.82	7.22	9.2
5/6/32	59.01	4.91	9.1

TOP TEN LOSSES 1928-1950 BY %

Day	DJIA Close	Points Change	% Change
10/28/29	260.64	− 38.33	− 12.8
10/29/29	230.07	− 30.57	− 11.7
11/6/29	232.13	− 25.55	− 9.9
8/12/32	63.11	− 5.79	− 8.4
7/21/33	88.71	− 7.55	− 7.8
10/18/37	125.73	− 10.57	− 7.8
10/5/32	66.07	− 5.09	− 7.2
9/24/31	107.79	− 8.20	− 7.1
7/20/33	96.26	− 7.32	− 7.1
11/11/29	220.39	− 16.14	− 6.8

LARGEST ONE-DAY NASDAQ GAINS AND LOSSES SINCE 1971 BY POINTS AND PERCENT

TOP TWENTY GAINS SINCE 1971 BY POINTS

Day	NASDAQ Close	Points Change	% Change
1/3/01	2616.69	324.83	14.2
12/5/00	2889.80	274.05	10.5
4/18/00	3793.57	254.41	7.2
5/30/00	3459.48	254.37	7.9
10/19/00	3418.60	247.04	7.8
10/13/00	3316.77	242.09	7.9
6/2/00	3813.38	230.88	6.4
4/25/00	3711.23	228.75	6.6
4/17/00	3539.16	217.87	6.6
6/1/00	3582.50	181.59	5.3
4/7/00	4446.45	178.89	4.2
10/31/00	3369.63	178.23	5.6
12/22/00	2517.02	176.90	7.6
11/14/00	3138.27	171.55	5.8
2/23/00	4550.33	168.21	3.8
1/10/00	4049.67	167.05	4.3
12/8/00	2917.43	164.77	6.0
3/3/00	4914.79	160.28	3.4
4/18/01	2079.44	156.22	8.1
1/7/00	3882.62	155.49	4.2

TOP TWENTY LOSSES SINCE 1971 BY POINTS

Day	NASDAQ Close	Points Change	% Change
4/14/00	3321.29	− 355.49	− 9.7
4/3/00	4223.68	− 349.15	− 7.6
4/12/00	3769.63	− 286.27	− 7.1
4/10/00	4188.20	− 258.25	− 5.8
1/4/00	3901.69	− 229.46	− 5.6
3/14/00	4706.63	− 200.61	− 4.1
5/10/00	3384.73	− 200.28	− 5.6
5/23/00	3164.55	− 199.66	− 5.9
10/25/00	3229.57	− 190.22	− 5.6
3/29/00	4644.67	− 189.22	− 3.9
3/20/00	4610.00	− 188.13	− 3.9
3/30/00	4457.89	− 186.78	− 4.0
11/8/00	3231.70	− 184.09	− 5.4
7/28/00	3663.00	− 179.23	− 4.7
12/20/00	2332.78	− 178.93	− 7.1
1/2/01	2291.86	− 178.66	− 7.2
5/2/00	3785.45	− 172.63	− 4.4
11/10/00	3028.99	− 171.36	− 5.4
4/24/00	3482.48	− 161.40	− 4.4
1/5/01	2407.65	− 159.18	− 6.2

TOP TWENTY GAINS SINCE 1971 BY %

Day	NASDAQ Close	Points Change	% Change
1/3/01	2616.69	324.83	14.2
12/5/00	2889.80	274.05	10.5
4/5/01	1785.00	146.20	8.9
4/18/01	2079.44	156.22	8.1
5/30/00	3459.48	254.37	7.9
10/13/00	3316.77	242.09	7.9
10/19/00	3418.60	247.04	7.8
5/8/02	1696.29	122.47	7.8
12/22/00	2517.02	176.90	7.6
10/21/87	351.86	24.07	7.3
4/18/00	3793.57	254.41	7.2
4/25/00	3711.23	228.75	6.6
4/17/00	3539.16	217.87	6.6
6/2/00	3813.38	230.88	6.4
4/10/01	1852.03	106.32	6.1
9/8/98	1660.86	94.34	6.0
12/8/00	2917.43	164.77	6.0
10/3/01	1580.81	88.48	5.9
11/14/00	3138.27	171.55	5.8
10/31/00	3369.63	178.23	5.6

TOP TWENTY LOSSES SINCE 1971 BY %

Day	NASDAQ Close	Points Change	% Change
10/19/87	360.21	− 46.12	−11.4
4/14/00	3321.29	− 355.49	− 9.7
10/20/87	327.79	− 32.42	− 9.0
10/26/87	298.90	− 29.55	− 9.0
8/31/98	1499.25	− 140.43	− 8.6
4/3/00	4223.68	− 349.15	− 7.6
1/2/01	2291.86	− 178.66	− 7.2
12/20/00	2332.78	− 178.93	− 7.1
4/12/00	3769.63	− 286.27	− 7.1
10/27/97	1535.09	− 115.83	− 7.0
9/17/01	1579.55	− 115.83	− 6.8
3/12/01	1923.38	− 129.40	− 6.3
1/5/01	2407.65	− 159.18	− 6.2
4/3/01	1673.00	− 109.97	− 6.2
3/27/80	124.09	− 8.13	− 6.1
3/28/01	1854.13	− 118.13	− 6.0
5/23/00	3164.55	− 199.66	− 5.9
4/10/00	4188.20	− 258.25	− 5.8
5/10/00	3384.73	− 200.28	− 5.6
4/19/99	2345.61	− 138.43	− 5.6

Based on NASDAQ composite, prior to Feb. 5, 1971 based on National Quotation Bureau indices

LARGEST WEEKLY DOW GAINS AND LOSSES SINCE OCTOBER 1928 BY POINTS AND PERCENT

TOP TWENTY GAINS SINCE 1928 BY POINTS

Week Ending	DJIA Close	Points Change	% Change
3/17/00	10595.23	666.41	6.7
9/28/01	8847.56	611.75	7.4
7/2/99	11139.24	586.68	5.6
4/20/00	10844.05	538.28	5.2
3/24/00	11112.72	517.49	4.9
10/16/98	8416.76	517.24	6.5
3/3/00	10367.20	505.08	5.1
6/2/00	10794.76	495.52	4.8
5/18/01	11301.74	480.43	4.4
1/8/99	9643.32	461.89	5.0
4/20/01	10579.85	452.91	4.5
10/22/99	10470.25	450.54	4.5
3/5/99	9736.08	429.50	4.6
5/17/02	10353.08	413.16	4.2
3/1/02	10368.86	400.71	4.0
11/6/98	8975.46	383.36	4.5
10/8/99	10649.76	376.76	3.7
3/30/01	9878.78	374.00	3.9
6/18/99	10855.56	365.05	3.5
10/27/00	10590.62	364.03	3.6

TOP TWENTY LOSSES SINCE 1928 BY POINTS

Week Ending	DJIA Close	Points Change	% Change
9/21/01	8235.81	– 1369.70	– 14.3
3/16/01	9823.41	– 821.21	– 7.7
4/14/00	10305.77	– 805.71	– 7.3
7/12/02	8684.53	– 694.97	– 7.4
7/19/02	8019.26	– 665.27	– 7.7
10/15/99	10019.71	– 630.05	– 5.9
2/11/00	10425.21	– 538.59	– 4.9
9/24/99	10279.33	– 524.30	– 4.9
1/28/00	10738.87	– 512.84	– 4.6
8/28/98	8051.68	– 481.97	– 5.6
8/31/01	9949.75	– 473.42	– 4.5
1/21/00	11251.71	– 471.27	– 4.0
3/10/00	9928.82	– 438.38	– 4.2
9/4/98	7640.25	– 411.43	– 5.1
10/13/00	10192.18	– 404.36	– 3.8
7/24/98	8937.36	– 400.61	– 4.3
1/9/98	7580.42	– 384.62	– 4.8
2/23/01	10441.90	– 357.92	– 3.3
2/25/00	9862.12	– 357.40	– 3.5
6/15/01	10623.64	– 353.36	– 3.2

TOP TWENTY GAINS SINCE 1950 BY %

Week Ending	DJIA Close	Points Change	% Change
10/11/74	658.17	73.61	12.6
8/20/82	869.29	81.24	10.3
10/8/82	986.85	79.11	8.7
8/3/84	1202.08	87.46	7.8
9/28/01	8847.56	611.75	7.4
9/20/74	670.76	43.57	6.9
3/17/00	10595.23	666.41	6.7
10/16/98	8416.76	517.24	6.5
6/7/74	853.72	51.55	6.4
11/2/62	604.58	35.56	6.2
1/9/76	911.13	52.42	6.1
11/5/82	1051.78	60.06	6.1
6/3/88	2071.30	114.86	5.9
1/18/91	2646.78	145.29	5.8
12/18/87	1975.30	108.26	5.8
11/14/80	986.35	53.93	5.8
5/29/70	700.44	38.27	5.8
12/11/87	1867.04	100.30	5.7
4/11/75	789.50	42.24	5.7
1/31/75	703.69	37.08	5.6

TOP TWENTY LOSSES SINCE 1950 BY %

Week Ending	DJIA Close	Points Change	% Change
9/21/01	8235.81	– 1369.70	– 14.3
10/23/87	1950.76	– 295.98	– 13.2
10/16/87	2246.74	– 235.47	– 9.5
10/13/89	2569.26	– 216.26	– 7.8
3/16/01	9823.41	– 821.21	– 7.7
7/19/02	8019.26	– 665.27	– 7.7
12/4/87	1766.74	– 143.74	– 7.5
9/13/74	627.19	– 50.69	– 7.5
9/12/86	1758.72	– 141.03	– 7.4
7/12/02	8684.53	– 694.97	– 7.4
9/27/74	621.95	– 48.81	– 7.3
4/14/00	10305.77	– 805.71	– 7.3
6/30/50	209.11	– 15.24	– 6.8
6/22/62	539.19	– 38.99	– 6.7
12/6/74	577.60	– 41.06	– 6.6
10/20/78	838.01	– 59.08	– 6.6
10/12/79	838.99	– 58.62	– 6.5
8/23/74	686.80	– 44.74	– 6.1
10/9/87	2482.21	– 158.78	– 6.0
10/4/74	584.56	– 37.39	– 6.0

TOP TEN GAINS 1928–1950 BY %

Week Ending	DJIA Close	Points Change	% Change
8/6/32	66.56	12.30	22.7
6/25/38	131.94	18.71	16.5
4/22/33	72.24	9.36	14.9
10/10/31	105.61	12.84	13.8
7/30/32	54.26	6.42	13.4
6/27/31	156.93	17.97	12.9
9/24/32	74.83	8.39	12.6
8/27/32	75.61	8.43	12.5
3/18/33	60.56	6.72	12.5
5/27/33	89.61	9.40	11.7

TOP TEN LOSSES 1928–1950 BY %

Week Ending	DJIA Close	Points Change	% Change
7/22/33	88.42	– 17.68	– 16.7
5/18/40	122.43	– 22.42	– 15.5
10/8/32	61.17	– 10.92	– 15.1
10/3/31	92.77	– 14.59	– 13.6
9/17/32	66.44	– 10.10	– 13.2
10/21/33	83.64	– 11.95	– 12.5
12/12/31	78.93	– 11.21	– 12.4
6/21/30	215.30	– 28.95	– 11.9
12/8/28	257.33	– 33.47	– 11.5
3/26/38	106.63	– 13.80	– 11.5

LARGEST WEEKLY NASDAQ GAINS AND LOSSES SINCE 1971 BY POINTS AND PERCENT

TOP TWENTY GAINS SINCE 1971 BY POINTS

Week Ending	NASDAQ Close	Points Change	% Change
6/2/00	3813.38	608.27	19.0
2/4/00	4244.14	357.07	9.2
3/3/00	4914.79	324.29	7.1
4/20/00	3643.88	322.59	9.7
12/8/00	2917.43	272.14	10.3
4/12/01	1961.43	241.07	14.0
7/14/00	4246.18	222.98	5.5
1/12/01	2626.50	218.85	9.1
4/28/00	3860.66	216.78	5.9
12/23/99	3969.44	216.38	5.8
4/20/01	2163.41	201.98	10.3
9/1/00	4234.33	191.65	4.7
7/2/99	2741.02	188.37	7.4
1/14/00	4064.27	181.65	4.7
2/25/00	4590.50	178.76	4.1
11/3/00	3451.58	173.22	5.3
1/21/00	4235.40	171.13	4.2
1/29/99	2505.89	167.01	7.1
10/20/00	3483.14	166.37	5.0
3/24/00	4963.03	164.90	3.4

TOP TWENTY LOSSES SINCE 1971 BY POINTS

Week Ending	NASDAQ Close	Points Change	% Change
4/14/00	3321.29	−1125.16	−25.3
7/28/00	3663.00	− 431.45	−10.5
11/10/00	3028.99	− 422.59	−12.2
3/31/00	4572.83	− 390.20	− 7.9
1/28/00	3887.07	− 348.33	− 8.2
10/6/00	3361.01	− 311.81	− 8.5
5/12/00	3529.06	− 287.76	− 7.5
9/21/01	1423.19	− 272.19	−16.1
11/22/00	2755.34	− 271.85	− 9.0
12/15/00	2653.27	− 264.16	− 9.1
12/1/00	2645.29	− 259.09	− 8.9
9/8/00	3978.41	− 255.92	− 6.0
3/17/00	4798.13	− 250.49	− 5.0
10/27/00	3278.36	− 204.78	− 5.9
2/9/01	2470.97	− 189.53	− 7.1
1/7/00	3882.62	− 186.69	− 4.6
6/15/01	2028.43	− 186.67	− 8.4
5/26/00	3205.11	− 185.29	− 5.5
7/23/99	2692.40	− 172.08	− 6.0
2/23/01	2262.51	− 162.87	− 6.7

TOP TWENTY GAINS SINCE 1971 BY %

Week Ending	NASDAQ Close	Points Change	% Change
6/2/00	3813.38	608.27	19.0
4/12/01	1961.43	241.07	14.0
4/20/01	2163.41	201.98	10.3
12/8/00	2917.43	272.14	10.3
4/20/00	3643.88	322.59	9.7
10/11/74	60.42	5.26	9.5
2/4/00	4244.14	357.07	9.2
1/12/01	2626.50	218.85	9.1
5/17/02	1741.39	140.54	8.8
10/16/98	1620.95	128.46	8.6
12/18/87	326.91	24.34	8.0
5/2/97	1305.33	96.04	7.9
1/9/87	380.65	27.39	7.8
8/3/84	246.24	16.94	7.4
7/2/99	2741.02	188.37	7.4
1/29/99	2505.89	167.01	7.1
10/5/01	1605.30	106.50	7.1
3/3/00	4914.79	324.29	7.1
3/8/02	1929.67	126.93	7.0
1/8/99	2344.41	151.72	6.9

TOP TWENTY LOSSES SINCE 1971 BY %

Week Ending	NASDAQ Close	Points Change	% Change
4/14/00	3321.29	−1125.16	−25.3
10/23/87	328.45	− 77.88	−19.2
9/21/01	1423.19	− 272.19	−16.1
11/10/00	3028.99	− 422.59	−12.2
7/28/00	3663.00	− 431.45	−10.5
12/15/00	2653.27	− 264.16	− 9.1
11/22/00	2755.34	− 271.85	− 9.0
12/1/00	2645.29	− 259.09	− 8.9
8/28/98	1639.68	− 157.93	− 8.8
10/20/78	123.82	− 11.76	− 8.7
10/6/00	3361.01	− 311.81	− 8.5
6/15/01	2028.43	− 186.67	− 8.4
9/12/86	346.78	− 31.58	− 8.3
1/28/00	3887.07	− 348.33	− 8.2
3/16/01	1890.91	− 161.87	− 7.9
3/31/00	4572.83	− 390.20	− 7.9
10/12/79	140.71	− 11.58	− 7.6
10/9/98	1492.49	− 122.49	− 7.6
5/12/00	3529.06	− 287.76	− 7.5
12/6/74	58.21	− 4.74	− 7.5

Based on NASDAQ composite, prior to Feb. 5, 1971 based on National Quotation Bureau indices

LARGEST MONTHLY DOW GAINS AND LOSSES SINCE OCTOBER 1928 BY POINTS AND PERCENT

TOP TWENTY GAINS SINCE 1928 BY POINTS

Month	DJIA Close	Points Change	% Change
Apr-99	10789.04	1002.88	10.2
Apr-01	10734.97	856.19	8.7
Mar-00	10921.92	793.61	7.8
Nov-01	9851.56	776.42	8.6
Oct-98	8592.10	749.48	9.6
Aug-00	11215.10	693.12	6.6
Feb-98	8545.72	639.22	8.1
Dec-99	11497.12	619.31	5.7
Jul-97	8222.61	549.82	7.2
Nov-98	9116.55	524.45	6.1
Nov-96	6521.70	492.32	8.2
Mar-99	9786.16	479.58	5.2
Apr-97	7008.99	425.51	6.5
Jun-99	10970.80	411.06	3.9
Oct-99	10729.86	392.91	3.8
Nov-97	7823.13	381.05	5.1
Dec-00	10786.85	372.36	3.6
Jan-97	6813.09	364.82	5.7
Jun-97	7672.79	341.75	4.7
Sep-97	7945.26	322.84	4.2

TOP TWENTY LOSSES SINCE 1928 BY POINTS

Month	DJIA Close	Points Change	% Change
Aug-98	7539.07	− 1344.22	− 15.1
Sep-01	8847.56	− 1102.19	− 11.1
Feb-00	10128.31	− 812.22	− 7.4
Jun-02	9243.26	− 681.99	− 6.9
Mar-01	9878.78	− 616.50	− 5.9
Oct-87	1993.53	− 602.75	− 23.2
Aug-97	7622.42	− 600.19	− 7.3
Aug-01	9949.75	− 573.06	− 5.4
Sep-00	10650.92	− 564.18	− 5.0
Nov-00	10414.49	− 556.65	− 5.1
Jan-00	10940.53	− 556.59	− 4.8
Oct-97	7442.08	− 503.18	− 6.3
Sep-99	10336.95	− 492.33	− 4.5
Apr-02	9946.22	− 457.72	− 4.4
Jun-01	10502.40	− 409.54	− 3.8
Feb-01	10495.28	− 392.08	− 3.6
Jul-99	10655.15	− 315.65	− 2.9
Mar-97	6583.48	− 294.26	− 4.3
Aug-90	2614.36	− 290.84	− 10.0
May-99	10559.74	− 229.30	− 2.1

TOP TWENTY GAINS SINCE 1950 BY %

Month	DJIA Close	Points Change	% Change
Jan-76	975.28	122.87	14.4
Jan-75	703.69	87.45	14.2
Jan-87	2158.04	262.09	13.8
Aug-82	901.31	92.71	11.5
Oct-82	991.72	95.47	10.7
Apr-78	837.32	79.96	10.6
Apr-99	10789.04	1002.88	10.2
Nov-62	649.30	59.53	10.1
Nov-54	386.77	34.63	9.8
Aug-84	1224.38	109.10	9.8
Oct-98	8592.10	749.48	9.6
Oct-74	665.52	57.65	9.5
Dec-91	3168.83	274.15	9.5
Jul-89	2660.66	220.60	9.0
Feb-86	1709.06	138.07	8.8
Apr-01	10734.97	856.19	8.7
Nov-01	9851.56	776.42	8.6
Apr-68	912.22	71.55	8.5
Apr-83	1226.20	96.17	8.5
May-90	2876.66	219.90	8.3

TOP TWENTY LOSSES SINCE 1950 BY %

Month	DJIA Close	Points Change	% Change
Oct-87	1993.53	− 602.75	− 23.2
Aug-98	7539.07	− 1344.22	− 15.1
Nov-73	822.25	− 134.33	− 14.0
Sep-01	8847.56	− 1102.19	− 11.1
Sep-74	607.87	− 70.71	− 10.4
Aug-74	678.58	− 78.85	− 10.4
Aug-90	2614.36	− 290.84	− 10.0
Mar-80	785.75	− 77.39	− 9.0
Jun-62	561.28	− 52.08	− 8.5
Oct-78	792.45	− 73.37	− 8.5
Jan-60	622.62	− 56.74	− 8.4
Nov-87	1833.55	− 159.98	− 8.0
May-62	613.36	− 51.97	− 7.8
Aug-81	881.47	− 70.87	− 7.4
Feb-00	10128.31	− 812.22	− 7.4
May-56	478.05	− 38.07	− 7.4
Jan-78	769.92	− 61.25	− 7.4
Sep-60	580.14	− 45.85	− 7.3
Aug-97	7622.42	− 600.19	− 7.3
Oct-79	815.70	− 62.88	− 7.2

TOP TEN GAINS 1928-1950 BY %

Month	DJIA Close	Points Change	% Change
Apr-33	77.66	22.26	40.2
Aug-32	73.16	18.90	34.8
Jul-32	54.26	11.42	26.7
Jun-38	133.88	26.14	24.3
Jun-31	150.18	21.72	16.9
Nov-28	293.38	41.22	16.3
Sep-39	152.54	18.13	13.5
May-33	88.11	10.45	13.5
Feb-31	189.66	22.11	13.2
Aug-33	102.41	11.64	12.8

TOP TEN LOSSES 1928-1950 BY %

Month	DJIA Close	Points Change	% Change
Sep-31	96.61	− 42.80	− 30.7
Mar-38	98.95	− 30.69	− 23.7
Apr-32	56.11	− 17.17	− 23.4
May-40	116.22	− 32.21	− 21.7
Oct-29	273.51	− 69.94	− 20.4
May-32	44.74	− 11.37	− 20.3
Jun-30	226.34	− 48.73	− 17.7
Dec-31	77.90	− 15.97	− 17.0
Feb-33	51.39	− 9.51	− 15.6
May-31	128.46	− 22.73	− 15.0

LARGEST MONTHLY NASDAQ GAINS AND LOSSES SINCE 1971 BY POINTS AND PERCENT

TOP TWENTY GAINS SINCE 1971 BY POINTS

Month	NASDAQ Close	Points Change	% Change
Feb-00	4696.69	756.34	19.2
Dec-99	4069.31	733.15	22.0
Jun-00	3966.11	565.20	16.6
Aug-00	4206.35	439.36	11.7
Nov-99	3336.16	369.73	12.5
Jan-99	2505.89	313.20	14.3
Jan-01	2772.73	302.21	12.2
Apr-01	2116.24	275.98	15.0
Dec-98	2192.69	243.15	12.5
Nov-01	1930.58	240.38	14.2
Oct-99	2966.43	220.27	8.0
Jun-99	2686.12	215.60	8.7
Sep-98	1693.84	194.59	13.0
Oct-01	1690.20	191.40	12.8
Nov-98	1949.54	178.15	10.1
Mar-99	2461.40	173.37	7.6
Jul-97	1593.81	151.74	10.5
Feb-98	1770.51	151.15	9.3
May-97	1400.32	139.56	11.1
Jun-98	1894.74	115.87	6.5

TOP TWENTY LOSSES SINCE 1971 BY POINTS

Month	NASDAQ Close	Points Change	% Change
Nov-00	2597.93	− 771.70	−22.9
Apr-00	3860.66	− 712.17	−15.6
Feb-01	2151.83	− 620.90	−22.4
Sep-00	3672.82	− 533.53	−12.7
May-00	3400.91	− 459.75	−11.9
Aug-98	1499.25	− 373.14	−19.9
Mar-01	1840.26	− 311.57	−14.5
Sep-01	1498.80	− 306.63	−17.0
Oct-00	3369.63	− 303.19	− 8.3
Aug-01	1805.43	− 221.70	−10.9
Feb-99	2288.03	− 217.86	− 8.7
Feb-02	1731.49	− 202.54	−10.5
Jul-00	3766.99	− 199.12	− 5.0
Apr-02	1688.23	− 157.12	− 8.5
Jun-02	1463.21	− 152.52	− 9.4
Jul-01	2027.13	− 133.41	− 6.2
Jan-00	3940.35	− 128.96	− 3.2
Dec-00	2470.52	− 127.41	− 4.9
Mar-00	4572.83	− 123.86	− 2.6
Oct-87	323.30	− 120.99	−27.2

TOP TWENTY GAINS SINCE 1971 BY %

Month	NASDAQ Close	Points Change	% Change
Dec-99	4069.31	733.15	22.0
Feb-00	4696.69	756.34	19.2
Oct-74	65.23	9.56	17.2
Jan-75	69.78	9.96	16.6
Jun-00	3966.11	565.20	16.6
Apr-01	2116.24	275.98	15.0
Jan-99	2505.89	313.20	14.3
Nov-01	1930.58	240.38	14.2
Oct-82	212.63	24.98	13.3
Sep-98	1693.84	194.59	13.0
Oct-01	1690.20	191.40	12.8
Jan-85	278.70	31.35	12.7
Dec-98	2192.69	243.15	12.5
Nov-99	3336.16	369.73	12.5
Jan-01	2772.73	302.21	12.2
Jan-87	392.06	42.73	12.2
Jan-76	87.05	9.43	12.1
Dec-91	586.34	62.44	11.9
Aug-00	4206.35	439.36	11.7
May-97	1400.32	139.56	11.1

TOP TWENTY LOSSES SINCE 1971 BY %

Month	NASDAQ Close	Points Change	% Change
Oct-87	323.30	− 120.99	−27.2
Nov-00	2597.93	− 771.70	−22.9
Feb-01	2151.83	− 620.90	−22.4
Aug-98	1499.25	− 373.14	−19.9
Mar-80	131.00	− 27.03	−17.1
Sep-01	1498.80	− 306.63	−17.0
Oct-78	111.12	− 21.77	−16.4
Apr-00	3860.66	− 712.17	−15.6
Nov-73	93.51	− 16.66	−15.1
Mar-01	1840.26	− 311.57	−14.5
Aug-90	381.21	− 57.03	−13.0
Sep-00	3672.82	− 533.53	−12.7
May-00	3400.91	− 459.75	−11.9
Aug-01	1805.43	− 221.70	−10.9
Aug-74	62.37	− 7.62	−10.9
Sep-74	55.67	− 6.70	−10.7
Feb-02	1731.49	− 202.54	−10.5
Oct-79	135.53	− 14.45	− 9.6
Sep-90	344.51	− 36.70	− 9.6
Jun-02	1463.21	− 152.52	− 9.4

Based on NASDAQ composite, prior to Feb. 5, 1971 based on National Quotation Bureau indices

LARGEST YEARLY DOW AND NASDAQ GAINS AND LOSSES
DOW SINCE 1928 BY POINTS AND PERCENT

BEST FIFTEEN YEARS SINCE 1928 BY POINTS

Year	DJIA Close	Points Change	% Change
1999	11497.12	2315.69	25.2
1997	7908.25	1459.98	22.6
1996	6448.27	1331.15	26.0
1995	5117.12	1282.68	33.5
1998	9181.43	1273.18	16.1
1989	2753.20	584.63	27.0
1991	3168.83	535.17	20.3
1993	3754.09	452.98	13.7
1986	1895.95	349.28	22.6
1985	1546.67	335.10	27.7
1975	852.41	236.17	38.3
1988	2168.57	229.74	11.8
1983	1258.64	212.10	20.3
1982	1046.54	171.54	19.6
1976	1004.65	152.24	17.9

WORST FIFTEEN YEARS SINCE 1928 BY POINTS

Year	DJIA Close	Points Change	% Change
2001	10021.50	− 765.35	− 7.1
2000	10786.85	− 710.27	− 6.2
1974	616.24	− 234.62	− 27.6
1966	785.69	− 183.57	− 18.9
1977	831.17	− 173.48	− 17.3
1973	850.86	− 169.16	− 16.6
1969	800.36	− 143.39	− 15.2
1990	2633.66	− 119.54	− 4.3
1981	875.00	− 88.99	− 9.2
1931	77.90	− 86.68	− 52.7
1930	164.58	− 83.90	− 33.8
1962	652.10	− 79.04	− 10.8
1957	435.69	− 63.78	− 12.8
1960	615.89	− 63.47	− 9.3
1937	120.85	− 59.05	− 32.8

BEST FIFTEEN YEARS SINCE 1928 BY %

Year	DJIA Close	Points Change	% Change
1933	99.90	39.97	66.7
1928	300.00	97.60	48.2
1954	404.39	123.49	44.0
1935	144.13	40.09	38.5
1975	852.41	236.17	38.3
1958	583.65	147.96	34.0
1995	5117.12	1282.68	33.5
1938	154.76	33.91	28.1
1985	1546.67	335.10	27.7
1989	2753.20	584.63	27.0
1945	192.91	40.59	26.6
1996	6448.27	1331.15	26.0
1999	11497.12	2315.69	25.2
1936	179.90	35.77	24.8
1997	7908.25	1459.98	22.6

WORST FIFTEEN YEARS SINCE 1928 BY %

Year	DJIA Close	Points Change	% Change
1931	77.90	− 86.68	− 52.7
1930	164.58	− 83.90	− 33.8
1937	120.85	− 59.05	− 32.8
1974	616.24	− 234.62	− 27.6
1932	59.93	− 17.97	− 23.1
1966	785.69	− 183.57	− 18.9
1977	831.17	− 173.48	− 17.3
1929	248.48	− 51.52	− 17.2
1973	850.86	− 169.16	− 16.6
1941	110.96	− 20.17	− 15.4
1969	800.36	− 143.39	− 15.2
1957	435.69	− 63.78	− 12.8
1940	131.13	− 19.11	− 12.7
1962	652.10	− 79.04	− 10.8
1960	615.89	− 63.47	− 9.3

NASDAQ SINCE 1971 BY POINTS AND PERCENT

BEST TEN YEARS SINCE 1971 BY POINTS

Year	NASDAQ Close	Points Change	% Change
1999	4069.31	1876.62	85.6
1998	2192.69	622.34	39.6
1995	1052.13	300.17	39.9
1997	1570.35	279.32	21.6
1996	1291.03	238.90	22.7
1991	586.34	212.50	56.8
1993	776.80	99.85	14.7
1992	676.95	90.61	15.5
1985	324.93	77.58	31.4
1989	454.82	73.44	19.3

WORST TEN YEARS SINCE 1971 BY POINTS

Year	NASDAQ Close	Points Change	% Change
2000	2470.52	−1598.79	− 39.3
2001	1950.40	− 520.12	− 21.1
1990	373.84	− 80.98	− 17.8
1973	92.19	− 41.54	− 31.1
1974	59.82	− 32.37	− 35.1
1984	247.35	− 31.25	− 11.2
1994	751.96	− 24.84	− 3.2
1987	330.47	− 18.86	− 5.4
1981	195.84	− 6.50	− 3.2
1977	105.05	− 7.17	− 7.3

BEST TEN YEARS SINCE 1971 BY %

Year	NASDAQ Close	Points Change	% Change
1999	4069.31	1876.62	85.6
1991	586.34	212.50	56.8
1995	1052.13	300.17	39.9
1998	2192.69	622.34	39.6
1980	202.34	51.20	33.9
1985	324.93	77.58	31.4
1975	77.62	17.80	29.8
1979	151.14	33.16	28.1
1971	114.12	24.51	27.4
1976	97.88	20.26	26.1

WORST TEN YEARS SINCE 1971 BY %

Year	NASDAQ Close	Points Change	% Change
2000	2470.52	−1598.79	− 39.3
1974	59.82	− 32.37	− 35.1
1973	92.19	− 41.54	− 31.1
2001	1950.40	− 520.12	− 21.1
1990	373.84	− 80.98	− 17.8
1984	247.35	− 31.25	− 11.2
1987	330.47	− 18.86	− 5.4
1981	195.84	− 6.50	− 3.2
1994	751.96	− 24.84	− 3.2
1977	105.05	− 7.17	− 7.3

Based on NASDAQ composite, prior to Feb. 5, 1971 based on National Quotation Bureau indices

STRATEGY PLANNING & RECORD SECTION

CONTENTS

162 Portfolio At Start Of 2003
164 Additional Purchases
167 Short-Term Transactions
173 Long-Term Transactions
177 Interest/Dividends Received During 2003/Brokerage Account Data 2003
178 Portfolio At End Of 2003
180 Weekly Portfolio Price Record 2003 (First Half)
182 Weekly Portfolio Price Record 2003 (Second Half)
184 Weekly Indicator Data 2003
186 Monthly Indicator Data 2003
187 If You Don't Profit From Your Investment Mistakes Someone Else Will/Performance Record Of Recommendations
188 IRA: Most Awesome Mass Investment Incentive Ever Devised
189 Option Trading Codes & Top Sixty-Nine Exchange Traded Funds
190 G.M. Loeb's "Battle Plan" For Investment Survival
191 G.M. Loeb's Investment Survival Checklist
192 Important Contacts

PORTFOLIO AT START OF 2003

DATE ACQUIRED	NO. OF SHARES	SECURITY	PRICE	TOTAL COST	PAPER PROFITS	PAPER LOSSES

PORTFOLIO AT START OF 2003

DATE ACQUIRED	NO. OF SHARES	SECURITY	PRICE	TOTAL COST	PAPER PROFITS	PAPER LOSSES

ADDITIONAL PURCHASES

DATE ACQUIRED	NO. OF SHARES	SECURITY	PRICE	TOTAL COST	REASON FOR PURCHASE PRIME OBJECTIVE, ETC.

ADDITIONAL PURCHASES

DATE ACQUIRED	NO. OF SHARES	SECURITY	PRICE	TOTAL COST	REASON FOR PURCHASE PRIME OBJECTIVE, ETC.

ADDITIONAL PURCHASES

DATE ACQUIRED	NO. OF SHARES	SECURITY	PRICE	TOTAL COST	REASON FOR PURCHASE PRIME OBJECTIVE, ETC.

SHORT-TERM TRANSACTIONS

Pages 167–176 can accompany next year's income tax return (Schedule D) Enter transactions as completed to avoid last minute pressures.

NO. OF SHARES	SECURITY	DATE ACQUIRED	DATE SOLD	SALE PRICE	COST	LOSS	GAIN

TOTALS: Carry over to next page

SHORT-TERM TRANSACTIONS *(continued)*

NO. OF SHARES	SECURITY	DATE ACQUIRED	DATE SOLD	SALE PRICE	COST	LOSS	GAIN

TOTALS: *Carry over to next page*

SHORT-TERM TRANSACTIONS *(continued)*

NO. OF SHARES	SECURITY	DATE ACQUIRED	DATE SOLD	SALE PRICE	COST	LOSS	GAIN

TOTALS: *Carry over to next page*

SHORT-TERM TRANSACTIONS (continued)

NO. OF SHARES	SECURITY	DATE ACQUIRED	DATE SOLD	SALE PRICE	COST	LOSS	GAIN

TOTALS: Carry over to next page

SHORT-TERM TRANSACTIONS (continued)

NO. OF SHARES	SECURITY	DATE ACQUIRED	DATE SOLD	SALE PRICE	COST	LOSS	GAIN

TOTALS: Carry over to next page

SHORT-TERM TRANSACTIONS (continued)

NO. OF SHARES	SECURITY	DATE ACQUIRED	DATE SOLD	SALE PRICE	COST	LOSS	GAIN	TOTALS:

LONG-TERM TRANSACTIONS

Pages 167–176 can accompany next year's income tax return (Schedule D). Enter transactions as completed to avoid last minute pressures.

NO. OF SHARES	SECURITY	DATE ACQUIRED	DATE SOLD	SALE PRICE	COST	LOSS	GAIN

TOTALS: Carry over to next page

LONG-TERM TRANSACTIONS *(continued)*

NO. OF SHARES	SECURITY	DATE ACQUIRED	DATE SOLD	SALE PRICE	COST	LOSS	GAIN

TOTALS: *Carry over to next page*

LONG-TERM TRANSACTIONS (continued)

NO. OF SHARES	SECURITY	DATE ACQUIRED	DATE SOLD	SALE PRICE	COST	LOSS	GAIN

TOTALS: Carry over to next page

LONG-TERM TRANSACTIONS (continued)

NO. OF SHARES	SECURITY	DATE ACQUIRED	DATE SOLD	SALE PRICE	COST	LOSS	GAIN	
								TOTALS:

INTEREST/DIVIDENDS RECEIVED DURING 2003

SHARES	STOCK/BOND	FIRST QUARTER	SECOND QUARTER	THIRD QUARTER	FOURTH QUARTER
		$	$	$	$

BROKERAGE ACCOUNT DATA 2003

	MARGIN INTEREST	TRANSFER TAXES	CAPITAL ADDED	CAPITAL WITHDRAWN
JAN				
FEB				
MAR				
APR				
MAY				
JUN				
JUL				
AUG				
SEP				
OCT				
NOV				
DEC				

PORTFOLIO AT END OF 2003

DATE ACQUIRED	NO. OF SHARES	SECURITY	PRICE	TOTAL COST	PAPER PROFITS	PAPER LOSSES

PORTFOLIO AT END OF 2003

DATE ACQUIRED	NO. OF SHARES	SECURITY	PRICE	TOTAL COST	PAPER PROFITS	PAPER LOSSES

PORTFOLIO PRICE RECORD 2003 (FIRST HALF)
Place purchase price above stock name and weekly closes below

STOCKS → Week Ending	1	2	3	4	5	6	7	8	9	10
JANUARY 3										
10										
17										
24										
31										
FEBRUARY 7										
14										
21										
28										
MARCH 7										
14										
21										
28										
APRIL 4										
11										
18										
25										
MAY 2										
9										
16										
23										
30										
JUNE 6										
13										
20										
27										

PORTFOLIO PRICE RECORD 2003 (FIRST HALF)

Place purchase price above stock name and weekly closes below

STOCKS Week Ending	11	12	13	14	15	16	17	18	Dow Jones Industrial Average	Net Change For Week
JANUARY 3										
10										
17										
24										
31										
FEBRUARY 7										
14										
21										
28										
MARCH 7										
14										
21										
28										
APRIL 4										
11										
18										
25										
MAY 2										
9										
16										
23										
30										
JUNE 6										
13										
20										
27										

PORTFOLIO PRICE RECORD 2003 (SECOND HALF)
Place purchase price above stock name and weekly closes below

STOCKS / Week Ending	1	2	3	4	5	6	7	8	9	10
JULY 4										
11										
18										
25										
AUGUST 1										
8										
15										
22										
29										
SEPTEMBER 5										
12										
19										
26										
OCTOBER 3										
10										
17										
24										
31										
NOVEMBER 7										
14										
21										
28										
DECEMBER 5										
12										
19										
26										

PORTFOLIO PRICE RECORD 2003 (SECOND HALF)

Place purchase price above stock name and weekly closes below

	Week Ending	STOCKS 11	12	13	14	15	16	17	18	Dow Jones Industrial Average	Net Change For Week
JULY	4										
	11										
	18										
	25										
AUGUST	1										
	8										
	15										
	22										
	29										
SEPTEMBER	5										
	12										
	19										
	26										
OCTOBER	3										
	10										
	17										
	24										
	31										
NOVEMBER	7										
	14										
	21										
	28										
DECEMBER	5										
	12										
	19										
	26										

WEEKLY INDICATOR DATA 2003 (FIRST HALF)

Week Ending	Dow Jones Industrial Average	Net Change For Week	Net Change On Friday	Net Change Next Monday	S&P Or NASDAQ	NYSE Advances	NYSE Declines	New Highs	New Lows	CBOE Put/Call Ratio	90-Day Treas. Rate	Moody's AAA Rate
JANUARY 3												
10												
17												
24												
31												
FEBRUARY 7												
14												
21												
28												
MARCH 7												
14												
21												
28												
APRIL 4												
11												
18												
25												
MAY 2												
9												
16												
23												
30												
JUNE 6												
13												
20												
27												

WEEKLY INDICATOR DATA 2003 (SECOND HALF)

	Week Ending	Dow Jones Industrial Average	Net Change For Week	Net Change On Friday	Net Change Next Monday	S&P Or NASDAQ	NYSE Advances	NYSE Declines	New Highs	New Lows	CBOE Put/Call Ratio	90-Day Treas. Rate	Moody's AAA Rate
JULY	4												
	11												
	18												
	25												
AUGUST	1												
	8												
	15												
	22												
	29												
SEPTEMBER	5												
	12												
	19												
	26												
OCTOBER	3												
	10												
	17												
	24												
	31												
NOVEMBER	7												
	14												
	21												
	28												
DECEMBER	5												
	12												
	19												
	26												

MONTHLY INDICATOR DATA 2003

	DJIA 4th from Last Day Prev. Mo.	DJIA 2nd Trading Day	Point Change These 5 Days	Point Change Rest Of Mo.	% Change Whole Period	% Change Your Stocks	Prime Rate	Trade Deficit $ Billion	CPI % Change	% Unemployment Rate
JAN										
FEB										
MAR										
APR										
MAY										
JUN										
JUL										
AUG										
SEP										
OCT										
NOV										
DEC										

INSTRUCTIONS:

Weekly Indicator Data (page 184-185). Keeping data on several indicators may give you a better feel of the market. In addition to the closing DJIA and its net change for the week, post the net change for Friday's Dow and also the following Monday's. A series of "down Fridays" followed by "down Mondays" often precede a downswing. Tracking either of the S&P or NASDAQ composites, and advances and declines, will help prevent the Dow from misleading you. New highs and lows and put/call ratios (www.cboe.com) are also useful indicators. All these weekly figures appear in weekend papers or *Barron's*. Data for 90-day Treasury Rate and Moody's AAA Bond Rate are quite important to track short- and long-term interest rates. These figures are available from:

> Weekly U.S. Financial Data
> Federal Reserve Bank of St. Louis
> P.O. Box 442
> St. Louis MO 63166
> **http://research.stlouisfed.org/publications/usfd/**

Monthly Indicator Data. The purpose of the first four columns is to enable you to track the market's bullish bias near the end, beginning and middle of the month, which has been shifting lately (see page 136, 137). Prime Rate, Trade Deficit, Consumers Price Index, and Unemployment Rate are worthwhile indicators to follow. Or, readers may wish to use those columns for other data.

IF YOU DON'T PROFIT FROM YOUR INVESTMENT MISTAKES, SOMEONE ELSE WILL

No matter how much we may deny it, almost every successful person in Wall Street pays a great deal of attention to trading suggestions—especially when they come from "the right sources."

One of the hardest things to learn is to distinguish between good tips and bad ones. Usually the best tips have a logical reason in back of them, which accompanies the tip. Poor tips usually have no reason to support them.

The important thing to remember is that the market discounts. It does not review, it does not reflect. The Street's real interest in "tips," inside information, buying and selling suggestions, and everything else of this kind, emanates from a desire to find out just what the market has on hand to discount. The process of finding out involves separating the wheat from the chaff—and there is plenty of chaff.

HOW TO MAKE USE OF STOCK "TIPS"

- The source should be **reliable**. (By listing all "tips" and suggestions on a Performance Record of Recommendations, such as below, and then periodically evaluating the outcomes, you will soon know the "batting average" of your sources.)
- The story should make sense. Would the merger violate anti-trust laws? Are there too many computers on the market already? How many years will it take to become profitable?
- The stock should not have had a recent sharp run-up. Otherwise, the story may already be discounted and confirmation or denial in the press would most likely be accompanied by a sell-off in the stock.

PERFORMANCE RECORD OF RECOMMENDATIONS

STOCK RECOMMENDED	BY WHOM	DATE	PRICE	REASON FOR RECOMMENDATION	SUBSEQUENT ACTION OF STOCK

INDIVIDUAL RETIREMENT ACCOUNTS: MOST AWESOME INVESTMENT INCENTIVE EVER DEVISED

IRA INVESTMENTS OF $2,000 A YEAR COMPOUNDING AT VARIOUS RATES OF RETURN FOR DIFFERENT PERIODS

Annual Rate	5 Yrs	10 Yrs	15 Yrs	20 Yrs	25 Yrs	30 Yrs	35 Yrs	40 Yrs	45 Yrs	50 Yrs
1%	$10,304	$21,134	$32,516	$44,478	$57,050	$70,265	$84,154	$98,750	$114,092	$130,216
2%	10,616	22,337	35,279	49,567	65,342	82,759	101,989	123,220	146,661	172,542
3%	10,937	23,616	38,314	55,353	75,106	98,005	124,552	155,327	191,003	232,362
4%	11,266	24,973	41,649	61,938	86,623	116,657	153,197	197,653	251,741	317,548
5%	11,604	26,414	45,315	69,439	100,227	139,522	189,673	253,680	335,370	439,631
6%	11,951	27,943	49,345	77,985	116,313	167,603	236,242	328,095	451,016	615,512
7%	12,307	29,567	53,776	87,730	135,353	202,146	295,827	427,219	611,504	869,972
8%	12,672	31,291	58,649	98,846	157,909	244,692	372,204	559,562	834,852	1,239,344
9%	13,047	33,121	64,007	111,529	184,648	297,150	470,249	736,584	1,146,372	1,776,882
10%	13,431	35,062	69,899	126,005	216,364	361,887	596,254	973,704	1,581,591	2,560,599
11%	13,826	37,123	76,380	142,530	253,998	441,826	758,329	1,291,654	2,190,338	3,704,672
12%	14,230	39,309	83,507	161,397	298,668	540,585	966,926	1,718,285	3,042,435	5,376,041
13%	14,645	41,629	91,343	182,940	351,700	662,630	1,235,499	2,290,972	4,235,612	7,818,486
14%	15,071	44,089	99,961	207,537	414,665	813,474	1,581,346	3,059,817	5,906,488	11,387,509
15%	15,508	46,699	109,435	235,620	489,424	999,914	2,026,691	4,091,908	8,245,795	16,600,747
16%	15,955	49,466	119,850	267,681	578,177	1,230,323	2,600,054	5,476,957	11,519,435	24,210,705
17%	16,414	52,400	131,298	304,277	683,525	1,515,008	3,337,989	7,334,781	16,097,540	35,309,434
18%	16,884	55,510	143,878	346,042	808,544	1,866,637	4,287,298	9,825,183	22,494,522	51,478,901
19%	17,366	58,807	157,700	393,695	956,861	2,300,775	5,507,829	13,160,993	31,424,150	75,006,500
20%	17,860	62,301	172,884	448,051	1,132,755	2,836,516	7,076,019	17,625,259	43,875,144	109,193,258

OPTION TRADING CODES

Option trading codes contain the stock ticker symbol, the expiration month code, and the striking price code.

For NASDAQ stocks with more than three letters in the stock code, the option ticker symbol is shortened to three letters, usually ending in Q. For example, Microsoft's stock symbol is MSFT, so its option ticker symbol is MSQ.

Each expiration month has a separate code for both calls and puts. Also, each striking price has a separate code, which is identical for calls and puts. In an option listing, the ticker symbol is first, followed by the expiration month code, and then the striking price code. For example, the Microsoft January 90 call would have the code MSQAR, and the Microsoft January 90 put would have the code MSQMR.

Expiration Month Codes		Striking Price Codes	
Call Code		**Code**	**Striking Prices**
January	A	A	5 105
February	B	B	10 110
March	C	C	15 115
April	D	D	20 120
May	E	E	25 125
June	F	F	30 130
July	G	G	35 135
August	H	H	40 140
September	I	I	45 145
October	J	J	50 150
November	K	K	55 155
December	L	L	60 160
		M	65 165
Put Code		N	70 170
January	M	O	75 175
February	N	P	80 180
March	O	Q	85 185
April	P	R	90 190
May	Q	S	95 195
June	R	T	100 200
July	S	U	7½ 37½
August	T	V	12½ 42½
September	U	W	17½ 47½
October	V	X	22½ 52½
November	W	Y	27½ 57½
December	X	Z	32½ 62½

Option Information Courtesy of Bernie Shaeffer, *The Option Advisor* (John Wiley & Sons)

TOP SIXTY-NINE EXCHANGE TRADED FUNDS

(Traded on the American Stock Exchange. See page 118 for Sector Seasonalities.)

Ticker	Exchange Traded Fund
DIA	DIAMONDS Series Trust I (30 Dow Stocks)
QQQ	Nasdaq-100 Index
FFF	FORTUNE 500 Index
FEF	FORTUNE e-50 Index
MDY	MidCap SPDRS
SPY	SPDRS S&P 500
XLY	Select Sector SPDR-Consumer
XLP	Select Sector SPDR-Consumer Staples
XLE	Select Sector SPDR-Energy
XLF	Select Sector SPDR-Financial
XLV	Select Sector SPDR-Health Care
XLI	Select Sector SPDR-Industrial
XLB	Select Sector SPDR-Materials
XLK	Select Sector SPDR-Technology
XLU	Select Sector SPDR-Utilities
VXF	Vanguard Extended Market VIPERs
VTI	Vanguard Total Stock Market VIPERs
BBH	Biotech HOLDRS
BDH	Broadband HOLDRS
BHH	B2B Internet HOLDRS
HHH	Internet HOLDRS
IAH	Internet Architecture HOLDRS
IIH	Internet Infrastructure HOLDRS
MKH	Market 2000+ HOLDRS (50 Big Caps)
OIH	Oil Service HOLDRS
PPH	Pharmaceutical HOLDRS
RKH	Regional Bank HOLDRS
RTH	Retail HOLDRS
SMH	Semiconductor HOLDRS
SWH	Software HOLDRS
TBH	Telebras HOLDRS (Foreign Telecoms)
TTH	Telecom HOLDRS
UTH	Utilities HOLDRS
WMH	Wireless HOLDRS

Ticker	Exchange Traded Fund
ICF	iShares Cohen & Steers Realty Majors
IYM	iShares Dow Jones US Basic Materials
IYD	iShares Dow Jones US Chemicals
IYC	iShares Dow Jones US Consumer Cyclical
IYE	iShares Dow Jones US Energy
IYF	iShares Dow Jones US Financial Sector
IYG	iShares Dow Jones US Financial Services
IYH	iShares Dow Jones US Healthcare
IYJ	iShares Dow Jones US Industrial
IYV	iShares Dow Jones US Internet
IYK	iShares Dow Jones US Non-Consumer Cyc
IYR	iShares Dow Jones US Real Estate
IYW	iShares Dow Jones US Technology
IYZ	iShares Dow Jones US Telecom
IYY	iShares Dow Jones US Total Market
IDU	iShares Dow Jones US Utilities
IGE	iShares Goldman Sachs Natural Resources
IGN	iShares Goldman Sachs Networking
IGW	iShares Goldman Sachs Semiconductor
IGV	iShares Goldman Sachs Software
IGM	iShares Goldman Sachs Technology
IBB	iShares Nasdaq Biotechnology
IWB	iShares Russell 1000
IWF	iShares Russell 1000 Growth
IWD	iShares Russell 1000 Value
IWM	iShares Russell 2000
IWO	iShares Russell 2000 Growth
IWN	iShares Russell 2000 Value
IWV	iShares Russell 3000
IWZ	iShares Russell 3000 Growth
IWW	iShares Russell 3000 Value
IWP	iShares Russell Midcap Growth
IWR	iShares Russell Midcap
IWS	iShares Russell Midcap Value
IVV	iShares S&P 500

SPDR *Standard & Poor's Depository Receipts,* **HOLDRS** *Holding Company Depository Receipts,*
iShares *Index Shares,* **VIPERs** *Vanguard Index Participation Equity Receipts*

G.M. LOEB'S "BATTLE PLAN" FOR INVESTMENT SURVIVAL

LIFE IS CHANGE: Nothing can ever be the same a minute from now as it was a minute ago. Everything you own is changing in price and value. You can find that last price of an active security on the stock ticker, but you cannot find the next price anywhere. The value of your money is changing. Even the value of your home is changing, though no one walks in front of it with a sandwich board consistently posting the changes.

RECOGNIZE CHANGE: Your basic objective should be to profit from change. The art of investing is being able to recognize change and to adjust investment goals accordingly.

WRITE THINGS DOWN: You will score more investment success and avoid more investment failures if you write things down. Very few investors have the drive and inclination to do this.

KEEP A CHECKLIST: If you aim to improve your investment results, get into the habit of keeping a checklist on every issue you consider buying. Before making a commitment, it will pay you to write down the answers to at least some of the basic questions—How much am I investing in this company? How much do I think I can make? How much do I have to risk? How long do I expect to take to reach my goal?

HAVE A SINGLE RULING REASON: Above all, writing things down is the best way to find "the ruling reason." When all is said and done, there is invariably a single reason that stands out above all others why a particular security transaction can be expected to show a profit. All too often many relatively unimportant statistics are allowed to obscure this single important point.

Any one of a dozen factors may be the point of a particular purchase or sale. It could be a technical reason—an increase in earnings or dividend not yet discounted in the market price—a change of management—a promising new product—an expected improvement in the market's valuation of earnings—or many others. But, in any given case, one of these factors will almost certainly be more important than all the rest put together.

CLOSING OUT A COMMITMENT: If you have a loss, the solution is automatic, provided you decide what to do at the time you buy. Otherwise, the question divides itself into two parts. Are we in a bull or bear market? Few of us really know until it is too late. For the sake of the record, if you think it is a bear market, just put that consideration first and sell as much as your conviction suggests and your nature allows.

If you think it is a bull market, or at least a market where some stocks move up, some mark time and only a few decline, do not sell unless:

- ✓ You see a bear market ahead.
- ✓ You see trouble for a particular company in which you own shares.
- ✓ Time and circumstances have turned up a new and seemingly far better buy than the issue you like least in your list.
- ✓ Your shares stop going up and start going down.

A subsidiary question is, which stock to sell first? Two further observations may help:

- ✓ Do not sell solely because you think a stock is "overvalued."
- ✓ If you want to sell some of your stocks and not all, in most cases it is better to go against your emotional inclinations and sell first the issues with losses, small profits or none at all, the weakest, the most disappointing, etc.

Mr. Loeb is the author of *The Battle for Investment Survival*, Fraser Publishing, Box 494, Burlington VT 05402.

G.M. LOEB'S INVESTMENT SURVIVAL CHECKLIST

OBJECTIVES AND RISKS

Security	Price	Shares	Date

"Ruling reason" for commitment	Amount of commitment $ _____
	% of my investment capital _____ %

Price objective	Est. time to achieve it	I will risk _____ points	Which would be $ _____

TECHNICAL POSITION

Price action of stock:
- ☐ hitting new highs
- ☐ in a trading range
- ☐ pausing in an uptrend
- ☐ moving up from low ground
- ☐ acting stronger than market
- ☐ _____

Dow Jones Industrial Average

Trend of Market

SELECTED YARDSTICKS

	Price Range		Earnings Per Share Actual or Projected	Price/Earnings Ratio Actual or Projected
	High	Low		
Current Year				
Previous Year				

Merger Possibilities	Years for earnings to double in past
Comment on Future	Years for market price to double in past

PERIODIC RE-CHECKS

Date	Stock Price	D.J.I.A.	Comment	Action taken, if any

COMPLETED TRANSACTIONS

Date Closed	Period of time held	Profit or loss

Reason for profit or loss

IMPORTANT CONTACTS

NAME	TELEPHONE	E-MAIL